THE BED AND THE THRONE

Northern and Central ITALY in the XVI Century

Cadore

Trent

Bergamo
Brescia
Vicenza
Treviso

Milan
Verona
Padua
Venice

Turin
Piacenza
Mantua
Mirandola
Ferrara

Parma
Modena
Bologna
Ravenna

Genoa
Faenza
Forlì
Rimini

Savona
Lucca
Urbino

Pisa
Florence

Siena
Perugia

Orvieto

Rome

Naples

0   25   50   100 mi.

Isabella d'Este, by Leonardo da Vinci

THE BED
AND THE THRONE

The Life of Isabella d'Este

George R. Marek

HARPER & ROW, PUBLISHERS
New York, Hagerstown, San Francisco, London

Endpaper maps by Alexander

107701

To M.

And you may then revolve what tales I have told you
Of courts, of princes, of the tricks in war . . .
And often, to our comfort, shall we find
The sharded beetle in a safer hold
Than is the full-wing'd eagle.

Cymbeline, *Act III, Scene 3*

Contents

INTRODUCTION

Why Isabella?

"Liberal and magnanimous Isabella" was the tribute the liberal and magnanimous poet Ariosto paid her; he used "magnanimous" in the prime sense of the word, "large of soul." Author, fabulator, and collector of the worldly-wise stories of his time, Matteo Bandello, wrote that she was "supreme among women." Castiglione, who wrote the manual which most widely instructed the conduct of late-Renaissance men and women, not to mention those who followed after, professed that "of her admirable qualities it would be offensive to speak unrestrainedly." She was, said the diplomat Niccolò da Correggio, "The First Lady of the world." Another poet addressed her as "glorious heroine." The great pope of her age, Leo X, let her know that she could treat him "with as much friendliness as you would your brother." Pietro Bembo, his secretary, Latin stylist, and poet fluent in three languages, deemed her "one of the wisest and most fortunate of women." In contemporary statements about her the word *grazia* appears again and again, meaning not so much "graceful" as a being endowed with grace.

Yet all this was said and written a long, long time ago. More than five hundred years have passed since the birth of Isabella d'Este, daughter of the proud-spirited house which ruled the state of Ferrara, and who was to become the ruler of the state of Mantua. Only scholars of the period, art detectives, museum curators, and those curious souls who poke into the corners of history's antique shop know her now. She was famous enough for Leonardo da Vinci—who did not much like women—to pause in his flight from Milan, sit down at her court, and draw a large sketch of her. Visitors to the Louvre, where the sketch is displayed in a special room, pause in admiration and say, "Now, who was *she?*" (I heard one man reply, "Probably his mistress.")

The state she governed no longer exists, and her city is a sleepy town, often as swaddled in fog as a baby in his winter blankets. In Isabella's time it was a "large" capital of 30,000 inhabitants, center of the state of Mantua. Today it is a small municipality of about 60,000 inhabitants. It has preserved some of its austere old elegance, but most of its treasures have been dispersed to the museums of major cities and those which remain are cavalierly treated. She was responsible for commissioning or collecting many of these treasures, but she was not herself a creative artist. She inspired and conferred with poets, but she was not herself a writer. She was a politician of extraordinary skill, but it cannot be said that she changed the course of history in the sense that Cesare Borgia or Pope Clement did.

Then, why write about Isabella? Why try to bring her into the light again?

As Falstaff was not only witty in himself, "but the cause that wit is in other men," so was Isabella not only strong in herself, but the cause that strength came to other women. She was one of the first women who can truly be called liberated. She broke the fetters forged by centuries of tradition and threw the links away. That necessity forced her to act is beside the point. She was able to do it. She was able to do it and remain soft-spoken, a voice gentle and low. She had no didactic purpose; she wanted to save herself, not the world.

She proved not only that the individual may rise above the *Zeitgeist*, an elevation as familiar as the ascent of a gull, but that the spirit of the time itself can be nudged, coerced, shaped, and pressured by an individual. Isabella was born at a time and into a world which was distinguished by passionate curiosity. This curiosity, this appetite for inquiry, stretched back into the past to discover the Laocoon and stretched forward to send, in 1492, three ships across the Atlantic. But to exercise it, to fire it by exchange of views, to hone it by conversation—what a talkative age it was!—was a prerogative of men. As to women—Vespasiano da Bisticci, a historian from the "progressive" town of Florence, expressed the almost general opinion. Women, he wrote, should observe two rules: "The first is that they bring up their children in the fear of God, and the second that they keep quiet in church, and I would add that they stop talking in other places as well. . . ."

Leon Battista Alberti, one of the most attractive polymaths of the

Renaissance, equally adept at painting, poetry, architecture, music, drama, mathematics, wrote a popular essay "On the Family" in which the spokesman is a Florentine merchant. He has this to say about wives:

> After my wife had been settled in my house a few days, and after her first pangs of longing for her mother and family had begun to fade, I took her by the hand and showed her around the whole house. I explained that the loft was the place for grain and that the stores of wine and wood were kept in the cellar. I showed her where things needed for the table were kept, and so on, through the whole house. At the end there were no household goods of which my wife had not learned both the place and the purpose. Then we returned to my room, and, having locked the door, I showed her my treasures, silver, tapestry, garments, jewels, and where each thing had its place. . . .
>
> Only my books and records and those of my ancestors did I determine to keep well sealed. . . . These my wife not only could not read, she could not even lay hands on them. I kept my records at all times . . . locked up and arranged in order in my study, almost like sacred and religious objects. I never gave my wife permission to enter that place, with me or alone. I also ordered her, if she ever came across any writing of mine, to give it over to my keeping at once. To take away any taste she might have for looking at my notes or prying into my private affairs, I often used to express my disapproval of bold and forward females who try too hard to know about things outside the house and about the concerns of their husband and of men in general.
>
> [Husbands] who take counsel with their wives . . . are madmen if they think true prudence or good counsel lies in the female brain. . . . For this very reason I have always tried carefully not to let any secret of mine be known to a woman. I did not doubt that my wife was most loving, and more discreet and modest in her ways than any, but I still considered it safer to have her unable, and not merely unwilling, to harm me.
>
> Furthermore, I made it a rule never to speak with her of anything but household matters or questions of conduct, or of the children. Of these matters I spoke a good deal to her. . . .

An exceptional, misogynist view? Surely not. Even Erasmus of Rotterdam, one of the most tolerant and humorous of Renaissance philosophers, offered in his *Colloquies* a dialogue between an abbot and a learned lady in which he has the abbot say: "Books destroy women's brains who have little enough of themselves."

Peter Burke, in *Culture and Society in Renaissance Italy*, gives a survey of what he calls "the elite," artists and writers, six hundred of them. "One 'variable' in the survey . . . appears to be almost invariable: their sex. Only three out of the 600 are women. . . . All are poets and all come at the end of the period."

Isabella captured a redoubt of a closed society. She was able to gain new respect and opportunities for her sex. Though she was not alone in this endeavor—the age boasted a few other remarkable women—she was especially adroit in helping to lift some of her sisters from medieval servitude and domestic subservience. That of course is not to say that she won on all fronts; we know that the struggle for equality continued and continues. But she was one of those who made the struggle possible. She opened the two sides of a hitherto largely unasked question. Civilization was the better for it.

We may document the change by contrasting previous quotations with one from Baldassare Castiglione's book *The Courtier,* by which he meant "The Gentleman" or, better, "The Cultured Man." Castiglione was an intimate friend of Isabella's and for a time served her as Mantuan ambassador to Rome. His book was published in 1528, when Isabella was fifty-four years old and regarded as "the First Lady of the world." *The Courtier* leaped into immediate popularity; it was a guide to a civilized conduct of life, a kind of how-to-win-friends-and-influence-people, written in a lively and charming style. Like the essays of Alberti and Erasmus, it is written in dialogue form, Castiglione using real persons as his interlocutors. Gasparo Pallavicino, Marquis of Cortemaggiore, serves as the devil's advocate and argues that it is perfectly silly for women to acquire learning. A woman—she is only an imperfect man, "a mistake of nature." Giuliano de' Medici answers: "I say that women can understand all the things men can understand and that the intellect of a woman can penetrate wherever a man's can."

Surely Castiglione had his admired Isabella in mind.

2

Three other reasons for writing Isabella's *vita sua* may be put forward. The first is the story of her marriage to Gianfrancesco Gonzaga of Mantua, a relationship which began in ignorance, grew into great love, and then declined into shame, bitterness, and, at the last, pity. It is not an unfamiliar story. Yet this unusual woman faced the problem in an unusual way, not by inviting other men to her bed, whether in revenge or for excitement. She saw other women issue such invitations, the Renaissance being almost as uninhibited sexually as is our age, but though the erotic roundelay swung continuously around her, her inclination lay in other directions. It was not "virtue" which made her act as she did, and to claim credit for it would never have entered her mind. She merely obeyed her impulses. She found a solution—and the tragedy did not destroy her. Though it hurt her deeply, she developed an antidote. The way she handled a sick marriage was remarkable.

The second reason: those of us who look with love at the artistic creations of her time will be interested in her as a collector. She lived for sixty-five years—1474 to 1539—and all but twelve of those years belong to the period known as the High Renaissance. She gathered a vast collection of the paintings, sculptures, medallions, silver, jewels, plates, tiles, books, manuscripts, and musical instruments of the period, as well as of the products of the antique. She lay siege to them in competition with the popes and the Medici, who had more money, but hardly more nerve.

Her taste was perceptive but not infallible. Though she recognized the genius of Mantegna, she did not really appreciate him at full value; he was the court painter of Mantua, a prophet in his own country. She says not a word about Piero della Francesca, whose frescoes adorned her parental home. Nor does she mention Pisanello, who before her time painted superb frescoes in her palace which, long thought to have been destroyed, have recently been rediscovered. Yet she appreciated the greatness of Leonardo, Michelangelo, Titian. Who can correctly judge a painting on which the varnish has hardly dried?

Isabella was a collector of conviction: she loved an object—or she hated it. She was urgently involved with the things she wanted and those she owned. Acquisition was to her a means of expressing herself, and the pursuit of art gave her a resource for self-assertion. This shopping fever is a characteristic common to collectors. As Aline Saarinen writes in *The Proud Possessors*, they "were not only possessors: they were also possessed."

Finally, Isabella's history may help us to regard more clearly that miraculous age of the Italian Renaissance. It was an age laced with light, loud with laughter, lusty in its zest for life, where a genius seemed to live in almost every house at every corner. We judge it now by the shapes of a thousand sculptures and by the colors held fast on a thousand canvases, by the churches and palaces strong enough to have survived a hundred stupid onslaughts, by its narrative inventions from which Shakespeare borrowed, by the beautiful

appurtenances which enhanced living and which ranged from dae-
dal jewels to symbolic soup plates. No wonder we think of the age
with envy and longing. We forget the slimy puddles between the
shining lakes. Who remembers that Sixtus IV let the people in the
papal states starve during a famine while he hoarded his wheat
until he got an exorbitant price for it, that he appointed Torque-
mada as head of the Inquisition, that he made the sign of the cross
over a cannon? All we remember is the Sistine Chapel. Walking
over the Rialto Bridge, who remembers that men convicted of petty
transgressions were forced to run naked from San Marco, whipped
all the way, until they fell exhausted by a little statue underneath
the bridge called Il Gobbo (the hunchback)? The Swiss scholar
Jacob Burckhardt in his fundamental study, *The Civilization of the
Renaissance in Italy,* published in 1860, did point to such dark
spots, but in the main painted too roseate a picture; later writers
such as J. S. Symonds, Peter Burke, and H. E. Barnes have corrected this. Still the idealization remains. We have stars in our eyes
when we speak of the Renaissance. The achievement is before us;
what it cost lies behind. The evil that men do does not always live
after them. Isabella could lie like an ambassador and bribe like a
smuggler. No use hauling her over the coals for such machinations.
"The past," wrote Goethe, "loses one of the prime rights of man: it
can not be judged by its peers." We must simply record the facets
of her prismatic personality. And when in our imagination we
breathe the heady air she breathed, we should also inhale the smell
of its soiled linen. In short, to understand her as a representative of
her time is to understand the time better.

3

Isabella's life is extraordinarily well documented. She wrote to
everybody who was anybody, and in return she received no fewer
than 28,000 communications, some merely short memoranda, others
lengthy and gossipy letters. It is evident that the Estes and the
Gonzagas were aware of their historic importance and preserved
the evidence. Copies of her letters and of documents concerning
her fill 10,000 pages in the Mantuan Archive. Unfortunately some
letters one would like to have, particularly some secret notes to her

brother on government affairs, were burned. She did not, of course, write all her letters herself, her various secretaries performing the task for her, as was the custom among high-placed busy persons. But sometimes, when she wrote to her favorite friend, her favorite brother, her husband, she wrote herself, occasionally noting under the signature, "Written by her own hand."

In the late nineteenth and early twentieth centuries the head of the "Mantua-Gonzaga Archive," Alessandro Luzio, a scholar of exceptional devotion, examined this material, sorted most of it, and published in the course of a long lifetime something like 120 monographs on Mantuan matters and on Isabella specifically. He was aided in his researches by his associate, Rodolfo Renier, but neither shaped what they found into a full-length biography.

It was an English lady, Julia Cartwright, who in 1903 wrote the first and, though long out of print, still the standard book about Isabella. She was an enthusiastic biographer, but she managed to turn Isabella into a proper Victorian lady, almost a Louisa May Alcott character. A solid German biography by Jan Lauts was published in 1952, but was never translated into English. (A French edition is available.)

Like Cartwright and Lauts, I owe a scholar's gratitude to Luzio's research. It would have been possible to write this book without much inquiry beyond it. All the same, an associate, Miss Iris Carulli, worked for a long time in the Mantua Archive as well as in the Libreria Marziana in Venice and was successful in finding a few documents hitherto overlooked. My own efforts—which included several visits to Mantua—were aided by Cedric Gould of the National Gallery, London; Jennifer M. Fletcher of the Courtauld Institute, London; Dr. Livio Oliveri of the Istituto Italiano di Cultura, Hamburg; Count Enrico Galeazzi of the Vatican; Anna Maria Lorenzoni of the Mantua Archive; Frederike Klauner of the Kunsthistorische Museum, Vienna; Clifford M. Brown of Carleton University, Canada; Dorothee Dummer in Munich; and especially by Frances Lindley, sympathetically critical and critically sympathetic editor of Harper & Row.

I hope—perhaps the hope is overly ambitious—that the book offers the reader not only the portrait of a woman of some importance but affords as well a side glance at a period which in its moral laxity and intellectual daring, the cynicism of government and church, and the idealism of a few, the concentration of wealth and ubiquitousness of poverty, its scientific doubting and its unscientific superstitions, illuminates our own time.

GEORGE R. MAREK

New York, 1975

About the letters: Some of them I give in the translation made by Julia Cartwright, which I have edited here and there. Other documents I have translated freshly. In doing so, I made no attempt to mirror in English the style of fifteenth- and sixteenth-century Italian, though I retained some of the formal modes then in use, such as Isabella addressing her little son as "Most Illustrious" or her husband as "Your Excellency."

THE BED AND THE THRONE

Is It a Boy?

The instant a baby was born in the days of the Renaissance, the parents looked underneath. If it was a boy, they were happy. If it was a girl, they were less happy.

Whatever the economic level of the family, the male child promised to be more useful and provide sturdier satisfaction. In a peasant's field he would soon be strong enough to stack the hay. In a goldsmith's forge he would soon learn how to do the simple hammering. In a banker's house he would soon absorb the mystery of the Venetian ducats, the Florentine *grossi*, the Milanese *testoni*. The higher the social position of the family, the more urgent became the question "Is it a boy?" until in palaces and castles it became all-important. The duke promised a new altarpiece to the Virgin Mary should the issue be fortunate, while the duchess consulted the astrologer. Since the hub of life and the core of power lay in the family, since the gears of society were oiled by nepotism, what these illustrious parents prayed for was continuity, which only a male offspring could assure: the Sforza and the Medici, the Estes and the Gonzagas, the Borgias and the Montefeltros, were inheritable units whose names had to be preserved if their flags were to be kept flying.

A girl was not only less useful but she cost more. Would the father's income suffice to dress her attractively? Could a dowry be provided? A dowry, whether a token tribute or large enough to constitute a bribe, was almost indispensable. The story of Cinderella was a popular motif of Renaissance literature, but in real life there were few princes to seek out the maiden, poor and blushing, on the hearth. If a dowry could not be scraped up or if the girl was too ugly to attract a man, she would often be put into a convent; nunneries were less expensive than husbands. In the upper strata of society, the choice of a daughter's husband was the parents', or rather the father's, while the mother, whatever her secret thoughts, endorsed the command, exactly as in *Romeo and Juliet*. It was a rare Juliet who refused a Paris. A marriage contracted against the father's will had no canonical validity.

Few women took part in public affairs, and fewer still could enter the professions and become doctors or lawyers. Girls in modest homes were educated on a catch-as-catch-can basis, less trouble being taken with them than with boys. In wealthier homes girls were more carefully reared, but their marriages were arranged at the earliest possible age, and therefore those who were best educated stopped their studies soonest. Only rarely did a young girl have a room of her own. In a crowded house, often including poor relatives who had no other place to go, little quiet and less isolation were available in which the daughter of the house could read and learn. A treatise of 1519 recommended that the man have "a place in his house to himself, free from cumbrance of women," but said nothing of the woman. Carpaccio's painting *The Dream of Saint Ursula*, in which the girl is sleeping in solitary comfort in a splendid room, was perhaps intended to show Ursula's exceptional status. Such privacy was a privilege not easily obtained.

As the fifteenth century turned into the High Renaissance, faith became feebler, at least among the educated classes. The piety of Fra Angelico was replaced by the choreography of Botticelli. Scholars juggled the question mark freely. Reading Aristotle and Plato in new translations, thinking men faced the fact that other viable philosophies existed before the teachings of Christ, though attempts were made to reconcile and combine the antique and the Christian views of the world. They did so without difficulty, since the mind can make itself believe anything it wants to believe. Gregovorius, in his *History of Rome*, tells us that during the pontificate of Leo X "God was again called Jupiter," the cardinals "Senators," and that Leo was apostrophized as descending from Olympus as Apollo.

With the broad mass, however, who did not read but heard sermons, religion still played a vital role, a dual role, frightening and consoling. One might scoff at the local priest, but the Vatican still exercised a pervading spiritual as well as temporal power. The Vatican said a woman should obey. In Italian Christianity the Madonna was as revered and as beloved a figure as Jesus; perhaps it is not exaggerating to find her a *more* beloved figure. She symbolized the virtues prized in a woman: humility, quietude, patience in adversity, orderliness, and cleanliness, as indicated by the spotless towel in countless Annunciations. The models for these Madonnas were usually not known beauties. They were either unknown girls whose faces, seen by the artist on some sun-drenched walk, had captured his imagination, or they were portraits of a woman the painter loved. Filippo Lippi used his favorite mistress, a nun; Titian's Mary in the great Assumption he painted for the Frari Church in Venice was his wife, who shortly after died in childbirth. The Madonna not only represented soft submission; she served as well as an ideal of beauty. As such she was, in the pictorial imagination of the High Renaissance, related to Venus.* The age looked at the naked body with a new joyful stare. Titian could not keep up with the commissions for the many portrayals of Venus ordered from him: Venus and Amor, Venus and Adonis, Venus and Mars, Venus with a page playing a musical instrument, Venus ministered to by a flock of putti, but always Venus in the full pride of her nudity; even Giovanni Bellini, after a lifetime of painting gentle Madonnas, broke loose in his old age with *The Feast of the Gods,* though he did not live to complete the work.

Physicians believed, and this belief was taught in the universities, that females were subject to more diseases, abnormalities, and weaknesses than were males. The prejudice seemed plausible because as one looked around, men were distinctly more in evidence than women. A visitor from England wrote that Italian cities seemed to be peacock farms, with the peacocks "marching up and down" and the peahens huddled in a corner.

Frequent pregnancies did not increase a woman's sexual attractiveness nor her desire for sexual play. Contraceptives were little used, though poor couples practiced interrupted intercourse. The church classified this as a sin, and priests inquired about it when the parishioner came to the confessional. Attempts were made to teach women—and for that matter men too—the finer points of lovemaking, but such instruction was by its very nature addressed

---

* Sometimes the Madonna was pictured with attributes of Venus, such as the seashell on which Venus rode, as in Piero della Francesca's great *Madonna and Saints,* painted for Federico Montefeltro of Urbino.

chiefly to the educated, many of the books and treatises being written in Latin. Mario Equicola, one of the lesser poets of the Renaissance, as well as a historian and biographer, who later served Isabella as secretary in Mantua, published a book which purported to tell the reader all he or she wanted to know about sex, or almost all. He called the little sex manual *Di Natura d'Amore* and dedicated it to Isabella d'Este:

The very great sensation of pleasure which we derive from coitus—[Aristotle] tells us—can be traced to those parts of the body where the orifices are found and those parts where the veins lie near the surface. It follows then that those parts should be played with, tickled and stroked. The feeling of pleasure evoked by this gentle movement will spread through the entire body. Nothing can be compared to its exquisite sensation.

. . . In this act of touching, argue the physicians, women receive more satisfaction than men. Galen and Avicenna adduce proofs to this effect. The prophet Tiresias, judging the make-believe contest between Jupiter and Juno, declared that a man had three measures of passion to give, a woman nine. To me this does not seem probable, because if it were so women would chase men, while the contrary is true. . . .

Love-making if practiced in moderation, the use of our physical capacity to perform the love-act, exalts our minds and makes us capable of noble deeds. Let us do it less frequently in the summer, more frequently in the winter, moderately in spring and autumn. . . . It has always been considered praiseworthy to recommend abstinence and chastity. No doubt that is a holy action. But I am compelled to say what I think and so I say that abstinence and too much retention can cause melancholy and infirmity . . . alienation of the mind, loss of pulse with coldness . . . disturbance of digestion, loss of appetite.

The double standard prevailed. Courtiers, soldiers, and princes cohabited with mistresses regularly and openly after marriage, and with prostitutes occasionally, and a gentleman of some importance simply had to have a mistress: in addition to the diversion she supplied, she served him as a status symbol. In theory the church frowned on the practice, but the local bishop condoned it, as he himself was usually living in concubinage. Illegitimate children became the rule, not the exception, among the noble houses, and such children were often brought up by the wife, along with and equivalent to the legitimate offspring. A bastard carried no badge of infamy. And, if it seemed advisable for reasons of inheritance, an illegitimate child could usually be legitimized by crossing a cardinal's palm. In short, aside from the ever-present danger of the *malum francicum*, the "French disease," there was no reason why a

Renaissance man should limit his "capacity to make love" to one partner.*

The Renaissance woman had to be governed by a different code. Castiglione in *The Courtier* censured the standard, "according to which a dissolute life is not a fault or degradation in us [men], whereas in women it is such utter disgrace and shame that a woman who has been slandered once, regardless of whether the charge is true or false, is disgraced for ever." A woman caught in adultery could be cruelly punished. Niccolò III d'Este, Marquis of Ferrara, grandfather of Isabella, three times married, sired in addition to four legitimate children a brood of illegitimate ones variously estimated as seven to ten, though he himself boasted that during his reign of thirty-nine years he slept with eight hundred women and fathered twenty-seven children. The Ferrarese said: "Left and right of the Po—everywhere children by Niccolò." But when Niccolò discovered that his second wife, the beautiful Parisina Malatesta, was having an affair with his illegitimate son Ugo (a persistent legend, still current, relates that Niccolò discovered Parisina's infidelity by means of an intricate mirror arrangement by which he looked across the courtyard of the Este palace into her chamber), raging and grieving and cursing, he wandered through the palace the whole night, until at dawn he ordered both wife and son beheaded. He then commanded that any and every Ferrarese woman convicted of adultery was to be condemned to death. (He soon had to withdraw the order: it might have decimated Ferrara's female population.) Though it all happened half a century before Isabella was born, they used to tell her the story, sparing none of the gruesome details: how Parisina ran through the rooms of the palace screaming, how pitifully Ugo pleaded with his father, and how Niccolò would not speak to them.

Marital fidelity, then, was the text preached to women. It was not always and not quite taken seriously. The desire to captivate often proved stronger than moral precepts. While young girls daydreamed, married women learned how to appear obediently faithful, and yet sidestep their vows. They were encouraged by a frankness of sexual discussion which became ever bolder as the Renaissance unfolded. The badinage of educated society was permeated by a healthful bawdiness. Poems, plays, and novelle told

* Syphilis was not known in Italy until about 1495, but then it swept the peninsula with great rapidity.

titillating tales, the outspokenness of which was not to be matched until recent times.

Matteo Bandello, a Dominican priest, gathered together the 214 stories he had written during a long lifetime, very unpriestly stories of love, lust, and violence, and published them in three volumes. His book became an enormously popular compendium. (It was probably his version of the Romeo and Juliet story which Shakespeare used as his source.) One of Bandello's most famous novelle (Part III, Number 46) was "The Greek Girl and the Fisherman." A young and pretty Greek woman, married to a landowner, comes upon a young fisherman. The fellow is sitting there, having stripped off his trousers, and so the girl can observe that the "staff which hangs between his legs is large enough to ring church bells." Sitting on the bank of the river, he uses it as a fishing pole. Intrigued, the girl invites him to her house, where in quick succession "they perform three dances together." The story of the fortunately endowed young man is bruited about and presently most of the good ladies of the village receive a sample of his potency, including the wife of the mayor. None of the husbands ever finds out.

Bandello's story, he tells us, was read one summer night to "Madama of Mantua" (Isabella) and "the gracious Duchess of Urbino." Neither the ladies nor the damsels of their retinue were shocked.

A woman of the upper class, if she was reasonably attractive, made the most of her attractions, prompted not only by the timeless and universal instinct of vanity, but by the spirit specific to and characteristic of the time, which was to bestrew everything everywhere with gay color. Banish the somber, hide fears behind a gaudy arras, decorate every manifestation of life—such was the motto of the Renaissance, and it included the beautification of one's person. The holiest altar of Saint George and the unholiest sword of a Borgia glittered with gold, shone with emeralds, and captured light with lapis lazuli, "blue as a vein o'er the Madonna's breast." Color was all around, intense and flattering, and the clothes of men were as colorful as the clothes of women, both taking delight in the brocades and the taffetas designed by artists, often great artists. Here too a distinction was drawn between the sexes. While sumptuary laws applied to men and to women, their purpose being to keep people from dressing above their station and to stem the flow of money abroad for imported material, in practice the men could dress as they pleased and nobody bothered them, but the women were sternly admonished to limit their caprices. In Venice a law stipulated that a girl's brocade dress could use only enough material to cover her figure. The Venetian women, of course, got around the edict. They wore dresses using yards and yards of material, but gathered the excess material in front and carried it on their arm, and the fashion spread to all of Europe. (Later, when the Venetian government tried to capture some of the fashion trade, they set up a life-sized doll in Piazza San Marco to display the coming styles.)

In an ambience where color streaked the vestments of priests, glowed in the miniatures of the breviaries, decked the armor of the professional soldier as well as the accoutrement of his horse, and bounced from frescoed walls and ceilings, it was impossible for the self-respecting lady of the house to remain drab. She spent hours on her toilet, and her cosmetics were numerous and expensive. "In no country of Europe since the fall of the Roman Empire was so much trouble taken to modify the face, the colour of the skin and the growth of the hair, as in Italy at this time [1500]. All tended to the formation of a conventional type, at the cost of the most striking and transparent deceptions," wrote Jacob Burckhardt. The lady had at her disposal "beautifying water" to cleanse the skin, astringent plaster, eye shadow, nail polish, pumice for the teeth, strawberry paste for her complexion, and perfumed oils for the breasts, the nipples of which were rouged. Perfume was often made at home and was used by both men and women; for special occasions, such as receptions and pageants, even horses and mules were sprayed with perfume.* A girl paid most attention to her hair, because Italian men took particular delight in a woman's tresses. Since the majority of women were brunettes, it was fashionable to be a blonde.** The sun was supposed to bleach the color of the hair, and women spent many a day sitting patiently in the sun, hair spread out, face covered, because a suntan was decidedly not fashionable. False hair and hair pieces were widely used, and such aids were made either of silk or of real hair, often imported from the north and more expensive if blond. The headdress was elaborately

---

* Even money was sometimes perfumed. Some of the objects extant from the Renaissance, particularly jewelry, still give out a faint perfume.

** In a famous lecture given at Prato, the philosopher Agnolo Firenzuola attempted to define the elements of female beauty. He prefers blond for the hair, which should be long and curly, "brightness" for the complexion but not dead white, strongly marked eyebrows, a mouth which when opened should not display more than six upper teeth, and so on, in great detail.

worked, and after it was finished it was stiffened with gum. For the "conventional type" the hair was shaved off the forehead to make the forehead look higher, pulled back, and then built into a maze intertwined with ribbons and jewels. The jewelry was created by such men as the Pollaiuolo brothers, the Vivarini family, Ghirlandaio (son of a goldsmith), Benvenuto Cellini, and Michelangelo. The combination of hair and jewels—a mixture of nature's play and the artist's work—can be seen, for example, in the bewitching profile portrait by Antonio Pollaiuolo, in the Milan Poldi-Pezzoli, of a girl any man would fall in love with at first sight.

Obviously we have no means of knowing how faithful to nature are the portraits of these beautiful women, how much flattery lay on the artist's palette, or what part of the enchantment sprang from the artist's mind. Yet as one looks at the many and diverse portraits of women, ranging from an imaginary Laura by Giorgione to a "factual" Ginevra Benci by Leonardo, one is confirmed in the conviction that, to a greater or lesser extent, the artists thought of their models as nymphs of the bedchamber.

Contemporary literature dealing with women was sharply divided: novelists and satiric poets loved to present women as deceivers, either adorable or merciless, but deceivers all; while the lyric and heroic poets created creatures impossibly noble, impossibly self-sacrificing. Yet even in the glorification lies condescension: a woman is important not for what she does for herself but for what she does for her lover. In the Romances it is the man who goes adventuring while the fair Italian Penelope sits in the castle.

At the end of the fifteenth century a few advocates did arise to discuss "the value of women." Three such treatises have survived: they were issued within a fifteen-year span, suggesting that one writer was influenced by or copied from the other, and, by coincidence, they can be connected with Ferrara and Mantua, the scenes of our story. Eleanora d'Este possessed a book by one Bartolomeo Gogio, *De Laudibus mulierum* (In Praise of Women), dedicated to her in 1487, which consists of seven sections, Gogio rather overdoing his argument by devoting four to a "proof" that women were actually superior to men. He plays safe by using no contemporary examples: his women are mythological and biblical. A similar work was written in Mantua by Agostino Strozzi, entitled *La Defensione de le donne*. Mario Equicola followed with his *De Mulieribus* (circa 1501), dedicated to Margarita Cantelma, a close friend of

Isabella d'Este's; but his book might have been not much more than a lover's tribute, Margarita Cantelma being his mistress.

Like most sermons, these defenses of women preached to the already converted and probably were read by women rather than by men. By and large it remained true—in the hovel as in the castle—that the birth of a girl child was greeted with less satisfaction than that of a boy, and that the female remained a second-class citizen.

<h2 style="text-align:center">2</h2>

Yet in discussing a society as multilayered and fragmented as that of the Renaissance, we must allow for as many exceptions as are contained in a German grammar. Not all husbands made excursions to strange beds; not all unions mocked marriage vows. Isabella's father, Ercole I, the enterprising and able Duke of Ferrara and Modena, who was married to the pretty but rather bland Eleanora of Aragon, daughter of the king of Naples, had five legitimate children and three illegitimate children (perhaps more), but Eleanora told her daughter often how contented and happy she was with her husband and how graciously he catered to her wishes. Isabella adored her mother, and all the children, at least the legitimate ones, looked up to the father. Isabella's nephew Ercole II (the enthusiasm for mythology made the name "Hercules" fashionable), married to Renée of France, lived in continuous love and harmony with his wife.

Similarly, whatever the orientation of the age, it could point to a few women of brave achievement: Caterina Sforza was a veritable Amazon, riding to battle when she was seven months' pregnant; cruel and tough, she hated her husband, yet fought for him and defended his city, Forlì, with fanatic courage against his murderers and against Cesare Borgia himself; though in the end she was vanquished, all Italy admired her. Vittoria Colonna wrote good poetry and filled her life after her husband was killed—twenty-two years of it—with works of charity and by aiding and inspiring scholars and artists. Late in his life she was Michelangelo's great and good friend, perhaps the only human being he trusted. Lucrezia Tornabuoni, married to Piero Medici and mother of Lorenzo the Magnificent, was not only a fair poet but an excellent businesswoman. She bought the sulfur springs at Morba and developed them into a fashionable health resort, adding the profits to the Medici fortune. In addition to Lorenzo, she gave birth to and reared four other children.

Yet these were the exceptions, birds who soared high above the flock, rare and to be marveled at.

3

We have noted that usually the choice of a husband was not made by the girl but by her father. The higher the social position of the family, the truer this was. A daughter from a reigning house, a girl whose father was head of a state—her marriage was not made in heaven but in the council chamber. She was used as a means to an alliance, traded off for political purposes. The prettier she was, and the richer, the greater her political value and the sharper the trading. If she could not perpetuate her family's name, she could help in the accretion of her family's power. Matrimonial alliances could often secure frontiers better than stone walls.

In a fractioned Italy, in which the smaller principalities were constantly in danger of being gobbled up by the larger, threatened now by military expeditions, now by plots of poison and poignard, the game of friendship, false and true, and as variable as mountain weather, was being played by all sovereigns. The four largest powers were Florence, the Republic of Venice, Milan, and the Papal States, the latter comprising a huge territory which one pope after another sought to aggrandize. The pope did not shy away from the dirtiest of political ploys, in the belief that dirtiness is next to Godliness, provided it enriched the possessions of the Church. The smaller states formed unstable leagues and unstable enmities, so that Mantua was often at odds with Ferrara, Urbino with Gubbio, Parma with Milan. Each state was as cabined and confined as a conjurer's tent. For a long time the country could not even agree on a common language: they all spoke some form of Italian, yet in Florence they called it "Tuscan" and in Foligno "Umbrian," and many pretended they could not reconcile the differences in the dialects. A ruling prince literally owned his realm:* he owned the

* Florence and Venice were "republics," though not in the sense in which we understand the word. Genoa, too, was nominally a republic, though actually a vassal state belonging to Milan. The southern territory centering in Naples

land, he owned the mines, he owned the fish in the river, and he owned his people, having complete authority to impose taxation, authority to punish crimes, authority to lead them to war. Quite a few of the princes ruled wisely, promoting the general welfare; yet, barring natural disasters, drought or pestilence, the best part of welfare flowed into the ruler's coffer. The larger the territory, the more copious the flow. Italy's earth and Italy's water produced most of Italy's wealth. Each prince's task was first to protect, then to enlarge, his territory. If marriage bonds or negotiated alliances proved ineffective, he summoned the soldier. An army was to be had for the paying, led by professional fighters, the condottieri, who were the experts at organizing the alarums and excursions, while the soldiers did the dirty work.

Here was the dark side of the bright age, the age in which the eighteenth-century poet Alfieri said, "The plant known as Man grew to its full flowering." The plant had thorns.

Ferrara was a small state, governed by the Estes since the thirteenth century. It had become vigorous under Isabella's grandfather, the child-producing Niccolò. Ercole I, his third son and Isabella's father, had succeeded him at the age of forty, and proceeded to strengthen the state further by regulating its finances, developing industry and agriculture, and undertaking a bold building program. He planned broad roads, straightened streets, and solidified fortifications. He even had a public park constructed, an exceptional boon to city dwellers. Historians point to Ferrara as the first example of consistent urban planning in Europe. Ercole supported the University, founded in the fourteenth century, which now, in the middle of the fifteenth century, was led by Guarino da Verona, professor of Greek and rhetoric, whose fame was so great that students used to stand for hours in freezing weather waiting to enter the room where he would lecture. This dedicated teacher would help poor students from his own purse, though he was not a rich man, and he invited pupils and friends to come and enjoy a dinner of "beans and conversation." In addition to Guarino, Ferrara University continued to attract a group of remarkable talents, among

---

was a monarchy, the "Kingdom of the Two Sicilies." Milan was a duchy, as was Ferrara. A number of smaller states, "owned" by their sovereigns (Savoy, Monferrato, Urbino, Verona, etc.), accounted for the split condition of a country which experienced almost all forms of government.

them the humanist Pico della Mirandola and the celebrated Philippus Aureolus Paracelsus, the brilliant physician who, in spite of his bombastic behavior and unbelievable boasting, did come forth with the revolutionary idea of treating disease by specific medicines rather than by bloodletting and purging.

Ercole's personal income, derived from monopolies, liens, custom duties, and other sources, was enormous, and though he had to pay the expense of a large standing army, he had enough money left over to spend on pageants and festivals, jousts and hunts, theater and works of art. He loved the theater. He was hardly one of the outstanding patrons of art—he was a bit too careful with his ducats —but he knew its representational and touristic value. Ferrara became a city worth visiting. Dosso Dossi's portrait of Ercole* shows a strong face, clean shaven, tight lips, an assertive nose; it gives the impression of a man who thought pretty well of himself. He is dressed as a soldier, but he was less of a soldier than a diplomat, skilled at weaving those secret alliances which formed the fabric of Renaissance policy.

He was already forty-three years old when Eleanora, after two miscarriages, gave birth to their first child. It was a girl. The mother wrote to her friend Barbara Gonzaga of Mantua a letter in which joy is somewhat muted:

> Thinking of the love and esteem which unites us both, I should like duly to inform Your Magnificence of the blessing which God has bestowed on us through a birth. Consequently I hereby impart to you the news that God's grace has given us last Tuesday around the second hour** a pretty little baby girl, and that after the birth we feel well and are in good condition . . . . If we have said nothing to the others, except yourself and your daughter Madonna Margherita, who is like a sister to us, the reason lies in the fact that it is not customary to send any formal notice when a girl is born . . . .

The date was May 19, 1474. The girl was named Isabella.

* The painting was done not from life but nineteen years after Ercole's death. Dossi probably modeled it on an earlier portrait by Ercole Roberti.
** Probably about 9 P.M. In Italy the hours were then reckoned from 1 to 24, starting at sunset.

II

Preparation of a Princess

A little girl from a great house: either she had to learn practically nothing, growing up to the task of making herself desirable to a man—or she had to learn a great deal. Isabella had to learn a great deal.

To boys and girls of middle-class homes, elementary schools were available, but education was not compulsory and most children went to school only between the ages of eight and eleven, being taught reading and writing. While exact figures are unavailable, the degree of literacy in the Italy of the fifteenth century seems to have been high.* In the commercial centers a few boys—no girls—went on between the ages of eleven and fourteen; there was still some propaganda around that girls, "unless they were to be nuns, should be taught not to read, but to sew." Children of noble families did not go to school. They were taught by private tutors, and the extent of their education depended on the father's decision.

In a family in which there are little sisters, one is usually "the beauty" and the other "the brains." Beatrice d'Este, born a year after Isabella, was the beauty, Isabella was the brains. Ercole early saw to it that she cultivated her mind. She was quite willing to do so, though of course nobody asked her.

Isabella's most important subject, aside from the fundamentals of reading, writing, and the catechism, was Latin. As a second language it was indispensable, the language in which most of the instructive and many of the entertaining books were penned, as well as the language in which one communicated with the bishops, scholars, and ambassadors who came to Ferrara from foreign coun-

---

* John Larner, in *Culture and Society in Italy, 1290–1420*, writes that it was claimed that 60 to 80 percent of the lay population in Florence was to some extent literate. He believes this figure to be exaggerated.

tries. Latin in books, Latin on the monuments, Latin for the official documents, Latin intoned at the morning Mass, Latin all around, giving voice to the worship of the antique. How could one enjoy those romps of Plautus which were enacted under the open sky at Ferrara as often in the original as in translation, how could one endure those long poetry readings on winter evenings, how could one take part in the process, which seemed so vital to every educated man and woman, of excavating the ancient stones from the ground on which one walked, in short how could one partake of the "rebirth," the "renaissance" of the ancestral world, if one's knowledge of the language was limited? Battista Guarino, son of the famous scholar, was Isabella's first Latin teacher and drilled her in the irregular verbs—Isabella was no older than five. Shortly they progressed to Cicero's *Epistles* and, after a year or two, haltingly read the *Eclogues* of the beloved Virgil—verses suitable for a young girl—and, as Isabella's facility grew, the *Aeneid,* which she could hardly understand. Being the tutor of a princess is a delicate position, but both Battista and his successor Jacopo Gallini seem to have enjoyed it, in later years reminding Isabella that they had "good days" together when they turned the pages of the Latin grammar and when they construed the *Aeneid* "with rare grace and fluency." One wonders what effect the pressure of teaching exerted on the little girl. Did all that studying help develop her intellectual keenness, her critical faculty, and her ability to think a problem through? Or were the demands made on her responsible for instilling in her character a certain disdain, an intransigence toward those who knew less or were less endowed? In after years, she was always ready to display her learning, and she let no one forget that she was reputed "to speak Latin better than any woman of her time."

As a child she was given instruction in music, learned to sing, to play the lute and the viola, and acquired some facility on the portable reed organ, an instrument which was highly prized and which one can see in many a Renaissance painting, played by a preoccupied angel. She did not have much talent for music, as she herself confessed; when the poet Gian Trissino wrote that her voice "lured the Sirens from their rocks and charmed wild beasts," he was evidently paying her a poet's compliment. They tried to teach her French, too, but she didn't take to it, and in later years she refused to speak it even when doing so could have helped her politically. She thought the language ugly.

What an extraordinary little girl she must have been! Her vari-hued personality was shaped by contrasting influences: she had but to run five minutes away from her home and she was in the middle of an untouched field, where she could pluck as many flowers as she wanted, or lie still and dream. Beyond that field stood a forest, thick and dark; they told her to be careful—it was full of wild boars. No boar ever came near the little princess, but the promise of danger made the excursion more tempting. A few miles off flowed the broad Po; there she was taken to fish and swim. Yet when she returned home she sensed danger less understandable but more real than the hoofbeat of a strange animal. Somebody was threatening her father: she could hear the hoofbeats of the horses of the soldiers when she woke up in the morning—they were riding around the castle in a continuous watch. Ercole told her not to worry, but to read her Virgil.

The Castle was an austere building, as ancestral dwellings were wont to be. It was huge (it still seems huge in modern Ferrara, dominating the city), and therefore it was a good place in which to play hide-and-seek. Her mother's room was her favorite spot, where, as close to the fireplace as possible, she could listen to stories of ghosts and witches. The Castello served as both a fortress and a home; imposing from the outside with its stern walls and crenellated towers, it was plain enough when you got inside, and it displayed luxury only on festive occasions. On weekdays the food was simple, simply served. However broad the pomp when somebody came to visit, when the family was alone the servants bustled about in plainest clothing, and until the year of Isabella's birth the pages at court slept on straw in dark rooms. Then linen bedsacks were ordered not so much out of consideration for their comfort as to prevent their dragging wisps of straw through the palace. In Eleanora's bedroom Isabella could look at several paintings by such artists as Rogier van der Weyden (who had worked in Ferrara and showed Italian artists how better to use oil in painting) and Pisanello; when she went into her father's study she saw above his desk a crucifix by Jacopo Bellini, and when she was allowed to play in the great official apartments, Piero's frescoes surrounded her. Isabella no doubt much preferred the summer palace, just outside the city, which had been built only five years before her birth and which was called with wishful thinking Schifanoia (Banish Boredom), as Frederick the Great was to call his Potsdam palace Sans Souci. Schifanoia was indeed a fairy tale of a place, filled to the brim with curiosities a child was not allowed to touch, but which she could admire: fascinating miniatures, illuminated little prayerbooks, strange majolica plates from Faenza which displayed an artificial fish or a three-dimensional snake and which were more suitable for show than for dining, jeweled caskets, crystal reliquaries, bronze medals by that master medalist Sperandio, painted chests which contained glittering fabrics fine for dressing up in, huge tapestries from Flanders; while such walls as were not covered by tapestries shone with new-finished frescoes by Francesco Cossa, depicting the year-round pleasures to be squeezed from life, month by month. March is for pruning trees, April—dedicated to Venus—the time for making love, May the time for excursions, led by Apollo, into forests and fields, and so on.*

Still another place Isabella loved—in later life she referred to it nostalgically—was the villa of Belriguardo (Beautiful View) on the banks of the Po. It was said to contain as many rooms as the year has days; that is probably exaggerated, but her father was always ordering improvements and enlargements, and there were rooms enough for Cosimo Tura and later for the gentle Ercole Roberti to beautify.

Her most frequent playmate when she went fishing on the bank of the Po or riding in the forest—always, to be sure, watched by a small retinue—was her little sister. Even as a baby Beatrice was beautiful and gay, looking like a blissful putto, ready to be painted into an altarpiece for the Madonna or serve as helper to Venus. "What an exquisite child!" everybody said.

Isabella in her own right was an attractive child, a bit on the pudgy side, but with lively eyes and of lively grace. When she was seven her father asked the Duke of Urbino to lend him his dancing master, one Ambrogio, who was a Jew. Ambrogio taught Isabella

---

* Alas, only seven of these frescoes remain visible and those imperfectly. In the eighteenth century the palace was turned into a tobacco factory, and not only Cossa's murals but those by Cosimo Tura and others were covered with whitewash. In the middle of the nineteenth century the work of restoring them began, but at first this work was done ineptly and at best what remains now seems pale and weary. Only when one remembers how much Renaissance art has been destroyed and yet how much remains can one form an idea of the wealth produced in those two centuries.

how a princess should move, sit, behave, but although the girl
loved to dance, and danced before she received formal instruction,
she preferred reading even to dancing, while Beatrice disliked
reading, disliked Latin, and had to be forced to stay indoors and
learn anything at all.

When finally, a year after Beatrice, the longed-for male heir was
born, great was the rejoicing and long the festivities, and little Isabella must soon have realized that a girl was a girl but a boy was
something else again. He was to become Alfonso I, the third Duke
of Ferrara and Modena. Ercole was forty-five when Alfonso came
into the world, but that wasn't the end of making children. Three
years later another son was born, Ippolito, who was at once destined for a churchly career, as was the custom; thanks to Ercole's
heavy contributions to the coffers of Pope Innocent VIII, Ippolito
was made an archbishop at the ripe age of eleven and a cardinal at
fourteen and eventually became one of the most learned and most
profligate prelates of his time. The next year came another son,
Sigismondo.

Surrounded by the court's dwarfs and buffoons and cavaliers, by
manuscripts and books which were so large that a child could
hardly carry them, surrounded by music and by the pageantry of
Catholicism, Isabella might have had the wealthy little girl's conventional "happy childhood"—she *did* have a happy childhood—had
it not been for the discord and derangement inherent in her time.
She could only have had a dim recollection of the September day
when she was two years old and, her father being absent, her
mother suddenly gathered her three little children and, pale and
frightened, locked herself with them in the most secure room of the
Castello. Eleanora had been warned. Ercole's nephew Niccolò, an
illegitimate son of Ercole's brother, had pressed a claim to Ferrara.
It had been ignored. He had sat in Mantua brooding revenge. Now,
with his uncle away, he thought his chance had come. With seven
hundred soldiers he marched into Ferrara and proclaimed himself
sovereign. He threw the city into a turmoil, but the invasion turned
out to be a dilettantish effort: not enough soldiers, not enough
bribes. Ercole's troops proved loyal and conquered the invaders,
while the people of the city declared themselves for Ercole. Niccolò
was captured, condemned, executed, and then—how characteristic
of Renaissance politics!—buried with full military honors. Nothing

was ever said of the fact that Ercole had tried previously to get rid
of his troublesome nephew by having *him* poisoned.

Yet Ercole, who fundamentally was a peace-loving ruler, did not
remain long at peace. The Pazzis, ruthless rivals of the Medici,
planned to kill Lorenzo the Magnificent. On Easter Sunday, 1478,
they attacked him in the Florence cathedral, but succeeded only in
murdering his younger brother Giuliano. The crime shocked an
Italy used to violence, and Florence at once proceeded against the
Pazzis. During the wild street fighting which ensued, the Floren-
tines, crying for revenge, hanged the Archbishop of Florence. Pope
Sixtus IV—who most historians think was behind the Pazzi conspiracy all along—took that as his cue to excommunicate Lorenzo and
declare war against Florence. Naples joined the pope. But Ercole,
believing that a papal victory would endanger Ferrara, took
Florence's part and indeed was presently appointed general of the
antipapal forces. Consequently, his was the strange fate of opposing his wife's father. The war lasted for two years and tore much of
Italy into bloody strips, until the Turks, always fixing their beady
glances westward, threatened to invade Italy. Then they all made a
hasty peace.

Two years later, in 1482, Girolamo Riario, the pope's nephew and
leader of the papal forces, suggested to his power-hungry uncle
that Ferrara was a prize worth taking. Once more, war. Now
Ferrante of Naples, changing sides, sent troops to help his son-in-
law; Milan and Florence took Ercole's part; Venice allied itself with
the pope, and after a year of indecisive and general killing, Sixtus,
threatened from north and south and by riots in Rome itself, made
peace. That didn't at all suit the Venetians: their troops had advanced to within four miles of Ferrara's walls, driving the peasants
into the city, where the besieged citizens faced starvation, and after
all that, the Venetians were not going to lose their advantage.
Sixtus promptly excommunicated them and joined his recent enemies, Florence and Milan, in driving the doge's soldiers back to
their water-lapped islands. Ferrara was saved. For a time Italians
could return to loving their artists and hating their neighbors.

The long and short of it was that through most of Isabella's childhood, behind the gay noise of lances clashing in jousts, of heralds
summoning spectators to pageants, of hunting parties galloping
over the fields, of lutes plucked in soft accompaniment to lovers'
plaints, of the professional laughter of buffoons trying to induce

their little audience to laugh, behind the pleasant sounds of living
well, war played its detonating obbligato. Even a child as protected
as a princess could not have been deaf to it, nor have failed to observe her father's worried look. Isabella learned as well something
of the putrescence of politics. Sitting at the dinner table and only
half-understanding the conversation, she heard her parents discussing Pope Sixtus. He spent such fortunes on his debauched nephews,
Pietro and Girolamo, that the Romans whispered that they were
really his sons, and Stefano Infessura wrote that they were his homosexual playmates. (Infessura wrote a famous history of fifteenth-
century Rome, but he hated the popes so passionately that his
accusations cannot be taken without question.) Sixtus financed his
wars by selling ecclesiastical titles to the highest bidder. At a time
when moderate freedom of thought and expression prevailed, he
suddenly approved the suppression of books the Inquisition deemed
subversive. And yet this most unscrupulous of pontiffs beautified
Rome by straightening and widening streets, improving its water
supply, adding 1,100 volumes to the 2,500 of the Vatican library,
and designing a lordly bridge over the Tiber, the Ponte Sisto. He
ordered the building of two exquisite churches, the little Santa
Maria della Pace, with its Raphael frescoes, and Santa Maria del
Popolo, as rich as a queen's jewel box. It was at his instigation, too,
that the Sistine Chapel was built, for the decoration of which he
summoned to Rome Italy's most eminent artists, whether their
homes lay in friendly or hostile cities. (Perugino, Signorelli, Pinturicchio, Ghirlandaio, Botticelli, and Piero di Cosimo were some of
them.) The glory and the infamy of the Renaissance met in Sixtus.

When Isabella was ten years old, Sixtus died, leaving debts of
some 150,000 ducats (about $3 million in today's equivalent).
Roman mobs broke into the Vatican granaries, hacking at Girolamo's palace, while the noble families met in armed clashes, each
trying to get the upper hand by choosing a new pope. A hasty conclave elected Pope Innocent VIII, a Genoese, as a compromise; he,
it was said, was not overly endowed with brains but seemed at least
an amiable man.

Isabella, now a teenager, began to understand what the world
around her was like. Yet Rome seemed far away and unreal, as far
away and as unreal as that strange monk in Florence called Savonarola, who demanded the "burning of worldly vanities." Real were
those Latin authors whose books she devoured with ever-increasing

zeal; real was Dante. Her mother owned a *Divine Comedy,* bound in blue velvet, the clasps of silver encrusted with rubies and diamonds, and sometimes when the book would be carefully lifted off the table, Isabella was allowed to fondle the binding if her hands were clean, and her mother would read with her some verses with an ancient sound to them.

2

Long before, she had had her first taste of travel. Incredible though it seems, Eleanora decided to take the three-year-old Isabella and the two-year-old Beatrice to visit their grandfather in Naples, leaving their infant brother at home. The occasion was the second marriage of Grandpapa, King Ferrante. That was probably just an excuse: Eleanora wanted to show off her two little girls—and, political considerations never absent, she wished to affirm anew the Ferrara-Naples relationship. Ercole approved. Then, too, she thought she would discuss with Ferrante her husband's idea, already broached, of selecting a husband for Isabella.

To undertake such a journey was indeed venturesome at a time when it took two days to ride from Perugia to Urbino, a distance of sixty-five miles, and one marvels at the enthusiasm with which the people of the fifteenth century voyaged over roads which the rains turned into mud ponds, and where marauders endangered possessions and life itself, and mosquitoes stung the voyager with vicious bites which could cause malarial infection. Yet off these intrepid people went, trotting over extreme distances, from Mantua to London, from Rome to Innsbruck. There were inns and hostelries available in some of the larger cities—in the fourteenth century one hears of tourist hotels in Venice, such as the Duck, the Melon, the Lobster, the Hat, and these were inspected for cleanliness by a special tourist police—but most of these inns were filthy, and the stretches between them offered no shelter to the traveler overtaken by darkness. Eleanora traveled with a protective retinue from court to court and had no need of public accommodations, yet it was a cumbersome venture and the journey could not have been completed in less than a month. But completed it was, and the grandfather was as delighted with his two grandchildren as grandfathers usually are. As a ruler Ferrante was as ruthless as they came in those ruthless years; as a man he was debauched and sexually cruel; as a family man he was all honey to his daughter and her little girls. They stayed for several months, and Isabella became the favorite of her Uncle Federigo (later king of Naples), who said that he would like to marry her, but she was a bit young for him. Beatrice was Ferrante's favorite, and when it came time to leave, he begged Eleanora to let Beatrice remain. In Naples she could be taught the refinement needful for a princess of the world. Beatrice remained; Isabella returned with her mother.

A few of us experience in our childhood the good fortune of knowing somebody who fulfills for us the function of an idol; that man or woman, to whom we look up in fresh wonder and innocent imitation, can guide the path of our interests more effectively than the preoccupied father or the too familiar mother. Little Isabella had her idol, the elegant and handsome Niccolò da Correggio. His mother was one of the illegitimate daughters of old Niccolò Este, and therefore a half-sister of Ercole's, and Correggio had been brought up at the Ferrara court. He may well have served as the model for Castiglione's man-of-the-world. He set the fashion for men's clothing, sounded the tone for courtly converse, knew all the rules of the tournament; but he was far more than a perfumed Osric, being a poet, or at least a versifier, of some ability, ready at short notice to produce a precisely rhymed sonnet, to spin a witty quatrain, or to improvise a quotable epigram. His Latin was of course impeccable.

Ercole took pleasure in Correggio's company, and both of them took a great interest in theatrical performances, especially of the twelve comedies by Plautus, the texts of which had been found early in the century. They decided to give the *Menaechmi* of Plautus, translated into Italian verse, and for this production elaborate scenery was constructed in the courtyard of the Castle, providing the many entrances and exits which a comedy of errors requires. Musicians, actors, costumers, and torchbearers were hired and instructed, and the text revised, with Correggio supervising everything and perhaps turning for a point or two to the little Latin scholar. Isabella, twelve years old, was present at all the rehearsals, her eyes shining, getting in everybody's way. Ferrara's populace was invited to the performance, which lasted for many hours, the play being interspersed with pantomimic mythological scenes, dances, songs, and rough jokes by the clowns. The date was January 25, 1486; it is considered a pivotal date in the history of the theater, being the first full-scale "modern" presentation of a play. After that success, performances were given every year except when war intervened.

Neither the excitement of theatrical performances nor his building projects, nor the problems of administration, let Ercole forget that he had two daughters, both attractive children, and that their natural destiny was to augment Ferrara's power. First, Isabella—to whom should she be promised? Of various possibilities, Mantua seemed both most practical and most desirable. There the Gonzagas had ruled for a century uninterruptedly and satisfactorily; Mantua was relatively safe from the upheaval of revolutions. In 1432 Gianfrancesco Gonzaga I had been elevated to the rank of "Marquis," a hereditary title. He is remembered because he summoned to Mantua and there supported Vittorino da Feltro, one of the great teachers of the Renaissance.

In a house called Casa Zojosa (Joyous House) Vittorino lived with his boys and taught them the Greek ideal of the cultivated mind in a cultivated body, shaping that ideal to suit the contemporary world so as to produce *l'uomo universale*, the universal man of the Renaissance. His teaching included such disparate subjects as Platonic philosophy and fencing, Christian ethics and wrestling. Vittorino lived simply, despised fame, took as pupils those he thought promising, no matter what their social status or the pleas uttered by ambitious parents, despised wealth, wore the same clothing in winter as in summer, and made the marquis support as many as sixty indigent scholars and supplemented the subvention from his own pocket. He died a pauper, and Gianfrancesco had to pay for his funeral, but some part of Vittorino's greatness lived on in his pupils.

Lodovico Gonzaga, Gianfrancesco's son, was one of them. He had been a fat and self-indulgent little boy; Vittorino made him reduce, gave him self-confidence, taught him discipline, instilled in him an appreciation for art and letters. The result was that Lodovico felt such reverence for his teacher that he refused to sit in Vittorino's presence, and when he succeeded his father, he collected a superb library, established a printing press, gave commissions to the architect Leon Battista Alberti, invited Donatello, and after several futile tries persuaded the dour and difficult Mantegna to come to Mantua, where the painter remained until his death, complaining, scowling, and painting masterpieces.

The only one of Mantegna's masterpieces still to be seen in Mantua is the decoration of the Camera degli Sposi (Hall of the Betrothed), created in honor of the betrothal of Lodovico's son, Federigo I. Here, in finely preserved frescoes, the Gonzaga family is assembled, a domestic scene so vivid, so lifelike, that the spectator feels himself an intruder. In a vernal landscape these elegant ladies and gentlemen perform a ceremony of welcome, all joy and courtesy, the courtesy embracing even the pet dogs and the pet dwarf. But as you look closer, not a few of those faces bear a mean, tough, greedy look, the look of the freebooter. If, before leaving, one glances at the ceiling, one perceives a different facet of the Renaissance imagination. There Mantegna painted a flowered balcony on the balustrade of which winged putti disport themselves, climbing precariously in and out of the apertures of the railing, one holding a laurel wreath, one an apple, the third a staff; several festively dressed ladies, a Negress among them, peer into the room, while an arrogant peacock surveys the scene. The center of this scene of dizzying perspective is the open sky painted in an endless vista, symbolizing, perhaps, that this sunny life was to continue forever. The painting was called by its contemporaries "The Eye of God"; God was a master of ceremonies.

It was Federigo's son, Gianfrancesco, a boy eight years older than Isabella, whom Isabella's parents considered as a candidate for her hand. Mantua's territory was smaller than Ercole's domain, but it lay between Ferrara and the Duchy of Milan and was bounded on the north by the Republic of Venice, a strategic buffer position which could serve as a protective shield against the Venetians, and suggested an alliance to Ferrara as a wise diplomatic move. Negotiations were begun and an inquiry sent to Federigo. Isabella was then six years old.

From the Gonzaga point of view, a marriage into the lofty Este family seemed equally desirable, not the least reason being that Ferrara's military defenses were efficient. And the Estes were socially superior to the Gonzagas because they could trace their ancestors back further.

Nevertheless, the prospective bridegroom's father wanted to know what kind of a girl this Isabella was. Was she presentable?

Was she gracious? Was she intelligent? Would she grow up capable of being the wife of a ruling prince? Federigo sent one of his trusted diplomats, Beltramino Cusatro, to Ferrara to inspect the proposed daughter-in-law. Cusatro reported:

Donna Isabella was conducted to our room and we involved her in conversation. I and some others asked her questions on different subjects, to all of which she replied with such good sense and so ready a tongue that I marveled that a child of six could give such intelligent answers. I had heard about her singular intelligence, yet I would not have believed the extent of it. Madonna [Isabella's mother] promised me her counterfeit painted from life, which is to be sent to Your Excellency. [April 1480]

Cosimo Tura did Isabella's portrait (now lost), for which he was paid six ducats (about $120), and Cusatro promptly dispatched it with a note, saying that "Your Highness and Gianfrancesco may see her face, but I can assure you that her extraordinary knowledge and intelligence are far more worthy of admiration." Cusatro's favorable impression was confirmed by another Mantuan visitor, who wrote the marquis that he saw Isabella dancing and that "the grace and elegance of her movements were amazing in one of her tender age."

Agreement between Ferrara and Mantua having been concluded, Isabella's engagement to Gianfrancesco was duly announced on May 28, 1480, nine days after her sixth birthday. It was, of course, an occasion for a great festival. Just before the engagement, Ercole had received an inquiry from the Sforza family in Milan. Would he consider Isabella's becoming the bride of Lodovico Sforza ("Il Moro"), who within a year was to assume the regency of Milan? The prospective bridegroom was twenty-three years older than the proposed bride. That didn't seem to matter. What mattered once again was alliance of power, Milan gaining as much from Ferrara as Ferrara from Milan. Ercole replied he was sorry—he must have been *very* sorry, because Milan was a lot more important than Mantua—but Isabella had already been promised, the agreement settled. Would the Sforza consider his other daughter, a year younger, but attractive? They would. Lodovico would have to wait for a few years and console himself with mistresses, but at the proper time he could conduct home that beautiful child, grown up. The Beatrice-Lodovico engagement was announced on the very same day as the Isabella-Gianfrancesco engagement, a day on which Ercole could well have been pleased with his matchmaking skill.

Acquaintance followed engagement. In the autumn of the year, the fourteen-year-old Gianfrancesco was sent to Ferrara, where he beheld, with little interest and some embarrassment, his future wife. He had nothing to say about her in his letter home, but plenty to say about the sumptuous reception, how Duke Ercole and a large band of knights rode out to meet him, how the duke dismounted and took him by the hand and personally led him to the city, while the trumpets blared and the drums rolled, and how he was then treated to an enormous meal. A little later they organized a very exciting hunt for him. Still later, a huge horse race, won—honestly or not—by a Gonzaga horse. He does say that once he "played a game" with Isabella, but what the game was he does not specify, and he quickly dropped what seemed to be a boring subject.

These official meetings and receptions were governed by a rigid ceremonial, according to the rank of the dignitaries. Two processions would ride to a previously designated location. A duke would dismount before a king and bend his knee, but if both men were of equal rank, neither would dismount, and the host would first speak to the guest from horseback. The fact that Duke Ercole dismounted to greet the son of a marquis indicates that he wanted to extend exceptional honors to his young visitor. The Renaissance gesture of welcome was traditional as well: the right hand held upright at ninety degrees from the wrist. (One sees the gesture in Mantegna's Camera degli Sposi, where Lodovico Gonzaga greets his son.)

Two years later, during the Venetian war, Beatrice and Isabella were moved from Ferrara to Modena, a safer city. Isabella fell ill there; a record of expenditures kept by Eleanora shows an entry (May 22, 1483) for the fees of two physicians sent to Modena. Eleanora, it is certain, was deeply troubled. Away from home, with a war going on, her child was seriously enough ill to warrant the summoning of two doctors. On that same May 22, Isabella wrote a letter to Gianfrancesco, acknowledging a few little gifts he had sent her "which had delighted her so greatly that she almost felt well again. . . . When they told me Your Excellency may be willing to come to Modena to find out if my condition had taken a turn for the worse, I would almost have been glad to be ill, just to see you here."

Though the letter is written in Isabella's handwriting, its stilted style indicates that somebody, probably her mother, dictated the polite inanities to her. Isabella recovered soon enough from her illness, which seems to have been a gastric disturbance; later in life she was again subject to intestinal upsets.

The next year Federigo Gonzaga died, and Gianfrancesco succeeded him as ruler of Mantua. He was eighteen. Gradually the relation between the two young people became closer, though distance separated them. They began to exchange little poems, and the gifts increased in costliness: tapestries, medallions—he sent her his portrait as a medallion—gold rings, pectorals, musical instruments for the court musicians, even one or two exotic animals to be exhibited in the garden of the palace. Isabella wrote that she heard her fiancé liked to ride wild horses; he ought to be careful, that was very dangerous. Eleanora wrote, in age-old mother-in-law fashion, that he ought not to be too lavish in his expenditures; one heard of money troubles in Mantua. Five hundred servants and more than six hundred horses—they gobbled up a wicked sum.

In spite of such advice, Gianfrancesco liked his future mother-in-law and wished to please her. She very much wanted to own a painting by Mantegna. That was easier wished for than done. True, Mantegna was in the employ of the Gonzagas, which meant theoretically that he was obliged to execute any commission his employer required. Practically, however, the artist was too famous and too recalcitrant to be dictated to. We have some evidence on this point. When the Duke of Milan wrote to Federigo that he would dearly love to own a Mantegna and sent a suggestion for a design, Federigo had to reply:

> I received the design you sent and urged Andrea Mantegna to turn it into a finished form. He says it is more a book illustrator's job than his, because he is not used to painting little figures. He would do much better a Madonna or something, a foot or a foot and a half long, let's say, if you are willing. . . . [1480]

Nothing came of this.

Now, when Gianfrancesco learned about Eleanora's wish, they tried once again. He sent a note to the painter, enclosing Eleanora's letter.

. . . We trust you will satisfy this lady and use the utmost diligence to finish the picture, and we beg of you to put forth all your powers, as we feel sure you will do, and that as quickly as possible, since we are most desirous to gratify the said illustrious Madonna. [Nov. 6, 1485]

A week later Gianfrancesco inquired again:

We do not know if you have yet put your hand to the work, so now we repeat that you must finish it as quickly as possible, seeing that we greatly desire this thing, in order to satisfy the wish of the said lady as soon as feasible. . . .

A month later Mantegna had just begun the work, Gianfrancesco spurring him on by telling him it was meant to be a Christmas present—and that "we will see to it that you are well rewarded and your labor not wasted."

Three days later:

. . . We are sure that in finishing this picture you will use such diligence as will do you honor, and that it will bring you no small glory. And as Lodovico of Bologna is going to Venice, you had better see him about that varnish, if you have not already spoken to him, that he may bring or send you some without delay.

The mixture of admonition, promise of reward, and personal appeal proved effective. Mantegna finished the picture, though probably not in time for Christmas, and Gianfrancesco took it to Ferrara. It is almost certainly the "Painting on Panel of Our Lady and Her Son with Seraphim by the Hand of Mantegna" described in a Ferrara inventory and now in the Brera Museum in Milan.

The wedding was first planned for 1486, when Isabella would be *twelve*. It was postponed a year and further postponed, at Eleanora's suggestion, because, said the mother, the health of her child was still not perfect and she was unable to undergo the strain of marriage and transplanting to a strange city. In the meantime, she invited Gianfrancesco to visit them "so that both of you can gradually fall in love." Perhaps Eleanora tried to postpone the marriage because she hated to face separation from her first-born; perhaps her hand could not stop caressing the face of that small eager girl. Certainly, after Isabella left, Eleanora wrote her more than once that she missed her terribly. For several years she left her daughter's room unused, the shutters closed; she would not enter the room.

The last matter to be settled was the size of the dowry. Here sentiment stopped and sharp bargaining began. From Mantua came one Girolamo Stanga, with full power to settle the business. He reported:

Their Excellencies [the Estes] propose to give good and beautiful jewelry valued at 8,000 ducats [$160,000]; then a silver service worth more than 2,000; further our own dishes, which are now in the hands of Francesco Baldi in Venice [probably a banker or pawnbroker], will be redeemed; further the ruby which belongs to Lorenzo in Florence; that altogether amounts to 7,000 ducats. She herself [Isabella] will bring 3,000 ducats. As to the rest of the sum, which will add up to 25,000 ducats, they will give us debentures written on Modena and payable within eighteen months. I know there are other gifts, in addition to the dowry, which Madama [Eleanora] proposes to deed to her daughter and which are worth between 8,000 and 10,000 ducats. It is certain that Their Excellencies love their daughter so much that they do not seem to be able to do enough for her. If Your Magnificence had heard the eloquent excuses of Their Excellencies, as they complained of the [cost of the] last war and the depressed times, you would have become convinced that they had every intention of doing more and giving more. . . .

In point of fact, all this amounted to a rather modest marriage portion, as marriage portions of noble houses went, and the suspicion lies near that Stanga was purposely trying to make it look as generous as possible, whether for selfish or kindly reasons it is impossible to say. Had he been bribed? Or had the Estes dazzled him? Ercole Este was not known to part lightly with a ducat. Eleanora's dowry had amounted to 80,000 ducats, nearly twice as much. A dowry of 100,000 was not exceptional. Anna Sforza brought Alfonso Este (Isabella's brother) 150,000 ducats. When Emperor Maximilian I consented to marry Bianca Maria Sforza, a stupid and unprepossessing girl, he got 400,000 ducats.

The trousseau, however, was a splendid one, and its preparation took many months. According to custom, a princess had to wear at her wedding the "belt of majesty." A Milanese goldsmith, Fra Rocco, was paid no less than 600 ducats ($12,000)—more than the price of a major altar painting—to fashion the belt. The two most precious materials used in painting were gold and ultramarine, and contracts for works of art often specified the use of these materials, the price of the object depending on it.* Ercole Roberti was charged with the task of obtaining enough gold, ultramarine, lacquer, and other materials to paint thirteen cassoni, the decorated cases which contained the bride's possessions. After a special buying trip to Venice, he used eleven thousand pieces of gold leaf for these paintings, and he supervised as well the construction and decoration of the nuptial bed and that of the coach in which Isabella was to make her entry into Mantua. The date of that entry was to be February 16, 1490, which the court astrologer recommended as favorable.

Mantua, too, made suitable preparations. Isabella's reception in Mantua was to be a regal one, and guests were invited from the papal and the French courts, from Florence and Milan, from Naples and Venice. Two weeks before her arrival, the export of foodstuffs was forbidden and all fish was requisitioned in order to feed the expected guests. Gianfrancesco issued a public invitation to any qualified knight to take part in a great tournament, the winner to be rewarded with 200 ducats. Altogether the bridegroom wanted to match the bride's luxury with his own, but that was somewhat difficult. Though that vast and sprawling palace contained art objects enough, he was not content, and he borrowed from his wealthy brother-in-law, the Duke of Urbino, silver vessels, majolica plates, and tapestries, including a famous series of Flemish tapestries which depicted scenes of the Trojan War. He gave various silversmiths various commissions amounting to 8,747 ducats. To raise money for the traditional "morning gift" from bridegroom to bride to compensate her for her loss of virginity, Gianfrancesco mortgaged three of his houses. Yet the tightness of cash in no way restricted his largess. He liked the grand gesture. We get an idea of the luxury with which he dressed through a memorandum in which he bids everybody look for a ruby which had fallen off one of his cloaks and "which is large and worth about a thousand ducats."

The wedding was performed in Ferrara on February 11. For the banquet in the castello, Duke Este displayed one of his prize possessions, the tapestries showing the Queen of Sheba's visit to Solomon; Eleanora had brought them with her from Naples, and they were used only on the most formal occasions. The guests dined off

* Ultramarine was expensive because it was made from ground-up lapis lazuli, which had to be imported from the Middle East. (See Michael Baxandall, *Painting and Experience in Fifteenth Century Italy*.)

a new dinner service, designed by Cosimo Tura, the dishes made of gold, engraved with drawings of griffins and dolphins, "good-luck" talismans. Cornucopias spilling fruit were held by sculpted genies. Temples made of sugar displayed banners painted with the Este and the Gonzaga arms. Poets recited verses while the food grew cold. Before the banquet, the bride rode through the principal streets of Ferrara, rider and horse weighed down by gold and jewels.

The following day the bridal couple set out for Mantua in a procession as elaborate as Mantegna might conceive. Isabella and her family—parents, brothers, three of her cousins—occupied a large bucentaur, a ship built in the Venetian style and used for state occasions, lacking mast or sails and usually rowed by forty men, the hull richly decorated with carvings and gold decorations. Four smaller ships of the same type acted as convoy, while fifty-one other vessels followed behind. Up the broad Po they moved westward to the point where the great river is joined by the Mincio, the river on whose banks Mantua lies. The flags flew, the heralds blew the long trumpets, and the people—the local chronicler recorded there were 17,000 of them, which would have been more than half the population of Mantua—stood on the banks of the river, cheering warmly in defiance of the cold weather.

On the fifteenth of February 1490, ignoring by a day the astrologer's recommendation, Isabella made her formal entry into Mantua.* The city had been hung with banners and whatever flowers could be gathered in the middle of the winter. At the port children dressed in white greeted Isabella with songs and recitations of poems. Isabella rode on a white horse, at her right her husband, at her left Guidobaldo Montefeltro, Duke of Urbino, who was married to Gianfrancesco's sister Elisabetta. Since Gianfrancesco's parents were dead, Elisabetta, three years older than the bride, acted as the official hostess at the tournaments, dances, torchlight processions, tributes recited by poets, hunting excursions, and boat rides on one of the three lakes formed by the Mincio. Each day a formal banquet was served inside the Palace, an informal one on the square outside, the tables spread for hundreds and the fountain flowing with wine.

---

* The fifteenth was a Monday, "moon day"; Tuesday (*martedì*) was "Mars day." Perhaps they believed that moon day was more suitable for the occasion than Mars day.

One guest the bridegroom very much wanted there was not there. Mantegna was not there. He had gone to Rome to work for Pope Innocent VIII, Gianfrancesco having given him leave to do so. Mantegna was unhappy in Rome, did not like working for the pope, thought he was being slighted, and above all worried about the unfinished series of enormous paintings he had left behind, *The Triumph of Caesar*. Would Gianfrancesco personally see to it that all the windows were tight and no rain could penetrate to spoil the canvases? Gianfrancesco assured him that the canvases were perfectly safe and patiently waiting for his return. At Christmas time a messenger galloped into Rome with a letter from Gianfrancesco: he begged Mantegna to return at once. He needed him to design the decorations and the pageants for the wedding feast. No time to be lost—would he come? Mantegna received the messenger in bed. He was ill; he could not travel. Was he really ill? We cannot know; we only know that the shy man hated official functions and that the ceremonies took place without his help.

Isabella now had to meet her new relatives. They presented a large and bewildering array. Among them were her husband's two brothers, Sigismondo, who was destined for the church without the least inclination toward any form of sanctity, and Giovanni, impudent, temperamental, no older than Isabella. Isabella liked him. There were two sisters, as well: Chiara, the elder, was married to Gilbert de Montpensier, a nephew of the French king; she lived in France but had duly appeared at the wedding; the younger sister, Maddalena, who was to die within the year, was married to Giovanni Sforza, Lord of Pesaro. Este uncles, Gonzaga cousins, various relatives through marriages arranged like her own—it was a group drawn from the corners of the peninsula, as often at loggerheads as at agreement, but now accoutered in brocade and jewels, exquisitely cordial with one another.

Of them all Elisabetta was to prove the most valuable friend. She influenced Isabella by showing her how a woman, more specifically a woman at the summit of the social pyramid, could enrich her life. Herself ailing, she was married to a man who was impotent, but she was content, she said, to live with Guidobaldo as sister and brother. He, too, was a gentle man, finding comfort in philosophy and art, and she treated him with never-ceasing tenderness. Her portrait painted by the young Raphael shows a poised face, in which the lips are compressed in sorrow, as though contradicting the tranquillity of the brow, and the eyelids are lowered over eyes that glance far off in resignation.

The two sisters-in-law formed a lifelong and loving friendship, and their letters to each other are bright missives of trust and candor. Isabella's positive disposition frequently cheered Elisabetta. Two years after her marriage, the eighteen-year-old Isabella, talking like an old aunt, advised Elisabetta, who was taking the baths at Viterbo, that "more important than the first bath was the resolution to banish melancholy. . . . Please force yourself to exercise on foot or on horseback. Seek pleasant company," and so on.

On the last day of carnival the wedding guests finally went home. Now, hardly grown out of childhood, Isabella was a married woman. Now she was the mistress of the huge, old, formidable, and ugly Gonzaga Palace, called La Reggia. Now she was the marchesa of the state of Mantua. And now she needed to learn how to please a man she scarcely knew.

III

In Love

The two strangers fell in love.

He strengthened in the sixteen-year-old girl her pride in herself; he, the first man she had known, awakened her and then confirmed in her the consciousness of her value as a woman. She was never to lose that sense of value, though for some time to come and traditionally she still asserted, "My lord wants this" and "It is my husband's wish"—and not only asserted it but did what he wanted done. She gave him as a countergift the unpremeditated gaiety of a girl who had as yet experienced little pain, the tenderness which youth bears to youth, the pleasure which the look and touch of beauty convey. Marriage made Isabella bloom. As to Gianfrancesco, who had married her because she was an Este, he found in her in their first year continuous delight.

She must have been pretty, though we can only guess at what she looked like. The poets who likened her to a "Venus reborn" do not help us, and by a curious fate all the portraits painted of her in her youth—and there were several—have disappeared. It is probable that she was not a sensational beauty, not comparable to one of the famous women before whom men fell silent, such as Lucrezia Borgia or Sanchia of Aragon. Her charm was compounded of mental as much as physical attributes. She was not inclined to live exclusively for and in the bedroom. That is not to deny that she paid as much attention as any doxy to her face, her hair, her complexion. She made the most of her endowment, not only with the help of cosmetics and clothes, but by the grace with which she played her lute, her proud stride, her statuesque posture as she sat on her horse, and the careful stage management of her public appearances. We know that she was continuously afraid of getting fat and often deprived herself of dishes she loved. She noted with a bit of *Scha-*

denfreude that her sister was growing stouter, "like our mother," while her own figure was still slim, and she dressed cleverly to accentuate its lines. She had succeeded in bleaching her long, fine hair to a light blond. Her eyes, as brown as fir cones in autumn, scattered laughter. She enjoyed—how could she not?—the admiration of famous men. "None more graceful, none more beautiful have I known," Ariosto wrote. That leaves it up to the imagination. I for one imagine her to have looked as a girl like one of the three Graces, the one who stands nearest Venus, in Botticelli's *La Primavera*. (Six exquisite women in that picture and they are all blondes!) Botticelli painted it when Isabella was three years old, so, of course, this is pure invention on my part.

Gianfrancesco was as ugly as Isabella was attractive. His lips were pursed and thick, his nose was snub and large, his eyes protruding and as round as billiard balls; he wore his hair long and soon grew a bushy beard and a drooping mustache, perhaps because he wanted to draw attention from his features. (A terra-cotta bust in Mantua shows him clearly.) But his body was lithe and athletic; he was a superb horseman. He was as interested in the care of the famous Gonzaga Barbary horses as his father and grandfather had been, and he spent much time in the stables. Much less intellectual than Isabella—he read little, his Latin was practically nonexistent, he had no stomach for philosophic discussions—he matched her in high spirits, at least in his youth. When he wanted to, he could turn on great charm; indeed, he was one of those ugly men women find irresistible. He was virile and highly sexed; he was stalwart and fearless as well, which was the expected stance for a soldier. That is what he was, a professional soldier, a condottiere, and as such he early gained a reputation. The year before he married, the Republic of Venice, foreseeing troubles to come, had appointed him captain of the Venetian army. The important appointment indicates that his skill at and knowledge of war were appreciated.

Such skill consisted, at least in part, of being able to raise an army of soldiers quickly, train them, and direct them against an army led by the opposing captain, using subterfuges, treacheries, circumventions, while shedding as little blood as possible. One condottiere respected the other; war was a contest for professionals. The prince, sitting high on his horse, would sometimes ostentatiously charge the enemy, courting a conspicuous death; but more often the sally was but a show and it was the little people who really got hurt, the peasant murdered for his wheat, the merchant plundered for his silk. Plundering was the recognized reward of war, the promise held out to the soldier who breached the fortress. The condottieri knew this; they knew all the tricks, were greatly valued, and extravagantly paid; one of the most highly regarded, Federigo da Montefeltro, earned as much as 45,000 ducats ($900,000) a year while in active service.

There was no war going for the moment; Gianfrancesco and Isabella could be together and were together, though Gianfrancesco was occasionally required to go to Venice for consultation. At such times Isabella invited her sister-in-law Elisabetta to visit her. The two explored the countryside, once going as far as Lake Garda, that enchanting lake artfully ringed by lemon trees and oleander. Grave and gay, they read books, played a card game called *scartino,* and discussed life. Life—it was at that moment pulsating through their world at a high beat. Elisabetta, who was to gather in Urbino some of the noblest spirits of the age—among them Bembo the poet, Bibbiena the scholar and playwright, Cristoforo Romano the sculptor, and a singer called "L'Unico Aretino" (The One and Only Arezzian)—believed that nothing was impossible for the searching mind to achieve. The steps man could climb had no final rung. The Greeks had fashioned their gods in the image of man; these new Italians fashioned themselves into gods. Elisabetta was quoting a writer she particularly admired, one "in whom Nature had united all her gifts . . . tall and finely molded, with something of divinity shining in his face." This was Count Giovanni Pico della Mirandola, poet, musician, architect, student of Plato and the Bible, fluent in half a dozen languages including Hebrew, and tolerant of all religions, which he tried to combine into one universal creed. Yet with all his erudition and good looks, this paragon was modest and lovable, as popular with men as with women. He had written a famous oration, "On the Dignity of Man," which stated the ambition of the age:

O highest and most marvelous felicity of man! To him it is granted to have whatever he chooses, to be whatever he wills. . . . On man when he came into life God the Father conferred the seeds of all kinds and the germs of every way of life. Whatever seeds each man cultivates will grow to maturity and bear in him their own fruit. If they be vegetative, he will be like a plant. If fleshly, he will become brutish. If rational, he will grow into a heavenly being. If intellectual, he will be an angel and the son of God.

When Isabella visited Elisabetta in Urbino, the two friends became even closer. After her return home, Elisabetta wrote her: "Your departure made me feel not only that I had lost a dear sister, but that life itself had gone from me." The feeling was echoed by Isabella. "I love you as much," she wrote to Elisabetta, "as if we had been born of the same mother." That mutual love never faltered. And now, more than ever, Isabella determined to cultivate her "intellectual seed."

In the first year of her marriage, Isabella was occasionally homesick. She wrote to her parents, her tutors, and to her pet clown, Fritella, who had loved her as a child and to whom she now sent a ducat and three lengths of satin. Her brothers came to visit her; she intended to return to Ferrara with them to see her parents, but Gianfrancesco, who wanted her with him every day and night, asked her to postpone her journey. She did so until November, when she found her mother deeply embroiled in preparing for Beatrice's wedding, aided by a whole solemn deputation from Lodovico Sforza. The hustle and bustle, the conferences concerning the wedding outfits and the ceremonies, excited her, and she found time to write to her husband only a little note:

My dearest Lord, —if I have not written before, it is not that you have not been continually in my heart, but that I had simply not a moment to spare as long as the Milanese ambassador was here. Now I must do my duty and tell you that I can have no pleasure when I am away from Your Highness, whom I love more than my own life. —One who loves Your Highness more than herself, ISABELLA DA ESTE DA GONZAGA. Ferrara, November 25, 1490.

Off went the note by special courier, and only three days later Gianfrancesco replied:

Since you feel that you cannot be happy away from me any longer, which is only natural, considering the immense love which we both feel for each other, it seems to me that, now you have satisfied your illustrious father and mother's wishes, as well as your own affection for your family, you might return home for our own happiness, and so I shall look forward to your arrival with impatience.

Even two years later, in August 1492, when Isabella was in Milan, she wrote, "I do not want to deny that I am having a wonderful time here. Yet when I think of the distance which separates us, I wish with all my heart that I could see you more often and

offer you my homage. Remember me with your love and write me
often that you are well."

A palace is not a home. Isabella almost at once set out to make it
into one. The food was atrocious, she found, and since Neapolitan
cuisine enjoyed a high reputation, she wrote to the Mantuan ambassador in Naples to hire a good cook for her, "for Maestro
Jasone, who officiates here, really leaves much to be desired." She
ordered new linen, bed covers, wall hangings, small rugs from
Venice, as well as Murano crystal glasses and a new Faenza dining
service, "large enough to serve forty guests." It would be pleasant,
she thought, to populate the place with pets. She purchased a lap
dog and ordered a Persian kitten. Imitating Elisabetta, she was determined to form that new home of hers into a center which poets
and artists, scholars and courtiers, would be glad to visit. Every day
she wrote invitations to those near and far, to Niccolò da Correggio, whom she admired more than ever, to Matteo Boiardo, who
was working on his poem *Orlando Innamorato* and sent her part of
the manuscript, to Antonio Tebaldeo, a young poet whose sonnets
were making a reputation, to Lodovico's son-in-law Galeazzo di San
Severino, with whom she carried on a lively debate as to the com-
parative merits of the fabled paladins Rinaldo versus Orlando. And
from her father's palace she summoned several Ferrarese artists.
The best of them, Ercole Roberti, got so seasick during his voyage
up the Po that he turned around and went back to Ferrara without
even saying goodbye.

For a time she kept up her childhood interest in Latin. She asked
her old teacher Guarino to recommend a new instructor to her. He
approved, "since a truly cultured woman is as rare as a phoenix,"
and recommended a Mantuan scholar, one Sigismondo Dolfo. She
didn't seem to like Dolfo, changed teachers, but soon gave the lessons up altogether. She was now too busy for cloistered pursuits,
too busy with Gianfrancesco.

Isabella and her friends not only discussed, exchanged views,
gossiped—they played. All kinds of games. Books on games (*Libri
di Ventura*—Books of Luck) are frequently mentioned in Isabella's
letters. The mathematician Luca Pacioli, professor at the University
of Pavia, wrote a book which he dedicated to Isabella and Gianfrancesco (who did not like games), the Latin title of which can be
translated as "Pleasant and Happy Treatise on Games in General,

with Special Reference to All Methods of Playing Chess, as Well as Other Pastimes."

They played chess. They played cards. They played charades. They played a form of Ping-Pong. They played a game in which they sat in a circle: the first player wrote a sentence, the next another without knowing what the first wrote, and so forth until all had participated. Then the whole thing was read aloud and the more double entendre it turned out to be the more successful the game.

Of course they danced, especially when a court function gave them the excuse for doing so. Italian dance steps were at first simple; when the French came they taught more intricate dances, and later the Spanish introduced such stately measures as the pavane. "Une belle dame qui danse à merveille" were the words with which Isabella was introduced to Louis XII. Music—it sounded often in the house, but was used prevailingly as accompaniment to song or verse. Isabella not only played the lute and the clavichord, but heard the sound of viols, zinkes, dulcimers, kitharas, rankets, and cromornes. We know that the Renaissance was not a musically jejune period, though we are far from knowing the names of as many practitioners of the art as we do the names of painters. Isabella did not "collect" composers, nor seek the acquaintance of virtuosi, though in her time there lived in Mantua a composer musically named Bartolomeo Tromboncino, who composed such beautiful madrigals that when he killed his unfaithful wife they decided to let him go unpunished.

The search for entertainment, the desire to lighten life, took forms less mellifluous than music. Every court had its jesters, its "whoreson mad fellows." Isabella kept a company of dwarfs, who were housed in a group of tiny, low-ceilinged rooms. These whimsical rooms, linked to other apartments by staircases with steps of reduced dimension, were meant more as a show for visitors than as a convenience to the inmates. Strange that a woman like Isabella could delight in the antics of these stunted creatures. They were skilled freaks, turning somersaults, juggling, dancing, and singing in falsetto voices, but their wit seems to have been fairly witless, at least as it has come down to us. Perhaps the jokes lose something in "translation" over the centuries. One Mattello (probably a made-up name, *matto* = crazy), whom she called "the Emperor of the madmen," used to don a priest's cossack, waddle into the hall, and harangue the company with unctuous sermons. Typically Italian, it would be even today: they were in awe of the Church but mocked the churchmen; they kissed the pope's foot and made mouths at him behind his back. When Isabella's brother Alfonso was ill, she sent Mattello to him at Ferrara; he would rather have had that visit, wrote Alfonso, than the gift of a castle. Shortly after, Mattello fell ill; Isabella nursed him and when he died grieved over the loss. She buried him in the Gonzaga family crypt. She had a female dwarf, too, "Crazy Catherine," who was an alcoholic and a bit of a kleptomaniac, hiding in her little room whatever she could steal. Isabella knew all about that, but overlooked it because Catherine was always merry and completely devoted to her mistress. Catherine could perform a trick: whenever she was asked, "Make water," she lifted her skirt and instantly did so in front of everybody. *That* was considered hilarious.

Whatever Isabella wanted she could have. She had only to express a wish and Gianfrancesco did his best to grant it. He had assigned her a separate wing of the Castello, the windows of which overlooked the lake. There she was to live for the next thirty years, until her husband's death, with her retinue, her "damsels," her attendants, her dwarfs. Her private apartments comprised three large rooms, from one of which a little stairs led to her *studiolo,* her study, which was tucked away in one of the towers of the Castle. This was her most personal domain, what in the beginning she called her "paradise," where she conducted her vast correspondence and worked at her accounts. One of the large halls on the ground floor she turned into her museum, which she was to call the *grotta;* visitors she thought appreciative were entertained there. Another stair led to three additional rooms; probably these housed her library.

Very early Gianfrancesco set up a financial arrangement for her. She did not have to ask him for money: she had a budget. We know this from a letter she wrote her father in 1502. Lucrezia Borgia, then married to Isabella's brother Alfonso, complained to her father-in-law that she was not being given sufficient means to live in the style to which she was accustomed. Ercole replied that Lucrezia's allowance exceeded that of his own daughter, and to prove the point asked Isabella to let him have specific details. These Isabella supplied at once:

My honored Lord and Father, —When I first entered this illustrious house I was assigned an annual allowance of 6,000 gold ducats, to pay for my clothes and outfit my retinue, and to help with marriage gifts for my damsels, as well as all that was needed for my servants—including two gentlemen; the Court supplying in addition the food for about a hundred persons. Afterward, in order that I might be free to increase or diminish my household, my illustrious consort voluntarily agreed, by the advice of his stewards, to take this burden off their shoulders, and give me another 2,000 ducats for the expenses of my whole company. Of this income 6,000 was raised by the toll of the mills, 1,000 by an excise duty, and for the other 1,000 I was given the house and lands of Letopaledano. So you see that in all I have 8,000 ducats a year. It is true that *by my own economy, and that of my servants,* the income of this estate has been increased by about 1,000 ducats, with which I have been enabled to buy the estate of Castiglione Mantuvano and the farm Bondenazzo, so that at present the rent brings in about 2,500 ducats a year. But I also have to feed about fifty more persons of my household. And it is true that my lord has given me other houses for my pleasure, such, for instance, as Sacchetta and Porto; but their income does not exceed their expenses, and sometimes I have to spend more money to keep them in repair. This is the sum and substance of what I can tell Your Excellency for your satisfaction, to whose grace I recommend myself forever. Mantua, May 23, 1502.

A yearly income ranging from 8,000 to 10,000 ducats ($160,000 to $200,000)—munificent, even if a hundred servants depended on it. If it proved sufficient for Isabella's needs, it proved insufficient for her desires.

2

First, there was the question of her costumes, for the apparel oft proclaimed the woman. It was not only a question of dressing as befitted the wife of a head of state; Isabella was passionately interested in personal adornment, in silks, brocades, satins, velvets, furs, fabrics shot through with gold and silver threads (real gold and silver), and of course in jewelry. Her letters exude the hedonistic pleasure she derived from rich materials, and she was always asking for news of the latest fashions. The standard garment of the Renaissance woman was a long dress covering the body and falling gracefully into many pleats; this was called a camora. The sleeves came separately, were made of different material, and presented the opportunity for the dressmaker's fancy and display of skill; they were often bestrewn with jewels and were prized as gifts. (Niccolò da Correggio designed a camora for Isabella, with gold links worked into a purple fabric. It was a sensational garment, and her sister Beatrice borrowed it to wear it at the wedding of Emperor Maximilian.) As a cloak one wore a sbernia (a contraction of "Hibernia" because the material was sometimes imported from Ireland), which was lined with silk or fur. Few Italian women wore elaborate hats—such as the ones sported by the nude Venuses of Lucas Cranach—they preferred little coquettish caps.

We get an idea of the extent of Isabella's demands for all such garments, festive or plain, if we peruse her "shopping list." The year happens to be 1515; it was by no means an exceptional year. Excluding jewelry and whatever she may have bought in Mantua, which no doubt was a lot, this is what she ordered in the first half of the year:

Date	Place ordered	
Jan. 7	Ferrara	6 gold caps, 2 lined with black silk, 2 with red, 2 with crimson.
11	Milan	A sable coat, "all sable."
Feb. 4	Ferrara	1 pair shoes white, silk lined, high heels.
		1 pair black velvet slippers.
		Fur sleeves.
5	Ferrara	25 ells black velvet for a camora.
March 11	Rome	Gold perfume bottle.
22	Bologna	2 bolts yellow silk. One thick, well-lined shawl.
April 3	Venice	2 ounces musk, 2 ounces ambergris, 200 pine seeds.
3	Venice	"Damascan" boxes for toiletries (ordered from Lorenzo da Pavia).
12	Bologna	2 bolts black silk, 4 ells fine cotton voile.
13	Bologna	250 bone buttons with black gold setting.
26	Bologna	4 ells fine cotton, for caps.
27	Bologna	½ bolt gold thread.
28	Bologna	Rosewater from Damascus. Black amber.
30	Bologna	8 ells fine cotton voile, 4 black and gold striped, 4 white and gold.
May 7	Florence	Ivory crown (sent to her by Machiavelli).
25	Correggio	2 bolts black raw silk.
		½ bolt white raw silk.
31	Ferrara	Turquoise and yellow watered silk, velvet for slippers.
June 19	Ferrara	220 gold buttons, 220 bone buttons.
21	Ferrara	1 ell yellow and cherry silk.
25	Ferrara	20 ells wide white-and-black silk ribbon.

In addition she bought within the space of a year and a half thirty-three pairs of shoes and a quantity of underwear, partly of silk, partly of a particularly fine quality of linen, woven in Rheims and called *tela di Rensa*.

As to jewelry—all wealthy women tried to outdo one another in its beauty and costliness, Isabella not the least ambitious among them. Often a jeweler was more appreciated than a painter and more considerately treated, though a good many famous painters designed jewelry as well. Ippolita Sforza wore a dress hung with gold and pearls to the value of 5,000 ducats ($100,000). The niece of François I did better: at her wedding the thirteen-year-old girl was so bedecked with precious stones that she could not walk but had to be carried. Bianca Maria Sforza wore a blouse with eighty pieces of the jeweler's art pinned thereon, each piece consisting of one pure ruby and four pearls. Isabella's jewelry became famous. She owned "the most beautiful emerald in the world," supposedly— but probably not—found in the grave of Cicero's daughter Tullia. She owned a brooch which was formed by a *spinella* (a stone imported from India), above which was fastened a pear-shaped pearl, topped off by a crown and a cornucopia of diamonds. She owned no end of gold belts, gold crosses, chains of coral, rosaries of amethyst and diamonds, bracelets, rings, head bands. She owned a Saint George made entirely of diamonds, the dragon at his feet being an irregularly shaped large pearl. Yet at no time could she vie with the possessions of the richest princes, their wives or mistresses, the collections of the Medici, the Sforza, and, wealthiest of all, the popes. Regretfully she had to return a fabulous ruby because "it was too large and too expensive." That was in September 1491. In April she wrote to a Mantuan agent in Venice, one Zilio, and sent him 100 ducats: "Please don't return any of this money [after paying for one of her purchases]. If there is any money left, spend it for a chain or anything that is new and elegant which you think I would like. And if the money is insufficient, advance your own. I will pay you back immediately and would rather remain your debtor than your creditor." Then follows a long list of things she wants: blue cloth for a camora, amber rosaries, black material for a sbernia—"but it must be of incomparably fine quality; don't mind the money even if it costs ten ducats an ell, as long as it is absolutely perfect. If it is not unique don't buy it." Indeed, the little Latin scholar had changed.

Toward the end of her first year of marriage, she was getting ready to attend her sister's wedding. There had been trouble. The troth had been pledged, terms, conditions, and date had long been agreed upon, when Lodovico Sforza announced that he could not get married on the stipulated date, May 1490, giving as his reason that at the moment the affairs of state weighed too heavily upon him. He was "too busy." Nobody really believed this, but Ercole and Eleanora Este, wanting to avoid a public scandal, or not to terminate relations between Ferrara and Milan, or perhaps guessing the real reason and hoping that Lodovico would come to his senses, decided to swallow the insult and say nothing. A postponement to July was agreed to. Early in July a messenger reached Ercole's court late one evening; he was pale and exhausted and he carried confidential letters from the bridegroom. What was in the letters? No one knew, except Ercole. Isabella was not told. Benedetto Capilupo, who was at Ferrara as the Mantuan legate and who later became Isabella's confidential secretary, wrote to Mantua that "every one was in a temper and the Duke seems very angry." The messenger left early the next morning. Ercole announced that once again the wedding was postponed. One may imagine what effect this had on the fifteen-year-old Beatrice—this being kept waiting almost at the church door, her sister safely married, herself apparently repudiated. Perhaps fortunately for her, Beatrice was anything but an introspective soul, and though she could not have helped being shamed, she may have shrugged her shoulders.

The reason for Lodovico's cruel dilatoriness was love, love for his mistress who, all who knew her agreed, deserved such devotion. Her name was Cecilia Gallerani, and Lodovico had lived with her for the past ten years in what amounted to marriage. He had given her a magnificent estate which Cecilia turned into a meeting place of artists and poets. She herself was a good poet and an eloquent writer, as adroit in Latin as in Italian. Springing from an aristocratic family, she could well have been a prince's consort; yet politically that was impossible and Lodovico knew it. But he could not bear to give her up, and when we look at her portrait we can quite understand the reluctance. This portrait Lodovico had ordered from Leonardo da Vinci as soon as the artist reached Milan in 1482.

It is *The Lady with the Ermine,* and Leonardo never painted a woman's face more enchanting than this, in which the Leonardesque smile lies more in the eyes than the lips.

Yet the marriage had to take place; the connection with Ferrara was too important to Milan to be severed; Lodovico's own position, always somewhat uncertain, could be seriously endangered. The date was finally fixed for January 1491. It was to be the wedding of the year: the less love the more pomp and glitter.

Lodovico made the most elaborate preparations. He dispatched a summons to all the artists living within the duchy to come forthwith to Milan, to design the wedding decorations; a refusal would be fined by 25 ducats and would incur the duke's "displeasure." They came and decorated the hall of the Milan Castello—a room 160 feet long—with frescoes depicting the history of the Sforza. Others designed the triumphal arches, the costumes for the pageant, the stage settings for the plays, a life-size effigy of Lodovico's father, sitting on a wooden horse. Lodovico sent Beatrice as a wedding gift a necklace of large pearls set in gold flowers with a pendant of rubies and emeralds; it was indeed an outstanding example of the jeweler's art. He wanted Beatrice sculpted at once: the portrait bust was formerly ascribed to Leonardo, but is almost certainly a work by Cristoforo Romano, who went from Milan to Ferrara to do it. It shows a pretty face, on the plump side, a tiny sensuous mouth, two careful curls winding down the soft cheeks, an expression childlike and petulant.

Anybody who was anybody was invited to the wedding. Lodovico wanted the occasion to show all Italy the wealth and power of the Milanese state. Roads were repaired, poor quarters of the city cleaned, bridges secured against the weight of the horses, city squares enlarged. Bramante improved a church, Leonardo's imagination played with the symbolic designs of heraldry, the armorers—working almost around the clock—hammered out shields, lances, and helmets which were to be displayed along the route of the procession, while an army of embroiderers stitched decorations on the coverings which were used to warm beds and walls. "Nothing is done by halves," wrote the Ferrara envoy to Ercole. Gianfrancesco and Isabella were to be guests of honor.

Gianfrancesco decided not to go. He judged that the Venetian Senate would not look with favor on his appearing at so official a function at the court of a man on whose brooding ambition and hard acquisitiveness the Senate frowned. Gianfrancesco was an employee of Venice, and Venice, herself deceitful, distrusted deceitful Lodovico, being particularly concerned with too firm an alliance of Milan-Ferrara-Mantua, an alliance which could encircle their domain. In fact, it was to be a double wedding: Anna Sforza, Lodovico's niece, was to be married to Alfonso d'Este, Ercole's eldest son, at the same time, and the implication of these double diplomatic moves was clear to the doge.

Isabella went. After all, what could prevent a sister from assisting a sister at her solemn moment? And if she was going to go, she had better make the right impression on the assembly. Throughout autumn and winter the couriers sped here and there carrying Isabella's orders for her wedding wardrobe. "She had nothing to wear," or so it seemed. The Venetian agent was bade to buy eighty perfect sable skins as lining for a sbernia, and if he could manage to get a whole skin, head and claws included, which could be used for a muff, so much the better. "The price is unimportant—let him search all through Venice to find the perfect furs." Next: she needed eight ells of the first-quality crimson satin for her cloak, she needed gold clasps, she needed a gold belt engraved with the Gonzaga crest, and so on and on. She sent to Milan to buy two skins of "Spanish cat" for trimmings, and at the last moment ordered another cloak, one of heavy brocade, from Genoa to be delivered by courier on her arrival. She planned to appear with a retinue of 114 people and ninety horses, and was miffed when Lodovico pleaded that he simply did not have room for so large a suite and asked her to limit herself to fifty people and thirty horses.

That year northern Italy suffered a particularly severe cold spell. A large section of the Po was frozen over, the valley covered with snow. Isabella's party started out in carts, traveling west until they reached the village of Brescello, where Eleanora d'Este and the bride had come to meet them. At this point the Po was navigable; here three bucentaurs and a fleet of smaller boats were waiting. But their voyage up the Po turned out to be an ordeal. Beatrice de' Contrari, Isabella's chief lady-in-waiting, wrote to Gianfrancesco back in Mantua:

The ship with the provisions stayed so far behind that this morning we had to breakfast with our gloves on [meaning they had almost nothing to eat] while a few of us, including myself, ate nothing at all. Around nine o'clock at night we reached Toresella—still without the provision ship. If Lady Camilla had not sent us something to eat for supper, I would have ended up as a saint in Paradise. When it was time to go to bed and we realized that all of us had to squeeze ourselves into that sad, noisy *bucentoro*, we felt like not going to sleep at all. My Lady [Isabella], the poor thing, froze without a fire and said she felt like dying. I felt such pity for her that I couldn't suppress a few tears. Finally she lay down and called me to crawl into bed with her. I did so to please her. But I wished it had been Your Excellency, instead of myself—it seemed a poor exchange and I was hardly able to warm her as Your Magnificence might have done. A fine foretaste of a wedding! If we will have to bear such hardships every day, I will make my testament. . . .

At length they reached Piacenza—on January 12, having started from Mantua on December 29, a long journey indeed!—slept in comfortable beds, warmed themselves, felt human again, and then proceeded to Pavia. They were now in Lodovico's territory, and there he himself was, encamped with courtiers and soldiers on the bank of the Ticino River, which joins the Po just below Pavia. As the party arrived, a great shout went up in the winter air and Lodovico ceremoniously led ashore first his bride, then Eleanora, and then Isabella. Lodovico, with his aquiline nose, double chin, and darting brown eyes, was not handsome, but he nevertheless made a figure likely to awe the women, decked as he was in a huge golden mantle, his head covered by a silver helmet surmounted by a Moor's head of solid silver, painted black. The party rode over the long covered bridge which was then almost 150 years old, and into Pavia's Castle. This edifice, they boasted, which was protected by walls 100 feet high and neighbored by an enormous park, was the noblest royal house in Europe, acknowledged a masterpiece of Lombard architecture. Faced in marble, it shone like an Alpine glacier in the winter sun. Once inside, Lodovico began to show them the treasures of which the Castle contained a suffocating abundance: frescoes telling the history of the Visconti and the Sforza, a portrait of Petrarch, who had once taught at Pavia University, a painting of ancestor Giangaleazzo receiving foreign ambassadors at a table laden with gold and silver dishes, large hunting scenes with wild boars and stags, as well as lions and tigers which never did exist in that part of the world, contrasting with biblical scenes painted by the melancholy Vincenzo Foppa. Lodovico led them through the armory with its collection of damascened breastplates, greaves, swords, helmets. He showed them the famous clock which Giovanni Dondi had taken sixteen years to construct and which told not only the time and the phases of the moon but also the movements of the planets as taught by Ptolemy. Most proudly he showed them the library, the illustrated breviaries, the text of the *Chanson de Roland,* the Latin and Greek manuscripts which he had corralled from as far as Hungary and Spanish convents.

Lodovico seems to have been more responsive to Isabella than to Beatrice. "I find myself highly honored and caressed by Signor Lodovico," she wrote to Gianfrancesco from Pavia, and her enthusiasm for his treasures was voiced in unstinted measure.

The wedding took place on January 17 in the Castle. Only a small company was present, the main festivities being planned for Milan, but Isabella's friend Niccolò da Correggio was there, handsome and superbly dressed as ever. An official proclamation announced that "that night the marriage was consummated," and Lodovico left the next morning for Milan to supervise the final preparations for the celebration. The ladies remained at Pavia for the better part of a week. Then they rode to Milan, to be met at the gate by a delegation of Milanese nobles and a hundred trumpeters. The crowds had come from all corners of Lombardy to watch the procession; the city was festooned with hangings of red and blue satin (the colors of the Sforza), the columns of the houses wreathed in ivy. Three tribunals were erected on the square before the Duomo, one occupied by musicians, one displaying the wedding gifts—mostly gold and silver plate contributed by the magistrates of Milan and other cities—and the third, in the center, for the bride and bridegroom to ascend, show themselves to the people, and receive the homage of the deputies. That night two hundred ladies were invited to a ball; Isabella danced the night through. Her looks, her bearing, and her dresses were judged glorious; a chronicler described her as "a creature come from Eden."

The climax was to be a three-day tournament. It was preceded by what from the description seems an endless pageant; it included a Mantuan troop clad in green and bearing gold lances, a float drawn by horses which were made to look like stags and unicorns, a troop of riders in black Moorish armor decorated with white doves, obviously a tribute to "Il Moro." Then, uttering wild cries, a group of "Scythians" galloped across the square on Barbary steeds, drew to an abrupt halt before the newlyweds, threw off their disguise, and revealed themselves as Milanese soldiers, while their captain thrust a golden lance into the ground and a giant soldier enveloped in a cloak painted with peacock's eyes proceeded to recite a poem praising Beatrice.

These warlike pageants, this delight in plumes and finery, this predilection for both loud noise and silent symbolism, this play of lances and of swords, these masques, charades, pastorals, and extravaganzas, this whirligig of wealth, a love of show often naïve— they were the extrovert signs of the age. The joy of the moment covered intimations of mortality. The best artists of the period lent their talents to festivities which were here today and gone tomorrow. Leonardo, the most introspective artist of those miraculous years, was no exception. Kenneth Clark in his study of Leonardo writes:

> In studying the architecture and even the painting of the Renaissance, we must always remember that one whole branch of each is almost completely lost to us—the architecture and decoration which was designed for pageants and masquerades. We know from Vasari how many of the greatest artists whose lives he records seem to have given a considerable part of their time to such ephemeral work. It was in these lath and plaster designs that a man could show his invention, his fantasy, unimpeded by cost and the painful process of construction; and we know that Leonardo did such work with pleasure.

That Leonardo took an active part in arranging the Beatrice-Lodovico pageant we know through the sheerest chance, an annoying incident which angered Leonardo sufficiently for him to record it. It is in the *Codice Atlantico* and reads:

> Item, 26 of January, being in the house of Messer Galeazzo di San Sev. [Severino—a brilliant and popular captain at Lodovico's court and Lodovico's son-in-law] ordering the festa of his joust, certain men-at-arms took off their vests to try on some costumes of savages, upon which Giacomo took up a purse which lay on the bed with their other clothes, and took the money that was inside it.

This Giacomo was an apprentice in Leonardo's household; Leonardo had caught him stealing once before but would not get rid of him, whether for sexual reasons or because he was efficient we do not know. Theft was punishable by death, if the prince so ruled. Presumably Giacomo got away with it.

The great joust was held and won by the Galeazzo whom Leonardo mentions. Legend has it that Gianfrancesco came incognito to Milan, that he entered the lists, was recognized by Lodovico, and was made welcome. Though it would not have been inconsistent with Gianfrancesco's character to flash such a surprise, the story is almost certainly invented. Isabella does not mention the presence of her husband; on the contrary, after all the tumult, she is ready to return to him—but not before she has visited that wonder of wonders, the Certosa of Pavia. This Carthusian monastery, though not yet completed, was already famous as a treasure house, with altarpieces, bronze grilles, choir stalls, and four stained-glass windows by Amadeo Borgognone, one of the finest of the Lombard masters. She simply *had* to see it, though no women were allowed to enter the monastery without a special dispensation from the pope. Lodovico arranged that in short order. He wrote to the prior that he wanted to show Isabella and Eleanora "the most remarkable things in our domain," among which "we count this our church and monastery." They were therefore to prepare a "fitting reception" for the two illustrious ladies and their retinue. "No excuse on your part can be allowed, since this is our will and pleasure. And above all, you will see that an abundant supply of lampreys is prepared." The prior knew an order when he read one. The records of the Certosa show that Eleanora and Isabella arrived on February 6 "with a suite of 400 horses and 800 persons; the expense of supplying them with confectionery, fish, and Malvasia wine amounted to 400 lire." Evidently the two ladies did not stint themselves.

Isabella then paid a short visit to her parental home. She was back in Mantua on February 17, after a relatively easy voyage, the cold having lessened, six days after the first anniversary of their wedding.

3

She returned from Milan with an impression which flooded her young soul: she had become deeply, not to say passionately, attached to Lodovico, her brother-in-law. Isabella loved her husband with the wonder of the new-married; in those first years she felt as tender to him as he to her. Yet the heart cannot be forced to be monogamous, and when she met Lodovico she was overwhelmed by the power which lay in this man, a force distilled from struggle, experience, guile, success, and wealth. He was dark and secretive and some twenty years older than Isabella—he had just turned forty when she met him—he was high-handed and generous; he was a complete commander and at the same time a man who could be deferential to a Leonardo or a Bramante, both of whom he had summoned to Milan. There Lodovico offered Isabella the most extravagant attention, and the young girl saw in him a fabled creature, imagined him as coming from a world different from the drier world of her father or the horse-loving world of her husband. Some of that portrait was drawn by her own dream, yet it was true that Lodovico lived on two planes, politically low, artistically high. The high thoughts he shared with Isabella. In art, he wrote her, "beauty of form is everything." Bernardino Corio, a contemporary historian, wrote that Lodovico cared so greatly for the arts "that they seemed to have descended from Heaven itself upon this excelling court." Isabella wrote that Lodovico had created "the home of art and understanding."

It is probable that their relationship was never sexually fulfilled. But the inferences of great mutual attraction are fairly clear: they determined to keep in touch, and before Isabella left they arranged for a weekly courier service (a trustworthy courier, of course) who would carry messages back and forth from Milan to Mantua, in letters penned on "heavy paper and heavily sealed with red wax." These letters are couched in careful language—both Isabella and Lodovico were circumspect—but they glow with the intimacy of kindred spirits. He complained that she did not write to him often enough: "My affection for Your Highness is greater than yours for me. Obviously, I think of you much oftener than you think of me, and I am certain that I write far more letters to you than you do to me" (September 1491). The riders would carry as well artichokes from Lodovico's estates and carp from Isabella's lakes. That was not enough: whenever she could, she went to Milan to see him. Gianfrancesco opposed these visits, advancing the same reason he had given in not attending the Beatrice-Lodovico wedding: it was unwise to show overt friendliness to a foe of Venice. All the same, she went. Once Lodovico entreated Gianfrancesco so earnestly that he allowed her to spend the carnival at Milan, though after she left he wrote her, "All Mantua complains of your prolonged absence." Little question but that Gianfrancesco was jealous: Lodovico was too full-blooded—with his sensual mouth, his "eyebrows like a blackbird's wings"—for a husband not to be concerned. Politically, too, Isabella took Lodovico's side, even after his actions had become inimical to Mantua's cause. When later, in 1498, Gianfrancesco openly broke with him, Isabella tried her best to reconcile the two men, sending Capilupo, her secretary, repeatedly to Milan to negotiate.

For a time the relation between Isabella and sister Beatrice became strained. A story that Beatrice sent Gianfrancesco one of her ladies-in-waiting "with whom to amuse himself" is almost certainly untrue, but the fact that such a story could gain currency indicates that something was amiss.

We will never know the whole truth of the matter, but of one thing we can be certain: Lodovico's admiration, affection, love—call it what you will—for Isabella awakened in her the ambition to imitate him and to surround herself with treasures. She had to be prudent: wealthy as she was, her wealth was insignificant compared to the wealth of a Sforza—the income of Milan has been calculated at about twelve times that of Mantua. She had to compensate by cleverness.

IV

Son of the Spider

Back and forth went the letters between Isabella and Lodovico, while he sent her gifts, including the rather peculiar one of "two fat oxen." Isabella, who loved to receive gifts, acknowledged them charmingly and signed herself "The one who will always admire you." Whatever Gianfrancesco thought of the matter, the politician in him got the upper hand over the husband. Diplomacy suggested that he change his attitude toward his brother-in-law. Lodovico's star was in the ascendant, his power expanding. Gianfrancesco felt he had to play along with this triumphant prince. Lodovico's heightened influence came about through a change in the papacy.

Pope Innocent VIII lay gravely ill, and practically every decent Italian was glad he was going to die. He had been ineffective in curing the corruption spread by his predecessor Sixtus; indeed, in some ways he had deepened the morass. Rome had become Sodom. Crimes were condoned, pardons purchased. One man committed incest with his two daughters, then killed them both, and was let off by paying 800 ducats. Things had to get better in a Rome so rife with violence, robbery, rape, and assassination that the Tiber had to be dredged each dawn to extract the dead bodies. Things had to get better in a Vatican in which the College of Cardinals had been increased to thirty-two by appointees who were as unworthy as princes of the church as they were financially worthy, some of whom went from morning mass directly to a reliable brothel. The candidate most anxious and most likely to become Innocent's successor was the clever, learned, enormously wealthy Cardinal Rodrigo Borgia. He was rich enough to bribe his way to the papal throne. And he was an intimate friend of Lodovico Il Moro. In 1492 Borgia became pope. Asked what name he wished to assume, he answered, "That of the invincible Alexander." Lodovico's brother,

Cardinal Ascanio Sforza, had been prominent in the pro-Borgia campaign. Obviously, it now became the better part of valor for Gianfrancesco to remain in Lodovico Sforza's good graces. Isabella became a means to an end.

Weighing one consideration against another, in the summer of 1492, he advised Isabella to accept a new invitation from Lodovico. By all means, go to Milan. She asked for time to outfit herself suitably for such a visit. Really, she couldn't be expected to be seen in dresses she had worn on her previous visit. "But, of course," she wrote to Gianfrancesco, who was in Venice—"if Your Highness thinks otherwise, I shall start tomorrow, even if I have to travel alone and in my chemise" (July 25, 1492). She didn't have to travel in her chemise, but set out on August 10, having ordered in a frantic hurry all she needed, including "a necklace of a hundred links." This necklace turned out to be such a masterpiece as to become the apogee of the jeweler's art. It was known throughout Italy as "*The* necklace of a hundred links." Halfway to Pavia she remembered that she had forgotten her best hat, a concoction of plumes and jewels. She sent a rider all the way back to Mantua, with the key to her black chest; he was to deliver the hat in Milan.

In Milan a pregnant Beatrice welcomed her sister, and Lodovico arranged dances and theatricals for her and showed her his treasury, which was heavily guarded and which he seldom showed to anybody. The Sala del Tesoro was a huge vaulted hall close to his apartments decorated with frescoes by Leonardo and Bramante, and here, locked in large chests, were thousands of gold ducats, which he kept in case he should suddenly need ready cash. Here, held flat by oak presses which Leonardo had designed, were heaps of gold and silver dishes and salvers. Here too was a collection of jewelry which included a ruby called La Spiga, "the ear of corn," worth 250,000 ducats; a diamond arrow called the Puncta; another ruby known as the Marone and worn by Beatrice as a brooch; and Il Lupo, "the wolf," consisting of a large diamond and three pearls valued at 120,000 ducats. This was the accumulation of a state the annual income of which exceeded 600,000 ducats. (The revenue of all of England in the fifteenth century was estimated at 700,000 ducats.) "Would to God that we who like so much to spend money had half as much," wrote Isabella.

She observed that all was not well with the marriage. It was not an unhappy one; Lodovico was rather fond of Beatrice, who outwardly—and especially to him—appeared as a laughing girl, "spending day and night in singing and dancing and all manner of delights," according to a Milanese chronicler. And Beatrice was dedicated to Lodovico, never even glancing at another man. Yet she could not satisfy his sexual appetite. Cecilia Gallerani was still his mistress, even after the wedding, and what was more, still installed in a suite at the Castello in a proximity which Beatrice found degrading. She trembled with fury every time she had to watch Lodovico walk over to Cecilia. At Beatrice's insistence, Lodovico eventually married Cecilia off to an obliging count, but that was not the end of his extramarital affairs. In 1495, four years after his wedding, Lucrezia Crivelli, one of Beatrice's ladies-in-waiting, came into his life. She too was beautiful enough to deserve to be painted by Leonardo: some art historians believe that Lucrezia served as the model for *The Virgin of the Rocks*.

Beatrice reacted to Lodovico's infidelities in ways consistent with her nature. She kept herself busy in a hectic round of riding, hunting (she narrowly escaped being killed by a wild boar), dancing, gambling (she was said to have won 3,000 ducats at cards at one session), designing fancy costumes, and most of all spending money. They called her "madly in love with luxury"—but it was the luxury of personal adornment. She shared little of Lodovico's and Isabella's interest in artistic possessions, but in her summer palace of Vigevano hung 424 dresses.

It is probable that Isabella realized how things stood. She saw her sister's perplexity in those hours when they were closeted together, and she tried to help her. We may guess that she advised Beatrice to interest herself in her husband's administrative concerns, as she herself had done at home. Beatrice followed Isabella's hint, for presently she was representing Lodovico as an ambassadress, and, except during her pregnancies, she discharged that function with élan, showing a diplomatic ability which nobody had suspected she possessed.

A curious situation: here was Isabella close to the man who attracted her, yet still very much in love with Gianfrancesco. Here was Beatrice, confused and a little puzzled by her sister, yet loving her and loving Lodovico. Here was Lodovico, borne high by success, but uneasy between the two women. It is clear that Isabella acted honorably and unselfishly: whatever pangs she may secretly have felt, she did her best to save the marriage. She appeared as a beneficent mediator. After her visit in 1492, the relationship of Lodovico and Beatrice became less beset with burrs. In spite of Lodovico's strayings, his affection for the "spoiled and pretty child" deepened. He drew toward her more tenderly and more sweetly—and there lay much tenderness in that willful soul. In the five years Beatrice still had to live, a better understanding, a more natural intimacy, prevailed. How much Isabella contributed to bring this about cannot be measured; that she contributed something is indubitable.

At the end of her visit to Milan, Gianfrancesco asked her to proceed to Genoa on a "good-will" mission; he wanted to establish a connection with the Mediterranean port. On entering the city, she encountered a curious local custom. She reported it to Gianfrancesco:

> At six o'clock we entered Genoa, amid the noise of guns and trumpets, and I was conducted to the house of Messer Cristoforo Spinola, where the governor's wife and sister-in-law and other noble ladies were waiting to receive me. Before I had time to dismount, a crowd of workmen gathered around me, and seized my mule, according to their custom here. They snatched the bridle and tore the trappings to pieces, although the governor interfered, and I willingly gave it up to them. I was never so frightened in my life, and was really afraid of some accident, but fortunately I did not lose my head. At length I was released from their hands, leaving my steed, a mule which Signor Lodovico had lent me, to be their prey. I must redeem it at a fair price, and shall have to buy a new set of trappings!

But more important than the visit to Genoa was her official visit to Gianfrancesco's employer, the Signoria of Venice. Gianfrancesco evidently deemed it prudent to send Isabella to assure the doge of continued Gonzaga loyalty, and Isabella, always eager to go somewhere and see new sights, did not need much urging. She set out in May 1493. After resting for the night on the island of Chioggia, she entered the famed city early the next morning, saw for the first time the hesitant blush of the Venetian dawn, heard the murmur of the gondolas cutting through the water as she passed between the protecting forts, and alighted in awe and wonder at the church of Santa Croce, where the doge, a deputation of the Senate, and the ambassadors of Milan, Ferrara, and Naples received her. She wrote to Gianfrancesco:

Here I landed and met the Prince and ambassadors coming out of the church, and kissed His Serene Highness's hand and exchanged courteous greeting, after which he led me to his bucentaur, which was loaded with gentlemen and ladies. There were ninety-three of these last, all richly attired and glittering with jewels, and I am sure that not one among them had less than 6,000 ducats' worth of precious stones upon her person. I sat on the Prince's right, and so, talking of many things, we rowed up the Canal Grande to the sound of bells, trumpets, and guns, accompanied by such a crowd of boats and people that it was impossible to count them. I cannot tell you, my dear lord, what loving attention and great honor are paid me here. The very stones of Venice seem to rejoice and be glad of my coming, and all for the love which they bear Your Excellency. Not only my own expenses, but those of my whole suite, are liberally defrayed, and two gentlemen have been deputed to provide for us. . . . Tomorrow the Doge and Signory are to give me an audience, and I will reply as you desired to the best of my ability. I do not describe the beauties of this place as you have been here so often, and will only say that it seems to me, as it does to you, the finest city which I have ever seen.

It was all very exciting, very flattering—and soon to be quite wearying. The next day Isabella was formally introduced by the doge at a sitting of the great council. She rose, bowed toward the doge, and made the expected little speech: she was happy to be able to assure His Serenity that Mantua was forever loyal to him and that her lord asked for no better fate than to live and die under the protection of the great Republic. The doge replied in equally rotund phrases. Then the old men filed past her. "I know," she wrote home, "that tomorrow's ceremonies will be no less boring, but I will bear it all cheerfully."

The morrow brought the traditional ceremony of the "wedding of Venice with the sea," the doge throwing a ring from the ship of state into the waters of the Adriatic. It was followed by an endless banquet. The weather was sultry, the speeches long, the food fishy. She ached by the time the day was done, and she sent off a little note to Gianfrancesco: "Have pity on me. I was never more tired and bored than I am with all these ceremonies." When was she going to be allowed to see something of Venice?

She managed it during the succeeding days. She visited the Church of Saint Zaccaria, gazed at its old suntanned campanile, and listened to the chant of the nuns; she went to Murano to watch the glassblowers at work; she inspected the new part of the doge's palace and saw Gentile and Giovanni Bellini painting the frescoes; she spent an hour or two exploring the oriental cave of Saint

Mark's, the "Church of Gold," straining her eyes to make out the meaning of the mosaics, and exclaiming in wonder over the "Blade of Gold," the retable which had been brought from Constantinople centuries ago. She met the Bellinis and asked Gentile if he would sell her a painting he was just finishing, the portrait of a doge. Gentile politely declined.

She returned by way of Padua, Vicenza, and Verona—cities which belonged to Venice—and went to one of her summer palaces to rest and escape the heat. It was certain now that she was pregnant.

On his next trip to Venice, Gianfrancesco heard his wife's praises sung. The doge, the senators, his Venetian friends, all told him how endearingly and tactfully Isabella had behaved, how much good she had accomplished, how much she had done to increase the confidence of the Venetians in their captain. Her husband loved her just then.

Later that year Beatrice, accompanied by her mother, journeyed to Venice on a similar mission, and they were similarly entertained and honored. When Isabella learned about it, she could not hide her jealousy. "Evidently," she wrote her mother, "they follow the same ceremonial routine for everybody." These tiny stabs of jealousy, usual between sisters, were perhaps inconsequential. Yet they were there, rooted in temperaments fundamentally diverse, or on Beatrice's part in her divining how her sister felt about Lodovico. "I have had a whole field of garlic planted for you," Beatrice wrote Isabella, a malicious reference to Isabella's stomach troubles, since garlic was considered a specific against intestinal upsets. "I am sending you a poem by Ariosto. You would profit from reading it," wrote Isabella to Beatrice, knowing that Beatrice would never read it. Beatrice envied Isabella's determined intellect; Isabella envied Beatrice her ability to live for the day (and no doubt her greater wealth). Yet over and above division lay unity, lay childhood closeness. Beatrice was the baby sister; Isabella may not have taken her very seriously, but she did love her, and Isabella's nature needed love. Complete trust and love prevailed between her and her brother Alfonso, though they quarreled now and then. As the two grew older, they grew closer, though they saw each other seldom, and though Alfonso, a blunt character, could not follow Isabella's higher flights of fancy.

2

She was now expecting her first child, with that tremulous mixture of anticipation and fear which every mother has known since she first felt something growing in her body, and observed that body, so carefully tended, assume an unfamiliar and inimical shape. Isabella was sure it was going to be a boy. To welcome him worthily she made elaborate preparations. A cradle of the most beautiful wood was constructed and decorated with gold and ultramarine. Special damasks and silks were imported to keep the baby warm in the Mantuan winter. A series of rooms was set aside, furnished and beautified, which were to house nurses and servants.

The baby was born on the last day of the year 1493, just before midnight chimed. It was a girl, and they named it Leonora, after Isabella's mother. Isabella was deeply disappointed; she wept, and at once she decided that the magnificent cradle was not to be used, nor was the baby to be put in the special rooms. The rooms were closed, the cradle put away. The following day she wrote Beatrice that "the little one is healthy though she is not what I wished for. But since God has so ordered it, I will love her."

But she could not. She never loved Leonora. And Leonora never loved her mother.

Before the birth of her child, Isabella had vowed that if all would be well she would make a pilgrimage to Loreto and Assisi. Gianfrancesco now urgently warned her against this voyage: trouble with the French king was growing acute; there might be a war. It was dangerous to move, and so far, and over mountainous territory. Nonsense!—she would go, she wanted to get away, and her friend Elisabetta would go with her. And she went. Not only that, but having once begun the journey, she decided to prolong it. When she was in Loreto, she received an invitation to visit Gubbio. Why not? She had always wanted to see that strange little city, called the "City of Silence," lying at the mouth of a gorge at the foot of the Apennines. Perhaps she wanted to buy the famed Gubbio ceramics of iridescent red luster. She wrote to Gianfrancesco for his permission—but he was so angry that he did not answer her letters. So she went without his permission, and stayed away from the end of March to the beginning of May. Not a word was said of the "pilgrimage"; she forgot religion for sightseeing.

It was the first rift in Isabella's marriage, the first of her purposeful absences.

3

The very qualities which gave the Italian Renaissance its strength—the diversity of its styles, which developed in territories so small as to appear to us almost suburban but were then so widely spaced that one seemed to have only a nodding acquaintance with another; the brave nonconformity of its thought; the acknowledgment of the value of a good life on earth, as against the medieval concept of a life hereafter; the importance assigned to the individual as an individual—these very qualities were responsible for disintegration. As a nation the inhabitants of this most attractive peninsula of Europe did not exist. They could not work together. It was the Italians themselves who subjugated Italy, not only by battling among themselves, but by opening the gates to the plunderer waiting outside their frontiers. Disunited and as suspicious of one another as the spaniels of a king, they became a prey to the French, the Spanish, the Germans, the Austrians, their country damaged, their citizens wrapping themselves in an every-man-for-himself, don't-trust-anybody, have-as-much-fun-as-possible cynicism. The artists and writers and philosophers carried on, while the invaders, consciously or not, took their creations and spread them throughout the European world. All that was written, built, painted, and sculpted in subsequent years in all of Europe was in some measure shaped by the Italian Renaissance, but Italy declined.

In spite of his wealth, his power, and the strength of will he manifested during the day, Lodovico Sforza did not sleep all that soundly. He had early assumed the regency of Milan from his nephew, the silly and sickly Giangaleazzo Sforza—"most incapable," the historian Guicciardini called him—and he never let go of his power, remaining Milan's ruler in fact if not in name. This usurpation embittered Giangaleazzo's wife, Isabella of Aragon, who hated Lodovico and hated Beatrice even more, and was constantly imploring her father, Alfonso II of Naples, to come north, make war on Lodovico, and bestow the dukedom on her and her husband. And Lodovico was afraid of Naples.

At the same time, the threat of conflict was moving toward Naples itself. Two centuries earlier, the French Duke of Anjou had been awarded Naples as a gift by Pope Urban IV for fighting the Hohenstaufen kings and saving the papacy; but France, busy with its interior problems, had not attempted any all-out efforts toward making good the claim to Naples. Now conditions within France had changed, and the Naples question came to the fore. While Naples confronted Milan with a view to restoring Galeazzo, France confronted Naples to enforce its ancient claim.

Further to complicate matters, the Borgia pope, Alexander VI, had shown his hand. It was a hand which clutched the stiletto more readily than the crucifix, though it was his beloved son Cesare who would be employed to wield the weapon. It had become clear in the first two years of Alexander's reign that the mission he had assigned to his son was to subdue as many Italian states as possible and add them to the papal territories. Alexander intended to achieve this, he announced, even if he had to kill ten thousand Catholics and call in the Turks to help. How could the princes ruling in their provincial castles guard themselves against the pope's determination? How could they save their possessions? Where would they look for help? To France, perhaps?

France had been formed into a nation by Louis XI, the "Spider King." Sitting in Paris, he had spun the threads which encircled the independent feudal lords—those dukes of Anjou, Orléans, Provence, and so on, each a great man in a small realm—and bound them fast to the crown. As the fifteenth century drew toward a close, France was one—one people, one government. The Spider's son, Charles VIII, who ascended the throne in 1483, judged that the time would soon be ripe when his united country could dare to enlarge and enrich itself by conquest. What prize could be more desirable than the land where a soft wind blew from an azure sky, the myrtle tree stood silent and high the laurel?

Charles prepared. He dreamed large dreams. But it might all have remained a dream if the Italians themselves, specifically Lodovico, had not nudged him toward acting on it. Charles's first demand was comparatively modest: he intended to proceed to Naples, there to press his claim to the Kingdom of the Two Sicilies, and he wanted unhindered passage for his army through Lombardy. Lodovico was delighted—such a move, he thought, would lift the Neapolitan incubus off his shoulders. He sent Galeazzo di Sanseverino, the able knight, to call on Charles VIII, bearing gifts of armor and perfumes in silver flagons. Charles welcomed him and invited him to select any of the court ladies who struck his fancy as a playmate for the night. The next day they got down to business, the sum and substance of which was that Charles was to be given the use of Milanese territory for his expedition.

Lodovico's emissaries were not the only encouraging visitors. Cardinal Giuliano della Rovere, the Borgias' implacable enemy, came to urge the French king to swoop down on Rome and depose Alexander. Savonarola mounted the steps of his chancel and, lifting hand and voice in ecstasy, proclaimed that Charles was destined by God to scourge abominable Florence and whip the godless pope.

Once having captured Naples, Charles schemed, he would use it as a jumping-off point to conquer the East: today Naples, tomorrow the world. Lodovico's dreams were equally fantastic: he would, with Charles's help, rule all of Italy, sooner or later. Thus three men—a proud usurper, a misshapen king, a crafty pope—played the game of "sovereignty" with loaded dice.

In March 1494 Charles's army moved: 22,000 infantry and 18,000 cavalry crossed the Alps, while a fleet sailed to Genoa. There a Neapolitan force met the ships: a battle ensued the bloodiness of which gave a foretaste of the slaughter to come. The French destroyed the Neapolitans. Charles halted at Asti, and Ercole Este and Lodovico went to meet him. They marveled at what they saw: he was a nothing of a man, small, spindly legs, a huge hook-nose, a black beard, shifty myopic eyes, a sallow complexion which made him look older than his twenty-four years. The son of the Spider looked like a spider. He stuttered and was so unlettered that he could hardly sign his name. His one abiding interest was women, a different one every night, and as Leporello did for Don Giovanni, he kept a catalog of those he slept with. This, then, was to be the conqueror of the world.* He had come to Italy with a staff which

---

* Frederick Rolfe (self-styled Baron Corvo) described Charles as "a conceited little abortion of the loosest morals even for a king." He wrote that Charles had twelve toes and he hid them "in splayed shoes which set the fashion in footgear for the end of the fifteenth century in Italy." The twelve toes business is doubtful.

included heralds, physicians, chamberlains, cooks, food tasters, pageboys, valets, singers, wardrobe keepers, ladies-in-waiting, ushers, buglers, drummers, harpists, oboists, and acrobats.

His progress was delayed by his contracting smallpox. It was a light case: he recovered, and in the autumn he marched through Milan, Florence, and south, nobody or hardly anybody lifting a sword to oppose him. In December he was in the pope's city. Charles negotiated with Alexander and was allowed to proceed. He finally reached Naples in February. He was hailed as a liberator from the Aragon rule, and for a while he lived up to this role, freeing political prisoners and reducing taxes. He and his soldiers breathed with delight the perfume of the orange blossoms, made plans to send back to France some of the best art treasures of Naples, and found plenty of willing women. (According to one theory, they imported the "French disease"; according to another, the French were infected by the Neapolitans; according to a third, syphilis had been brought from the New World and spread by Spanish soldiers.)

Only a few months went by before it became apparent that the conquest of Naples had been only the beginning, that Charles was determined to Gallicize all of Italy and to use its harvests to fill French stomachs. He treated Lodovico with insulting condescension and withheld the prize he had promised, the legitimatizing of Lodovico's rule in Milan. As it turned out, Giangaleazzo Sforza, the legitimate duke, died soon afterward—it was rumored that Lodovico had poisoned him, but it was probably a consequence of his sexual excesses—and so Lodovico obtained his desire without the help of Charles.*

The French intruders behaved everywhere as arrogantly as their king. The Italian people stirred fitfully and blamed their rulers. Isabella commented: "The rulers of this world ought to place greater value on the hearts of their subjects than on fortresses, treasures and weapons. The discontent of the people may cause more damage than the enemy in the field." Then, at last, the Italians awoke to the danger. Then at last—and even though temporarily—they united for defense. The former enemies formed a league, and it included

---

* Isabella d'Este visited Giangaleazzo's widow—how did Beatrice feel about her sister visiting her archenemy?—and described in a letter, written three months later, how the widow sat clad in black, her face hidden by a black veil, the room airless, its walls covered with black cloth. Isabella was greatly moved.

Milan, Venice, the pope, as well as Ferdinand of Spain and Maximilian I, "Emperor of the Holy Roman Empire," who had his own secret designs on Italy.

Venice took the lead: the Venetians were most skilled in such maneuvers. They kept sending delegates to Charles assuring him of eternal cooperation, while they treated the messengers from Naples who came imploring help against the French with watery coolness. All the while they worked on the details of the league. In February 1495 Gianfrancesco came incognito to Venice "to enjoy the carnival"; they renewed his contract as condottiere for five years at a yearly salary of 44,000 ducats, out of which sum he was to pay the mercenaries. At midnight on March 31 the treaty of alliance was solemnly signed by the doge.

Charles, of course, heard of these preparations. Yet life in Naples was just too pleasant, and it was not until May that he thought he had better go and see what this strange league was all about and how it could be torn apart. Leaving a small garrison behind, he began to travel north with his army. At the village of Fornovo, on the river Taro, near Parma, the allied army, estimated at 30,000 men, under Gianfrancesco, met the French. To help raise this army, Isabella had, at her husband's request, pawned her best jewels. She did it without demurring, much as she loved her jewels.

On July 5 the Battle of Fornovo, one of history's most curious battles, took place. The Italian allies outnumbered the French about three to one, but the French were better organized, better deployed, and their artillery was more modern than their adversaries'. Both sides committed incredibly stupid blunders. As soon as the Italian soldiers caught sight of the rich booty of a fleeing French regiment, they stopped fighting, dismounted, ignored the battle plan, and started plundering, endangering the entire operation. Torrents of rain, thunder and lightning, played an obstinate accompaniment to the clash. The river was overflowing, and the French began to push their enemies into the water. Many drowned in their heavy armor. But the French didn't follow up this advantage; they on their part became disorganized and fled. Confusion on both sides. Stupidity on both sides. Just what Tolstoy was to say four centuries later about the conduct of war. At the end of a day during which Gianfrancesco himself fought furiously, like a man who needed to justify himself—three horses were shot under him—both sides claimed victory. It was "the bloodiest battle Italy had witnessed in two hundred years." The allied losses were much heavier than the French, and many wounded and straggling Italians were mercilessly butchered by French servants and camp followers. Yet Charles, bereft of supplies, decided to retreat. After grueling marches in the heat of summer, the French reached Asti on July 11. The allies did not pursue them with their own shattered army.

To Isabella, Gianfrancesco sent a somewhat biased report of Fornovo, though his realization of the truth peeps out between the lines:

Yesterday's battle, as you will have heard from the heralds, was very fiercely contested, and we lost many of our men, amongst others, Signor Rodolfo and Messer Giovanni Maria; but certainly many more of the enemy were slain. [Not true.] And what we ourselves did is known to all, so that I need not speak of it here, and will only tell you that we found ourselves in a position of such peril that only God could deliver us. The chief cause of the disorder was the disobedience of the Stradiots [Venetian subjects of Albania], who gave themselves up to plunder, and in the hour of danger not one of them appeared. By the grace of God we and this army have been saved, but many fled without being pursued by any one, and most of the foot-soldiers, so that few of these remain. These things have caused me the greatest sorrow which I have ever known, and if by ill chance our enemies had turned upon us, we would have been utterly destroyed. Some French nobles were made prisoners by our company, amongst others the Comte de Pigliano and Monsieur le Bâtard de Bourbon.* The enemies departed this morning, and are gone over the hill toward Borgo San Domino and Piacenza. We will watch their course and see what we have to do. If others had fought as we did, the victory would have been complete, and not a single Frenchman would have escaped.

The league, interpreting the equivocal result for its own purpose, decided that Fornovo represented a great victory. They proclaimed so in loud praise and much ringing of church bells. After all, did they not get rid of the French? And the French did indeed sue for peace, Charles knowing that he was not going to be able to raise new troops fast enough.

Before Charles retreated to Lyons, he invited Gianfrancesco to call on him. Flattered, Gianfrancesco, making the grandiose gesture, returned some of Charles's possessions which had been captured during the battle: they included a portable altar, a reliquary supposedly containing a splinter of Christ's cross, as well as an

---

* Charles would have been taken prisoner had not the Bastard of Bourbon valiantly thrown himself between Charles and Gianfrancesco.

album of portraits of the women with whom Charles had shared a bed during his Italian sojourn. Gianfrancesco kept four of Charles's ceremonial costumes; he was going to give them to Beatrice. Oh, no, said Isabella: "Be assured that I would cede them only with my eyes full of tears—I expect an answer." Gianfrancesco did the expected and gave them to Isabella. Then suitably attired and perfumed, he called on Charles. He was later to rue the visit.

4

It was when Gianfrancesco went away from Mantua to do what he himself described as "great deeds"—and most of Italy subscribed to the description: he was the hero of the hour—that Isabella for the first time grasped the reins of government. She handled them well, demonstrating even at the age of twenty-one her sympathy with people, as well as her attention to detail and an instinctive gift for ruling. The Mantuans respected her, though there were a few complaints. She assured her husband that if discontent existed, it was isolated and needed not to be taken seriously. Just before the Battle of Fornovo she wrote him:

> The inventors of these malicious tales, who have not scrupled to disturb your peace of mind when you are occupied with the defense of Italy, showed little regard for my honor, or for those of my councillors. Let Your Highness, I beg of you, keep a tranquil mind, and attend wholly to military affairs, for I intend to govern the State, with the help of these magnificent gentlemen and officials, in such a manner that you will suffer no wrong, and all that is possible will be done for the good of your subjects. And if any one should write or tell you of disorders of which you have not heard from me, you may be certain that it is a lie, because, since I not only give audience to officials, but allow all your subjects to speak to me whenever they choose, no disturbance can arise without my knowledge.

The "malicious tales" to which she refers probably concerned charges of her using money earmarked for defense to add to her collection. No evidence as to the truth of this charge has been found. What money she did use was spent to improve relations between Mantua and Pope Alexander VI. Carp and the excellent Mantuan cheeses were sent in abundance to the Vatican, jewels to Giulia Farnese, the pope's mistress, a famed beauty whose golden hair reached to her ankles. Isabella also sent jewels and other gifts to Adriana Mila, a cousin of Alexander's, in whose house Alexander's daughter, Lucrezia Borgia, was living. She bought nothing, or not much, for herself. And it was perfectly true that she listened to anybody who applied to her.

She was growing up.

5

The Venetians rejoiced loudly once the French were safely over the Alps. They bestowed on Gianfrancesco the fulsome title "Captain General of the Republic," and increased his already large salary by 2,000 ducats, at the same time voting a pension of 1,000 to Isabella. She paid some of her debts and at once ordered new fabrics and jewels. Though the doge called Gianfrancesco "a modern Scipio," a few censorious voices were raised when he called on Charles and returned some of the booty. Yet at this triumphal hour it didn't seem to matter much.

During the Battle of Fornovo, when his life was in imminent danger, Gianfrancesco had vowed that should he be spared he would offer the Madonna a splendid new gift. The time had now arrived to redeem the pledge. At this moment he remembered an incident which had occurred shortly before Fornovo.

In Mantua lived a well-to-do Jew, Daniele Norsa. One exterior wall of his house was decorated with a fresco of the Madonna and saints. The painting offended Norsa's religious sensibilities, and he applied to the Mantuan bishop for permission to have it removed. Permission was duly granted. The painting was removed, and nothing much would have happened had not some evil prankster besmeared the wall with figures or caricatures of saints, together with scurrilous remarks about Catholicism. These graffiti appeared the night before Ascension Day, May 1495. In the morning, when the procession passed, the people saw the wall, became incensed, thought it the Jew's work, and started to throw stones at the house and menace Norsa. A government guardian restored order and whitewashed the wall. Norsa, still fearful, applied by letter to Gianfrancesco seeking protection. Gianfrancesco, already at camp, immediately sent orders that Norsa was not to be molested. Both he and Isabella were reasonably free of the hatred and suspicion people felt for the Jews, that strange and coherent group they could not understand.*

After Fornovo, however, Gianfrancesco had second thoughts. Shouldn't the Jew be made to pay for that tribute he himself had promised the Madonna? It was the least that could be asked of him in return for being protected. Aside from sheer parsimony, was Gianfrancesco superstitiously fearful that he might have offended the Madonna by permitting her fresco to be removed? Did he feel that putting Norsa to this expense represented some kind of compensation? Whatever his motives, he decreed that Norsa was to pay 110 ducats and that this sum was to be spent on a painting by Mantegna, glorifying the Madonna—and himself. Norsa paid.

The result is one of Mantegna's magnificent works, the *Madonna della Vittoria*, the Madonna of Victory. Gianfrancesco, clad in armor, is kneeling and smiling up at the Madonna. Behind Gianfrancesco stands Saint Michael, with the shining sword with which he fought for the Hebrew nation against the Prince of Hell, and behind him is a partly hidden old, sad Saint Andrew, carrying the cross to which he was bound in torture. These figures are balanced on the Madonna's left by Saint Longinus and Saint George. Relics of Longinus were supposed to be preserved in Mantua, and he was regarded as the city's patron saint. Saint George is gazing at Gianfrancesco, the traditional broken lance resting against his shoulder. But who is the kneeling female figure opposite Gianfrancesco? Logically and traditionally it should be Isabella. It is not. It is an old woman, simply dressed, who may represent Saint Ann or Saint Elizabeth or Osanna, a nun revered in Mantua. Above the Madonna a sprig of coral is suspended from a seashell. Coral protected one against the *malocchio*, the evil eye. The entire scene is set in a bower of leaves and fruits, through the openings of which one glimpses a jocund sky. In short, Mantegna produced a painting that expressed the period's pleasure in the beauty of nature and the beauty of man, in which young and old figures dressed as it were in their Sunday best were presented in colors which seem to have been ground from jewels.

* Isabella later roundly reproved an anti-Semitic preacher. She wrote to one of her vicars: "Tell the priest to do his job of preaching, hearing confessions, and other tasks necessary to the soul's health, but he is not to touch the Jewish question. I don't want him to preach sermons which are more scandalous than useful."

After Norsa had handed over the money for the painting, one might expect that he would have been left in peace. On the contrary. Gianfrancesco's brother Sigismondo and a Fra Girolamo Redini, a trusted adviser of the Gonzagas, now suggested that to house the picture worthily a new church ought to be built. What site could be more appropriate than the Jew's house? Let the house be pulled down—that would teach the Jew a lesson. Gianfrancesco at first resisted but soon enough gave in. Norsa's house was destroyed and a church built in its place. No document has been found to tell us whether Norsa was compensated or what happened to him afterward. Nobody seems to have bothered with so unimportant a matter.

A year after the battle, both church and picture were ready. Mantegna's painting was taken in procession from the artist's studio to the church. There, amid ceremonies which included the singing of lauds, children dressed as angels, a speech by the priest, the lighting of candles, and the placing of other votive offerings, the work was hung. Gianfrancesco was away. Isabella was in Mantua, but she was in the last stages of pregnancy and did not want to show herself. Shortly after, she gave birth to a girl, christened Margherita. The baby died.

V

Wife of a Hero

Isabella was the wife of a hero, and she imbibed with pleasure the compliments tendered the warrior's companion. She was proud too that she had kept Mantua in order while he was away. She believed in him heart and soul. She trembled for his safety. On the eve of the battle she had sent him a little gold cross which he was to wear around his neck and she had written him a typical wifely letter: "I beg you to take care of yourself, because I am always so afraid when I think that you are in the field, though I know that there is where you want to be." She followed this with a note purporting to come from their daughter, Leonora, one and a half years old:

Illustrious Prince and noble Signor, my sweet victorious father! Whether I am in my cradle or lie suckling in the arms of my sweet illustrious mother, wherever I am, I hear the chants and stories of your mighty deeds and the great victory of Your Excellency, who did beat and repulse the French and who did deliver all of Italy from the hands of the barbarians. I hear of the high fame and the great honors bestowed on you by the sovereigns of our lands, etc. . . . Your obedient daughter, still at her mother's breast.

And again she wrote: "I am sure you do your duty best and most efficiently by giving orders to others, not by fighting yourself."

Now that he was home again, she gazed at him with admiration, and she even wrote some poems in his praise, which however she tore up, judging them "feeble."

Gianfrancesco himself continued to trumpet Fornovo as a victory in the loud tone which seeks to obliterate doubt. "In all modesty [what modesty?] I must say," he wrote his brother-in-law Ippolito d'Este, "that this deed at arms not only recaptured Italy's honor, but Italy's freedom, and especially when one considers that no one except ourself has dared to oppose the French." Not everybody agreed. While the Venetian Senate officially swallowed the victory version, at least directly after the battle, while poets composed tangled rhymes of praise, while the great Sperandio designed a commemorative medal, a few realists took a cooler view.

In Bologna lived a lawyer, a curious, emaciated character with a long nose, whose passion was truth at any price and who feared neither prince nor priest. This Floriano Dolfo was a friend of Gianfrancesco, who, to do him justice, tolerated Dolfo's vinegar, perhaps as an antidote to the oversweet wine of flattery. Dolfo wrote:

Illustrious Signor: As a confirmation of the many lies which the people here are bruiting about, your letter of the 12th of this month was most welcome. I learned from it that Your Excellency has changed his profession and from being a historian has become a poet. It might have been better had you made this change *before* the battle, because then not quite so much flesh would have been butchered. Your Excellency either is laboring under a mistaken impression or all the eyewitnesses as well as the dead men are lying. Because all agree that the number of victims was far greater among the Italians than the French. Of course, your informants could easily excuse themselves, saying that they could not distinguish the bodies of the Latins from those of the barbarians, as they were all nude, headless, or disfigured by wounds, blood and filth. . . .

The letter made no impression on Gianfrancesco. Lauded by his wife, lauded by his world, he carried on with his favorite role of medieval knight, clad in spotless armor, forgiving his enemies. When presently Venice sent him to Naples to drive out a French garrison stubbornly entrenched there, he pursued the task with something less than zeal. The head of the French troops, Duke Gilbert Montpensier, fell ill; Gianfrancesco sent him his own doctor, along with gifts of fruit and delicacies. The fact that Montpensier was Gianfrancesco's brother-in-law, having married Chiara Gonzaga, did not serve as an excuse in Venetian minds. Relatives were unimportant; political relations were all-important. Worse still, Gianfrancesco set free the Bastard of Bourbon. He performed this gesture, contrary to Venice's interest, without consulting the doge, who would no doubt have said no. Nor did the doge approve Gianfrancesco's paying that visit to Charles, bringing with him a troupe of Mantuan musicians to serenade the king. More and more the Venetians were beginning to dislike Gianfrancesco's high-handed behavior. They were saying on the Rialto that their captain was flirting with the enemy. Was it so? Venice had too often indulged in such flirtations herself not to believe that it could be possible. Suspicion grew from gossip to belief.

Suddenly and unexpectedly Venice acted.

The blow fell on June 24, 1497. Gianfrancesco had gone to Venice. As he approached his house there, Giorgio Brognolo came out to meet him and told him that the Council of Ten, Venice's highest tribunal, had voted the day before to dismiss him. He was finished as captain, dishonored as leader, disgraced as soldier. Impossible! Gianfrancesco at first could not believe it. Marino Sanuto, a historian who kept a kind of Pepys's diary of goings on in Venice,* wrote that Gianfrancesco rode down the Grand Canal "with great arrogance" and demanded an audience with the doge. He was refused.

Isabella was in Verona officiating at a tournament as a guest of Venice. The Senate sent word that she was to be treated with all courtesy and consideration: not a syllable to her of her husband's fate. Of course the news leaked, and everybody except her knew about it, including her brother Alfonso, who got on his horse and rode in haste from Ferrara to Mantua, there to await his sister. When she returned and heard the news, they sat in her studio and wondered how they could help. Isabella was totally confused. She could not believe what had happened. Gianfrancesco had immured himself in one of his villas. He blamed everybody for conspiring against him, particularly Lodovico Il Moro, Galeazzo di San Severino, and Pope Alexander. Sanuto noted:

> I hear that he is very gloomy and goes clad in black, and wears an iron ring on his collar, which he has vowed not to lay aside until he has been on a pilgrimage to Loreto. And there is sorrow throughout the Mantovano, and the people, who had been happy and smiling before, are now sad and out of heart.

Was the Venetian Senate justified? Did they have proof of disloyalty or did they merely wish to cut an arrogant commander down to size? The matter is unclear. In November Lodovico wrote to Isabella saying that he had in his hands incontrovertible evidence of

---

* He recorded political scandals, fires, murders, marriages, bankruptcies, movements of ships, visits of important people, carnival performances, etc., in 58 large volumes. He was going to use these diaries, written in a lively, informal style, for a History of Venice. After some twenty years the Venetian Senate appointed Pietro Bembo as official historian. Sanuto was pensioned and told to make his diaries available to Bembo. It broke his heart.

Gianfrancesco's secret dealings with the French and that he had withheld this evidence only out of love for her, but this assertion is not completely to be taken at face value, Lodovico having his own reasons for wishing to pry Gianfrancesco loose from Venice.

In the political pattern of the subsequent years, as changeable as a kaleidoscope, only one recurrent formation can be descried—and that is Gianfrancesco's own shiftiness. This shiftiness played against and was reflected by the shiftiness of friend and foe. On horseback, sword in hand, he felt whole and comfortable; in the council chamber he was uncomfortable, a vacillating prince. His instability became falsehood, his irresolution false-heartedness. Untrue to himself, untrue to Italy, and in time untrue to Isabella, he shrank in stature, selling his great ability as a warrior to the highest bidder—and failing to deliver value for value received. It is entirely possible that his dismissal by Venice was based on guilt, which was shortly to be confirmed, though we cannot be sure that the Signoria's action was not the very act which pushed him into it, that in fact he became disloyal after he was accused of disloyalty.

Whatever the truth, her husband's disgrace dealt a severe shock to the trusting wife. Doubts assailed her. She who had felt so secure with him now began to question his motives. And now she had to recognize a new and increasing peril. The French were once again threatening all Italy; the Borgia pope was threatening Mantua.

2

Charles VIII died three years after Fornovo, only twenty-eight years old, worn out by lust. But Louis XII of France harbored the same ambition toward Italy as his predecessor, with the difference that his first target was to be Milan and he went about his plan more circumspectly than Charles had. He was of course able to find some legal pretense for his claim on Lodovico's dukedom; but what really motivated him was his loathing of Lodovico Sforza, whom he called "that Signor Lodovico" with a deprecating wave of his hand. He spent the better part of two years getting ready. He first negotiated with England and Spain, making reasonably sure they would not pounce on France while he was foraging in Italy, and he then turned his attention toward winning the two powerful forces within Italy to his side, Venice and the pope.

Nothing, Louis knew, could tempt Alexander except the prospect of extending the Vatican's influence, not so much for the glory of the Church as for the glory of his children. This hard man hugged his children to his bosom with idolatrous weakness, his lips wet, his eyes moist. No bribe was too large, no plot too dark, no crime too cruel provided it advanced their interests. We may believe Guicciardini, who admired Alexander's strength and his administrative skill, but—

he was possessed by an insatiable greed, an overwhelming ambition and a burning passion for the advancement of his many children who, in order to carry out his iniquitous decrees, did not scruple to employ the most heinous means.

Four of his "many children" were given him by a Roman matron, Vannozza de'Cattanei, with whom he lived for some twenty years. Later, in the home of his cousin Adriana—the woman to whom Isabella prudently sent a few jewels—he met the great beauty Giulia Farnese. He promptly became enamored of her, married her off to Adriana's son, whose scruples, if he had any, Alexander smoothed away with a large dowry, made her his mistress—"the Bride of Christ" the Romans called her—and made her young brother, Alessandro Farnese, a cardinal.

Alexander loved his son Giovanni best. But one morning in 1497 Giovanni's corpse was dredged from the Tiber, his throat slit, nine other wounds all over his body. His purse was intact; nothing had been stolen.

Alexander went half mad with grief. According to Johann Burchard, a German who functioned as Alexander's "master of ceremonies," and who recorded with typically German punctiliousness all that he was witnessing, Alexander refused food and drink "from Wednesday evening till Saturday," moaned and resolved to "amend our life" and to renounce all nepotism. His good intentions had but a seven-day life. Soon his lust for Borgia power proved too great.

The murder of Giovanni has never been solved. At the time nobody accused his brother Cesare; but as his reputation came to be besmeared with terror, many began to believe that he had killed his brother out of jealousy. Modern research is inclined to believe that it was probably the only murder he did *not* commit.

At any rate, Cesare remained to carry out his father's plans for conquest, and his own. To realize these plans Alexander now turned his attention to France and began negotiating with Louis XII. In substance, these were the agreements reached:

1. Cesare was awarded a French dukedom—the territories of Valentinois and Diois—and he was henceforth known as "Valentino."
2. Cesare was offered a bride, the beautiful and rich Charlotte d'Albret, sister to the king of Navarre.
3. Louis was to contribute soldiers and matériel for Cesare's military expeditions against the principalities once held by the Church, take them by force, and depose their sovereigns. The plan included Imola, Forlì, Faenza, Pesaro, and Urbino (governed by Guidobaldo and his Elisabetta, Isabella's friend). He intended as well to expand the papal territory by annexing Arezzo (belonging to Florence)—and Mantua.
4. Louis wanted to get rid of his wife, whom he had been forced to marry and who was deformed and ugly. He wanted to marry Anne, the widow of Charles VIII, who was beautiful and—what was more important—the owner of Brittany, thus preventing Brittany's withdrawal from the French crown. For this he needed and obtained an annulment from the pope.
5. Louis's adviser and friend, Georges d'Amboise, Archbishop of Rouen, was made a cardinal.
6. Alexander pledged strict neutrality in Louis's coming expedition against Milan.

The terms of this convenant were faithfully carried out, though "faithfully" is not an adverb one should apply either to Alexander or to Louis. As soon as the rumor of it spread, Cardinal Ascanio Sforza, Lodovico's brother, fled in haste from Rome. He understood. He understood that Alexander had broken with Lodovico, the very man who had supported his election, and that it was all up with the Sforzas.

Naturally, with the optimism which drowns judgment, Lodovico did not think so; he believed he could win against the combination of pope and king. He looked for help in the struggle. His overtures to Venice proved fruitless; they evaded committing themselves. To be sure, the Signoria hated the pope, but they hated Lodovico more. He appealed to Ercole of Ferrara. At first Isabella's father did not answer; he then offered to send a pitifully small troop of soldiers to Milan, and finally decided to stay out of the fray altogether because "he was now an old man." The only ally Lodovico could find was Emperor Maximilian, who was far away and unpredictable.

Gianfrancesco showed himself at his most indecisive and most venal. Louis XII offered him the leadership of French troops. At the same time, Lodovico said, "Come to our side and be our captain and we'll pay you more than the French." There followed endless secret negotiations, Gianfrancesco teetering from one to the other, unwilling or unable to come to a decision and using his vacillation as well as the knowledge that he was needed—not only for his military skill but for the fear that the name of the victor of Fornovo would instill in the enemy—to exact more money, more guarantees of security, and a high-sounding title. The matter of the title assumed an undue importance, for some unknown reason; it is easy to understand that a title would mean a lot to a man uncertain of himself, but it is difficult to understand why either Louis or Lodovico did not give him whatever title he wanted. Surely they could have found a means to cancel it if Gianfrancesco failed.

During these negotiations, Isabella found herself in a most difficult position. No question about it, her heart was with Lodovico. Their friendship was as close as ever, so close, indeed, that those in the know, both in Milan and in Mantua, were sure they were having an affair. Just recently Lodovico had invited her to visit a Milanese cloth merchant and choose whatever fabrics she desired. He had insisted that she take the most expensive, with gold and silver interwoven, costing 40 ducats a length. (She chose fifteen lengths—a gift worth $12,000.) Now, while the military talks were proceeding and though Lodovico had much to occupy his mind, he arranged to have two of the most learned Dominican scholars visit her in Mantua. (One of these was the prior of Santa Maria delle Grazie, the church in the refectory of which Leonardo was still, and with exasperating slowness, painting *The Last Supper*.) They were going to debate a theological question. Isabella enjoyed the debate so much that—she wrote Lodovico—though she lacked the professional skill for disputation, she was constantly on the point of taking part. Even her husband, who took not the slightest interest in such matters "and was used more to combat at arms than combat at words," was delighted. Lodovico answered that "with her mind and understanding, she could well have taken part in the debate" (May 1498).

"With her mind and understanding" she saw the political situation more clearly than he did. Yet her heart pressed her in opposition to her mind and led her to urge Gianfrancesco to come to Lodovico's side. It was a counsel prompted more by love than by logic, although her dislike of Alexander, her fear of Cesare, and her suspicion of the French no doubt had something to do with it. She must have felt intense impatience mixed with shame when in April of 1498 she received a remarkably outspoken letter from her husband's confidant, Girolamo Redini (the one who had acted against Norsa), now stationed in Rome:

. . . It seems to me that the better they in Rome understand and praise your personal virtues, courtesy, and all the other good qualities of Your Excellency, the more they regret that these qualities are absent from [the government of] Mantua. I am not writing you to curry favor with you. I write to bestir your heart and soul. . . .

I am not surprised that the Venetians dismissed him, I am not surprised that his brother [Sigismondo] is not yet cardinal, I am not surprised that they call him untrustworthy and say that he has neither stability nor brains. But I would be absolutely astonished, indeed I would call it a miracle, if the poor man would still be considered for any honorable undertaking. True, he has been betrayed by his own [friends], libeled, cruelly mocked here and in other places. That pains me to my soul and I can only hope that now God will become his mentor, and the Madonna. It is imperative that he show himself wise, that he show that he has determination and is not as weak as they picture him here, and that he act in a steadfast manner. He must give the lie into the very throat of the scoundrels who say that when he is in his cups he babbles forth all secrets. Pardon me, my Illustrious Lady, if I transgress my authority. If I give you pain, it is only because of the love I bear you. Have patience! These are not things about which one can keep quiet. You must be warned. Be cautious *in futurum*. . . .

Rome, April 22, 1498

Two months later Gianfrancesco signed a three-year contract with Lodovico at a salary of 40,000 ducats. An enormous stipend! The question of the title remained unresolved. Should Lodovico not satisfy him on that point, Gianfrancesco had the option to cancel the agreement.

At the end of June Lodovico announced that he was coming to Mantua to talk over details. The proposed visit got Isabella, the hostess, all excited. She wanted a splendid reception, and her own resources did not suffice, she thought. She borrowed plate and tapestries from Niccolò da Correggio and bustled about to make everything presentable. Should she assign her own rooms to the guest? What wines and dishes did Lodovico prefer? she asked

Benedetto Capilupo, who was in Milan. (The answer was white wine for breakfast, demisec but not "smoky"; for the main meal a light clear red. For food, anything she liked to serve.) Lodovico came with a train of a *thousand* courtiers, straining the resources of Isabella's court, and departed. Everything was in order.

But it was not. No later than October Gianfrancesco approached the doge, behind his wife's back, to inquire whether Venice would consider taking him back. Since Venice had thrown its lot in with France and the pope, this was nothing less than a betrayal of his agreement with Lodovico. An infuriated Isabella sent a secret messenger to Lodovico, informing him of her husband's intention. Lodovico stormed and threatened, broke off diplomatic relations with Mantua, let all Italy know what he thought of the "Mantuan trader," presently cooled off—and then resumed negotiations. On November 3 the contract was taken out of the archive, signed anew, and Gianfrancesco was granted the official title of "Captain General" of the troops of Milan and Emperor Maximilian. Isabella played an instrumental role in this second change of allegiance. Lodovico wrote her thanking her for her assistance; he knew that she had "labored diligently to bring about this happy result." The reaction in Venice was the expected one: "Everyone agreed," Sanuto wrote, "that the Marquis has treated our Signoria scurvily. The Pope is reputed to have remarked that we are well rid of a great fool." On the first of January, 1499, Maximilian's envoy solemnly delivered the baton and flag of the Holy Roman Empire to Gianfrancesco, while Isabella witnessed the investiture from a platform.

In that year of 1499, a year of whispers and broken oaths, a year the motto of which might well have been *semper infidelis*, when the news transpired in February that Venice had formed an alliance with France, Louis's purpose became clear, the plan decipherable: to destroy Lodovico and cut up the state of Milan. Isabella, who was visiting her father in Ferrara, left at once for Mantua to give her husband the bad news, to confer as to what next to do, and above all to save Mantua itself, toward which the doge—as well as Cesare—was now glancing. Gianfrancesco, realizing how powerful were the forces arraigned against Mantua, once more tried to change sides: he made overtures to Louis, using his sister Chiara, the widow of Montpensier, as a go-between. Louis was more than willing to welcome him; what did he care about Gianfrancesco's morality if he could harness his ability? In point of fact, what eventually happened was that Gianfrancesco aided neither the French-Venetian-papal side nor Lodovico, but continued to balance one against the other.

The stage was set, then, for the new invasion of Italy, for which essentially the pope's policies were responsible, as five years previously Lodovico had been. The French troops began to swoop down on Milan. They found their task ridiculously easy: village after village, little city after little city, capitulated, until Milan itself gave up. Lodovico fled across the snow-covered Alps in disguise until he reached Innsbruck and Maximilian, and Louis entered Milan in a triumphal procession on October 6. His soldiers emptied the Treasury, burned tapestries, stole the gold vessels, but he himself put on a gracious and forgiving mien. One of the first things he did was to invite Gianfrancesco to come to Milan; the two went hunting, and when a great feast was held on the twentieth of October to celebrate the French victory, Gianfrancesco led the formal dance, his partner one of Milan's most beautiful women, "la bianca Lucia." The Venetians considered that shameful.

It was at this moment that Isabella expunged from her heart her loyalty to Lodovico and renounced her love.

Whatever pain the decision gave her, she now knew that Lodovico was beyond help and that her first duty, as well as her desire, lay toward the state of which she was princess. What could be done to preserve Mantua from a fate similar to Milan's? Her political thinking took over. She knew that only by playing along with Louis could she save her state and her position. She determined to charm Louis. Her fame as a woman had reached him; it was not too difficult to capture his interest. She began at once: letter after letter went to the French king, redolent of perfumed compliments. The shipments of carp and cheeses, the baskets of peaches and caskets of wine, which used to go to Lodovico now arrived on Louis's table. When the French ambassador accused her of still being pro-Sforza, she wrote her envoy in Milan, Donato de Pretis, a letter which was obviously meant to be shown the king:

We wish you to convey—if only in jest—to the Royal Ambassador our invitation to come here and visit us and demand our pardon for what he said about our being pro-Sforza. Let His Excellency accept our offer and . . . he'll convince himself that we are true French. After that he won't need to apologize for his opinions. We confess frankly, being free of falsehood, that at one time we were very fond of Duke Lodovico, as fond as one can imagine, both for reasons of kinship and because of the affection and honors he showered on us. But after he began to treat our illustrious consort badly, our affection began to diminish. . . . We were always in accord with the aims of His Majesty, the Most Christian King [Louis], and now that he has shown such honors to our consort we are indeed a good Frenchwoman. If the Ambassador comes here he will see that we are most kindly disposed and that we are clothed in lilies [the symbol of France]. . . .

October 16, 1499

To which the French ambassador replied (in French):

Madame, I beg you most humbly to forgive the bad opinion I held of you. Now that you are a good Frenchwoman, I am your very humble servant.

November 2, 1499

They were both lying.

No sooner had Louis returned to Paris, leaving Milan under the command of General Gian Trivulzio, than the situation changed. Trivulzio governed ineptly, levied excessive taxes, the occupation forces behaved scandalously, and Lodovico managed to get together an army of sorts, helped by Gianfrancesco, who through messengers traveling to Innsbruck kept him informed of Milanese conditions. One of these messengers, disguised as a friar, was caught by the Venetians and tortured on the rack, and he confessed. Nevertheless, in February 1500 Lodovico once more took possession of his city, while Trivulzio thought it prudent to retire his forces to the western frontier of the duchy. Isabella, that "good Frenchwoman," was delirious with happiness over Lodovico's new luck. She wrote to Cardinal Ascanio Sforza that she longed to fly to Milan to help her friends. He replied with measured irony that her friends would prefer to see Gianfrancesco with some soldiers.

Yes, Gianfrancesco was coming, his troops were ready. But he never went. He kept the soldiers in fighting order but standing still in Mantuan fortresses. The "captain" never raised the anchor. He was playing the waiting game, staying in harbor, to watch which way the winds of war were going to blow.

He did not have long to wait. Louis replaced Trivulzio with the highly competent Marshal La Trémoille. He raised fresh troops, the French rallied and reoccupied Milan, and Lodovico attempted to flee; he was caught and thrown into prison. The unhappy man lingered on for eight years. He died in oblivion, aged fifty-seven. As far as we know, in all that time he never wrote to Isabella nor Isabella to him.

France and Venice now remained in firm charge. Louis XII once more came to the great Lombard city; Isabella once more became French, "clothed in lilies."

She had given asylum to Milanese refugees, including some relatives of Lodovico and, strangely enough, to Lodovico's enemy, Isabella of Aragon. That unhappy widow—she signed herself henceforth "unique in misery"—had to cede her oldest son to Louis, who took him to France as a hostage. She remained in Mantua until she retired, lonely and powerless, to Bari. Later Isabella welcomed Lodovico's two mistresses as well; she recommended Cecilia Gallerani to Louis as a "lady of rare gifts and charm," while Lucrezia Crivelli continued to live for many years with her two sons in a castle outside Mantua. Louis wisely forgave Isabella her meddling; she claimed that she had done so because she could not bear to see these innocent victims suffer. No doubt it was the truth.

She had managed to gain an all-powerful advocate at the king's court, Georges d'Amboise, now duly become cardinal; Louis relied on him to such an extent that the king's courtiers used to pronounce as a kind of password, "Laisser faire à Georges!" D'Amboise, Isabella heard, was a great admirer of Mantegna. She or Gianfrancesco commanded Mantegna to paint a picture for him at once. D'Amboise declared he valued it more than 2,000 ducats. He would do anything he could for the donor of so extraordinary a gift.

However busily Isabella solicited French favor, however unashamedly she used her charms on the king, buried in her heart lay grief for Lodovico's fall. She thought of that Sala del Tesoro, now empty and befouled with dirt; she thought of the manuscripts of Pavia now dispersed, the jewels spirited away to Paris, Beatrice's gold-embroidered camora now bedecking a sergeant's mistress, the cameos used as stakes in dice games.

Louis invited her to the great festival held in Milan which celebrated the final French victory. Leonardo had constructed a mechanical lion for the occasion; when it opened its mouth, it spewed forth fresh lilies. She smiled. She danced. She admired the lion. She captivated Louis. Did she do so only to safeguard Mantua? Perhaps not altogether. It was easy to like Louis, who, flinty in the field, was soft and ingratiating in the palace, a man who could unbend and take eager part in parlor games. He was the very opposite of Charles: *beau personnage et homme de plaisir,* he was called, gay, chivalrous, quick-witted. A friendship, and perhaps more than a friendship, developed between the two. How could Isabella help being flattered? Chiara let her know that Louis was greatly taken with her and promised not to harm her or to proceed against her state.

Gianfrancesco was not let off quite so easily. He was fined the sum of 50,000 ducats ($1 million) as reparations. He agreed to pay and then tried to wiggle his way out and have the fine reduced. An angry Louis declared that he would cede Mantua to Venice. They were eager to grab it and were just waiting for the word. Gianfrancesco once again got his troops in readiness and swore that he would die fighting for every foot of his territory. After some anxious weeks the matter was arbitrated, Venice was disappointed, and Gianfrancesco stowed his sword away. Presently Louis appointed him one of the "Knights of the King," Gianfrancesco paid, and Mantua remained independent. In all these parleys of peace Isabella played her part.

3

But the danger had not passed. There was still Cesare Borgia.

He could love neither man nor woman, be tender neither with child nor with mistress, act in good faith neither toward an allied nor toward a vanquished prince. Yet he was not a monster, not a precursor of Hitler, not a degenerate like Nero. Capable of generosity, artistic appreciation, and self-denial, he was driven with the force of a man escaping from hell by one obsession, hacking his way through a midnight forest with one need, the passion for power. He dreamed of it, schemed for it, and fought for it. He fought for it both at the head of his armies and with his bare hands. He did not know what fear was. All means justified his end. Symonds admired "the brilliant intellectual qualities of this consummate rogue." As many historians have condemned him as have excused him. Machiavelli, who devoted much analysis to him in *The Prince,* described him with un-Machiavellian fervor as "splendid and magnificent . . . so bold that there is no enterprise so great that it does not seem to him small."

Cesare undertook three major campaigns. In the first, in January 1500, he marched across the Apennine mountains, laid siege to Forlì and Imola, captured Caterina Sforza, and exhibited her to the Roman mob. But then he withdrew, receiving insufficient support from Louis, who was busy with Milan. He set out again in October, having increased his forces to 14,000, and Faenza surrendered. So did most of the castles in middle Italy, delivering a huge territory into papal hands. But there remained Urbino, an important city which gave access to the Adriatic. The Montefeltros, Guidobaldo and Elisabetta, were allies of the pope, and Guidobaldo had lent his artillery to Cesare's army. A firm friendship bound the couple to the Borgia family. They felt quite safe. Cesare had embraced Guidobaldo and sent him gifts.

In June 1502 Cesare once more proceeded. He was going against the city of Camerino. Leonardo was now in his service as chief engineer. Suddenly, and with less warning than a rattlesnake gives, he swerved and changed his course toward Urbino. The ailing duke fled barely in time; he had no other choice. Isabella, who was enjoying the June days in the country, received the news with horror. She wrote to Chiara:

We were here, very quiet and contented, enjoying the company of the Duchess of Urbino, who has been with us since carnival, and often wishing that you were here to complete our happiness, when news of the unexpected and perfidious seizure of the duchy of Urbino reached us. The Duke himself arrived here with only four horsemen, having been suddenly surprised and treacherously attacked, so that he narrowly escaped with his life. We were quite stunned by the blow, and are still so bewildered and unhappy that we hardly know where we are, as Your Excellency will understand; and so great is my compassion for the Duchess that I could wish I had never known her.

Guidobaldo told them that he had fled at midnight, saving "nothing but my life, my doublet and my shirt." He had been completely overwhelmed by Cesare, his "friend," who materialized out of nowhere and was even then on the outskirts of Urbino. Isabella now generously aided Guidobaldo. After staying with her for a while, he and Elisabetta moved on to Venice, where they were hospitably received.

Cesare had the great art collection of Urbino loaded on a train of mules and sold it to pay his mercenaries. Sanuto estimated the value of the booty at 150,000 ducats, which may be exaggerated.

Having done his work at Urbino, Cesare then subjugated Camerino. The few unconquered sovereigns, such as those of Perugia, Bologna, Gravina, Siena, trembled at what was to come.

In October of that year these lords organized a conspiracy against Cesare. Four of the leading conspirators met in Senigallia, a town on the Adriatic. Cesare rode into Senigallia, offered conciliatory terms, invited them on New Year's Eve to a conference in the governor's palace, toasted the new year of peace and forgiveness, embraced them, shook hands all around—and then had them arrested. Two were strangled that very night; two others were imprisoned and executed two weeks later.

Yet in all this cruelty a curious paradox appeared: Cesare governed the conquered lands well and wisely. He appointed good, honest men as his deputies and watched them closely. He himself worked as hard as any man. The people of some of the conquered cities praised this inexplicable centaur, half demon, half genius.

That he spared Mantua, that the Gonzaga state remained upright when all around the Italian states were toppling, was entirely due to Isabella's skill. It was an accomplishment to be marveled at. She diagnosed the premonitory symptoms and she early determined to get along with him, though she harbored no illusions as to his character and seems to have believed that he did murder his brother. Be careful of every word you say to Cesare, she warned Gianfrancesco, because "he does not scruple to conspire against those of his own blood." She reported Cesare's moves to Gianfrancesco with the accuracy of a good war correspondent. At the same time she kept sending him presents, perfumes, prize dogs, silver dishes, falcons, all gift-wrapped in glittering phrases. A few days after the affair at Senigallia she sent him a hundred beautiful masks to congratulate him on his victories. This was her letter:

Most Illustrious Lord, —Your kind letter informing us of Your Excellency's fortunate progress has filled us with that joy and delight which is the natural result of that friendship and affection which exists between you and ourselves, and in our illustrious lord's name and our own we congratulate you on your safety and prosperity, and thank you for informing us of this, and also for your offer to keep us informed of your future successes. This we beg you of your courtesy to continue, since, loving you as we do, we are anxious to hear often of your movements, in order that we may rejoice in your welfare and share your triumphs. And because we think that you should take some rest and recreation after the fatigues and exertions of these glorious undertakings, we send you a hundred masks by our servant Giovanni, being well aware that so poor a gift is unworthy of your acceptance, but as a token that if in our land we could find an offering more worthy of your greatness, we would gladly send it to you. If these masks are not as fine as they should be, Your Excellency must blame the masters of Ferrara, since owing to the law against wearing masks in public, which has only lately been revoked, the art of making them has been in a great measure lost. We beg you to accept them as a token of our sincere good will and affection for Your Excellency. . . .

It was an appropriate gift, since Cesare was in the habit of wearing a mask when he walked in Rome. He acknowledged the gift in an effusive letter which assured Isabella that

. . . these masks are above all precious to us because they afford a fresh proof of the singular affection which we know that you and your illustrious lord cherish for us, and have already shown in other ways, and now testify again by the long letter which accompanies them. For all this we thank you infinitely, although the greatness of your merit and of your goodness toward us is beyond words, and claims recognition by deed. . . .

What Isabella really had in mind appears in a letter she sent Gianfrancesco at this moment. "The Duke [Cesare] is proceeding toward Perugia," she wrote. "Under the pretense of congratulating him, I'm sending him a mounted messenger, who is to try to find out his next moves."

At one time in his drive north Cesare asked Gianfrancesco whether "he could house his troops in Mantuan territory." Gianfrancesco asked Isabella to deal with this transparent request. She did, with honeyed compliments and due procrastination, convincing Cesare that Mantua, little Mantua, would cause him more trouble than it was worth. It was not the place for his "glorious troops." All the same . . .

Every sound of horses' hoofs, every sparkle of metal in the sun, every cry of the watchman in the night, must have frightened Isabella. From one dawn to the next she could not know whether Elisabetta's or Caterina's fate was to be hers, when Cesare was once more to shift his ground, abjure announced intentions, and appear before the protecting wall, battering an opening with one of Leonardo's new machines. How hard to bear was this uncertainty! How hard to bear it was, as she wrote her husband, that now no one could be trusted. Over and over again she warned Gianfrancesco, more loose of tongue than she, to watch himself. "Rumor has it that in the presence of His Most Christian King and the Pope

Your Excellency let slip a few derogatory words against Valentino [Cesare]. Whether you did or didn't, he'll hear about this." Take precautions: do not admit unknown persons to your presence, "make sure your servants are reliable, so that no one can sneak the Borgia poison into your food." She wanted to send him a reliable food taster.

On July 23, 1501, she dictated this letter to be sent to Gianfrancesco in Milan, where he had gone to confer with Louis, and wrote a postscript in her own hand: "My Lord, Your Excellency, do not mock this letter. Do not say women are cowardly and always beset with fear. The evil of certain people is much greater than my fear or the courage of Your Excellency. I ought to have written this letter myself, but the heat is so awful that I think we will die if it lasts longer. . . ."

While Gianfrancesco was away, Cesare sent a messenger to Mantua. Isabella could make neither head nor tail of why he was there or what he wanted. She tried to sift him but in vain. By and by it dawned on her that he had come to spy. Isabella's succoring of the Urbino couple had made her suspect to Cesare. She asked Gianfrancesco to write her a letter, a pleasant, charming letter, praising Cesare with many words—"even if Your Excellency thinks the contrary"—which she could show the messenger. Gianfrancesco immediately sent such a letter. Isabella thought it was not good enough. She set to work to write a better one, crumpled and dirtied the paper so that the letter would look the worse for having traveled, forged her husband's signature, and showed the missive to Cesare's spy. The letter (lost) is supposed to have assured Cesare's delegate that he need not worry, even though publicly the Gonzagas seemed to have pleaded the cause of the Montefeltros. After all, was she not his sister? It was done only to send them on their way comforted, and to keep up appearances among relatives. Isabella then told her husband what she had done and implored him not to breathe a word to anybody, including Elisabetta. Anyway, she said, the spy departed seemingly satisfied.

The men and women living in high places learned to speak with a double tongue and write with a divided pen. Isabella became a master at flimflam, throwing perfumed dust in her enemy's eyes. What else could she do? They all did it. Seldom did they dare to confess openly what they thought, as when Gianfrancesco wrote his youngest brother Giovanni: "As far as we can foretell, we deem it certain that all of us, one after the other, will perish. We are like men led to the gallows who must helplessly watch others being hung before our eyes." It was more usual not to write so frankly, even to one's own brother, or to write in cipher, or to use harmless phrases which bore another meaning to the initiated. *Andare* could mean "to go"—or to perish; *bere* could mean "to drink" or to be poisoned.

On May 17, 1500, Isabella gave birth to a healthy baby: it was a *boy*. At last the longed-for heir had appeared. Her joy, her satisfaction, and her dynastic pride were great, though the celebrations were somewhat muted because of the "troubled state of Italy" (Isabella's words). The elaborate cradle was unwrapped, the special rooms filled with spring flowers, the palace hung with tapestries sent from Ferrara, a new staff of maids hired. The boy was named Federico. Who were to be the godfathers of this illustrious child? The choice was political; the parents asked Emperor Maximilian among others, as well as—it is hard to believe—Cesare Borgia. Both accepted, and both stood at the child's cradle, though only by proxy. Whatever Isabella's maternal feelings may have been—she probably acquiesced readily enough, since she was willing to try *any* conciliatory move to save Mantua—and whatever Cesare's intention for the future, he accepted the role of godfather with the creamy civility which floated on top of his envenomed cruelty:

I heard of the fortunate and much-desired birth of Your Excellency's little son with exultation as great as if it had been my own, and gladly accept the honor you propose to do me, begging that you will depute one of your councillors to represent me at the font and will give my congratulations to your most illustrious consort, hoping this babe may be the first of a numerous race of sons destined to perpetuate the name of two such noble and glorious parents.

May 24, 1500

Rumor, upon whose "tongues continual slanders ride—stuffing the ears of men with false reports," now circulated that this handsome baby was not Gianfrancesco's child. Whose, then? Louis XII's name was mentioned. "Everybody" knew that Isabella had visited him in Milan; "everybody" commented on the apparent pleasure she had found in Louis's company; "everybody" said the baby looked like the French king. He himself wrote Isabella that he felt Federico was his child. Was this merely royal badinage? Was it just a polite way of assuring her of the king's protection for the inheritor? No certainty exists, but the weight of psychological evidence goes against Louis's being the father. Once Lodovico's image faded from Isabella's mind and once she had met Louis XII, she may have fallen under the spell of his gallantry. The lady who protested that she was a "good Frenchwoman" when she was not may have turned prevarication into truth. But as to committing adultery—? We must leave the question unanswered.

It is certain only that Isabella, who adored Federico, spoke to Gianfrancesco always of "our son" and reported to him the infant's progress or lack of it: the one-year-old "today tried his first steps without being held," and "he enjoyed it no end though he swayed like a little drunkard," or the eight-year-old was "a little slow in learning to read, which worries me . . . send him an admonitory letter." It is certain, also, that Gianfrancesco never voiced a doubt as to his paternity and that he loved Federico; but he loved his four daughters as well, especially the first-born Leonora, whereas Isabella felt close and intimate toward none of them. For her it was always the sons; Ercole born in 1505 and Ferrante in 1507—and above all Federico, over and over again Federico, the exaltation and later the humiliation of her life.

Yet, following custom, she saw nothing wrong with using Federico as a political asset. The child was hardly two years old when she proposed to have him affianced to a baby of equal age, none less and none other than the daughter of Charlotte d'Albret and Cesare Borgia. It was actually Cesare who first made the suggestion. Planning far ahead, he no doubt thought the connection a way of obtaining Mantua without cannons. Planning less far ahead, Isabella no doubt thought the proposal would stave off a Borgia rape of her state. It was a diplomatic move to gain time, and it is just possible that she didn't mean it seriously. As ceremonious negotiations were begun and slowly pursued in the most ductile of languages, Isabella very, but *very* secretly conferred with a Don Emanuel from Spain about a possible Spanish bride for Federico.

At the same time Louis, though openly allied with Cesare, secretly didn't trust him. He let the Mantuan ambassador understand, again by secret intimation, not by open word, that Isabella would be wise to protract the Federico betrothal talks with Cesare, since "Only God knows what is going to happen."

Cesare insisted that Guidobaldo and Elisabetta Montefeltro be expelled from Mantua. If Gianfrancesco and Isabella were to remain his friends, the exiled couple must not be thus comforted. More, he planned to have their marriage dissolved, make Guidobaldo a cardinal, and thereby render the beloved ruler null and void. As long as they stayed in Mantua they were too close to Urbino for comfort. At Cesare's request Louis wrote an official letter to Gianfrancesco commanding him to send the Montefeltros away. La Trémoille whispered to the French legate in Genoa, who smuggled the word to Isabella, that she needn't take that letter too seriously.

The only person who walked a straight path was Elisabetta Montefeltro. She had lost her country; she was not going to lose her husband. Capilupo wrote Isabella that Elisabetta, now in Venice, was going to stay with Guidobaldo "if they both had to die in a hospital." Isabella tried to help her. With encouraging letters. With visits from trusted people who went to Venice. With money. Yet she kept assuring Cesare that she was on his side—she wrote, "because we love you as we do, we want often to hear of your deeds, so that we may rejoice over your good fortune" (and similar drivel) —and she was astonishingly successful in convincing Cesare. She convinced him even when Gianfrancesco's young brother, Giovanni, took part in an anti-Borgia uprising. She had "nothing to do with Giovanni, nothing whatever." Cesare evidently believed it. She had once again taken over the governing of Mantua, Gianfrancesco being in France with Louis, and she pursued her foreign policy of stepping nimbly from left to right. She smiled and her eyelids fluttered, but her eyes were wide open.

Yet while she perused reports from Rome, received the ambassador from Venice, was closeted with the legate from Ferrara whom her father had sent, had her friend Niccolò da Correggio give her the latest behind-the-scenes account of the Milanese colloquy between Louis XII and Cesare (a vivid letter from Niccolò has been preserved), supervised the beginning of Federico's education, wrote twenty letters a day, and always and forever speculated how to keep Cesare at bay—while she filled the roles of a sovereign, a diplomat, and a mother, she longed to be a wife again, to recover the first years of her marriage. She was alone, and she missed her husband. She missed him as a woman in need of an embrace. She implored Gianfrancesco to return from France, and she used their little son as an inducement:

> After I sent my last letter, Federico wished to have supper with me, which he did with the most charming grace in the world, and afterward, as he was at play with ten gold ducats before him, I made someone knock at the door and pretend that a poor beggar was asking for alms. Upon which he took up a ducat at once, and without any prompting, desired the money to be given him, saying: "Tell him to pray to God for me and also for my Papa." This delighted all who were present. I hope this childish inspiration will have the effect of soon bringing you home, where your presence is eagerly desired.
>
> December 2, 1502

The little story does not ring true—but no matter. Gianfrancesco had promised to return by Christmas; he could not—or perhaps he would not—and he remained at the French court until the end of January 1503. But in the spring of that year the French army of occupation met severe reverses in Naples. Louis acted promptly, sending strong troops to quell the uprising which had been prompted and financed by Spain. In July Gianfrancesco, after only five months in Mantua, started southward in the company of La Trémoille. Once more Isabella was left alone, responsibility in her soft quick hands.

4

Even though she was alone, there was yet one indulgence she did not have to deny herself. The episode of the "Sleeping Cupid" was an incident in Isabella's life which sheds light on Renaissance ethics in general and Isabella's character specifically.

A member of the Medici family, Lorenzo di Pierfrancesco, who traded a bit in works of art, commissioned a young and unknown sculptor to make a Sleeping Cupid in the antique style. Lorenzo, a man inclined to tricks—G. F. Young, in his history of the Medici, calls him "mean"—and in mentality and character far below his cousin Lorenzo the Magnificent, suggested to the sculptor that he give the figure an antique finish and make it look like a genuine, excavated-yesterday antique. It was done; the figure was sent to Rome and sold to a dealer for 30 ducats. The dealer first showed it to Cardinal Ascanio Sforza, who thought the piece beautiful but

had some doubts that it was a genuine antique. He couldn't make
up his mind to buy it. One of Isabella's Roman agents inspected it
and reported it as a fine piece of work, well worth buying, but in-
dubitably "modern." The dealer then brought it to Cardinal
Raffaello Riario, the wealthy churchman who had once won 14,000
ducats from the son of Pope Innocent in one night's gambling session. When Innocent had attempted to get the money back on the
grounds that his son had been cheated, Riario said sorry, he had already allocated the money to the Palazzo della Cancelleria* he was
then building. This Riario, then, who knew a great deal about cards
and not so much about art, bought the statue for 200 ducats as an
antique. After a while he learned the truth; angrily demanded his
money back, and got it, being a cardinal. The dealer then sold the
Cupid to Cesare Borgia, who in turn gave it to Guidobaldo of Urbino. The gift turned out to be an Indian gift with a vengeance:
when Cesare conquered Urbino, the Sleeping Cupid was one of the
hundreds of works of art trundled downhill on muleback and into
Cesare's treasury. By this time everybody knew the name of its
sculptor: Michelangelo Buonarroti. He had been twenty years old
when he carved the Cupid, but he had now become famous
through a Pietà he had sculpted for Saint Peter's in Rome.

At several points we have noted Isabella's love for her sister-in-
law Elisabetta of Urbino and Elisabetta's husband. She had exposed herself to danger by sheltering them when they were driven
from their high paradise. Yet this did not prevent Isabella from
reaching for certain works of art which belonged to the Montefeltros and were now in Cesare's grasp. She wanted a part of the
booty, in particular Michelangelo's Cupid, which she described as
"without an equal among the works of modern times." She wanted
it—and that desire overrode all other feeling. Indeed, it never
seemed to have entered her head that she was doing anything of
doubtful morality.

How did she go about getting the statue? Less than a week after
the fall of Urbino, she had it figured out. Instead of appealing to
Cesare directly—which of course she could have done—she used her
brother Cardinal Ippolito d'Este as an intermediary. She knew that
Ippolito was well liked by the pope and consequently by the pope's
son. She knew that a personal appeal by a member of the Church

---

* The noble palace is still standing at the corner of the Corso in Rome. It is
well preserved. The courtyard may be the work of Bramante.

might be effective. She knew, too, that Cesare was beginning to consider the advantages of a betrothal between Isabella's son and his daughter and might therefore be inclined to do her a favor, if she asked it nonchalantly. She fired off a letter to Ippolito, sending it by an "express courier"; the letter is a minor masterpiece of cunning:

Most Reverend Father in God, my dear and honored Brother, —The Lord Duke of Urbino, my brother-in-law, had in his house a Venus of antique marble, and also a Cupid, which were given him some time ago by His Excellency the Duke of Romagna [Cesare]. I feel certain that these things must have fallen into the said Duke's hands, together with all the contents of the palace of Urbino, in the present revolution. And since I am very anxious to collect antiques for the decoration of my studio, I desire exceedingly to possess these statues, which does not seem to me impossible, since I hear that His Excellency has little taste for antiquities, and would accordingly be the more ready to oblige others. But as I am not sufficiently intimate with him to venture to ask this favor at his hands, I think it best to avail myself of your most revered Signor's good offices, and beg you kindly to ask him for the said Venus and Cupid . . . I am quite willing, if it so please Your Reverence, that you should mention my name and say that I have asked for them very urgently and sent an express courier, as I do now, for, believe me, I could receive no greater pleasure or favor either from His Excellency or from your most dear and reverend self, to whom I commend myself affectionately. —Your sister, ISABELLA, Marchioness of Mantua.

Mantua, June 30, 1502

It is perhaps superfluous to point out that Isabella knew that the Cupid was not an "antiquity," and that the demand for the Venus was a ploy to mask what she really sought.

Less than a month after she wrote the letter, a mule arrived in Mantua bearing both statues, driven by a muleteer and accompanied by one of Cesare's chamberlains, who ceremoniously presented the gift to Isabella.

Later, when the Montefeltros were restored to power, Guidobaldo asked Isabella for the return of the Cupid. You are joking, replied Isabella. She claimed in a letter the verbosity of which hides a bad conscience that Guidobaldo himself had given her permission to ask Cesare for the Cupid. Under no circumstances would she give up the beloved statue. Guidobaldo, who knew Isabella's collecting passion, pretended that her argument convinced him and that "as far as his property and his person were concerned she could count on him for anything she wanted." That was putting *bonne mine à mauvais jeux.* The Michelangelo remained in Mantua.

There visitors of succeeding generations marveled at its beauty and poets penned verses in its honor. At the sale of the Mantua collection to Charles I, the statue presumably went to England, and there, or somewhere, it was lost.

5

The political situation at the beginning of the sixteenth century was that of an Italy twice conquered and thrice divided. The French held Milan. Cesare held the middle states as papal territory. In the south Louis XII had entered into a secret agreement with Ferdinand of Spain, with the pope's approval. Naples was carved up between France and Spain. Florence, Ferrara, Bologna, and Genoa were "allied" to France, meaning that they had become tributaries. Only Venice preserved her independence. Mantua, while remaining free, flirted with Cesare on Mondays and with Louis XII on Tuesdays. Gianfrancesco's and Isabella's little buffer state stood like an island in a morass, a triumph of diplomatic wheedling, but Gianfrancesco served as captain to a foreign king. Mantua, then and later, was important just because it separated enemies, like a Belgium which had not been overrun.

Men who dared to oppose Cesare could not set their lives at a ducat's fee, but men of moderate wealth could live comfortably as long as their wealth or rank was not conspicuous enough to incite a pope's cupidity. The poor—they lived as the poor always live. Life went on with its housebound problems amid the outer stresses, as life always does. Isabella continued to exert her diplomatic skill. But soon she was forced to meet a new problem in her own house, a problem intimate and deranging.

VI

"You Loved Me Little"

While she still owned her husband's love, while she still could believe in him, and even though she saw the snags in the fabric of his character, Isabella lived her days exultantly. Perhaps she pursued her artistic interests with a bit more zeal than Gianfrancesco found comfortable. Perhaps he was made to feel that he stood outside the intellectual circle of friends who were beginning to gather in her studio. The conundrums, riddles, epigrams, and Aristotelian allusions they bantered back and forth meant nothing to him; he preferred hunting hidden bears to hunting for hidden meanings in ancient texts. Yet there was give-and-take between them. She was still the wife, happy in her wifeliness. She accepted as part of the prevailing political ritual those dubious approaches of his, now to one combatant, now to the other. At any rate, as a girl she had been taught that the female obeys the male, and in the first years of her marriage she saw no reason for breaking that rule, though circumstances and her own skill combined to assign her more of a "male" role than was customary for a pampered princess.

Of course life did not remain untroubled. In November 1496 Anna Sforza, her brother Alfonso's wife, died, leaving him bereaved and childless. Although Isabella had hardly known Anna, she felt very close to her brother and suffered for him, even as she hoped that "in the years to come he would console himself with another love." And despite her differences with Beatrice, she was profoundly touched by her sister's fate.

On the afternoon of January 2, 1497, Beatrice gave a party. Though she was in the last stages of pregnancy, she danced with the abandonment of unhappiness. That night she gave birth to a stillborn child, and shortly after midnight she herself was dead, a

girl hardly twenty-two years old, who died before she had really
learned to live.

Lodovico was overcome with remorse. Before dawn the next
morning, he wrote to Gianfrancesco:

Most Illustrious Relative and Very Dear Brother,
    My wife was seized with sudden pains yesterday at eight o'clock. At eleven,
she gave birth to a dead child, and half an hour after midnight yielded her soul
to God. So premature and cruel an end has filled me with such bitter and inde-
scribable anguish that I had far rather have died myself than lose what I held
dearest and most precious in the world. . . . I beg of you to send no one to
offer me consolation, as such would only renew my grief. I have not wished to
write to the Marchesa and leave you the duty of breaking the news to her as
seems best to yourself, knowing full well that her grief will pass all bounds. . . .
                              Milan, January 3, 1497, 6 o'clock

The bereaved husband shut himself up in a room with boarded
windows, refused to see anybody, wept, shaved his head, dressed in
a long black coat, and took his meals standing. He broke his liaison
with Lucrezia Crivelli, who was to bear him a son in May. Lodovico could not have been faithful to a wife in any fashion, yet he
worshiped Beatrice's memory, and was never again the man he had
been. "From that time on," wrote Sanuto, "the Duke began to be
sore troubled." It was the beginning of the end of the gaiety and
glory of Milan.

Isabella's grief, less theatrical, was as real and could not have
been unmixed with a trace of self-accusation. Gianfrancesco wrote
Lodovico that he "had never seen his wife so completely overwhelmed." Lodovico wrote Isabella begging her to seek consolation
"he himself could not find."

It was, however, characteristic of her that once her initial grief
had abated, she thought once more of acquisition. She knew that
Beatrice's jewels and Lodovico's plate, the silver and the gold, were
gone beyond recall, sold to equip French soldiers, carried off to
Paris, offered as homage to a damsel or a diplomat. But she remembered that there still must be somewhere in Milan a clavichord
Lorenzo da Pavia had made for Beatrice, a marvel of sound and
beauty. Could she get it? She wrote to one Antonio Pallavicino,
who had been one of the chief traitors among Lodovico's court, and
asked him to search. She was quite willing to deal with a man who
had betrayed her friend. He found the instrument, got possession of

it, and shipped it to Isabella, though the transaction took more than a year.

So Beatrice was gone, Lodovico was gone, and it was just at that melancholy time that Isabella was forced to realize that her husband's love was turning away from her, that Gianfrancesco was something less than faithful to her.

Isabella was no lily growing in a walled garden. She knew man's desire and its gratification, and she recognized that around her "marriage and its rights were more often and more deliberately trampled underfoot than anywhere else," to quote Burckhardt's estimate of Renaissance sexual mores. She had heard the stories of her grandfather's exploits; her own father had sired at least three illegitimate children. And were Lodovico's mistresses not responsible for her sister's death, at least indirectly? What about her husband's brother, the pleasant and equable Giovanni? He had entered into a splendid marriage with Laura Bentivoglio, a charming girl, and yet one heard of his infatuation with a Venetian courtesan, one of the *cortegiane oneste*, meaning only that she was well educated and choosy. But there lay a vast difference between knowing about it and having it happen to you. How could this happen to me, Isabella thought, who loved him so much? How could this happen to me who in the beginning seemed to please him so greatly?

It appeared that one of her own damsels had an "understanding" with her husband. When Isabella discovered this, she lost her composure, grabbed the girl by the hair, and tore at it while the girl howled in pain. Isabella shouted, "Now go and play the nymph with my lord!"

But then Isabella got hold of herself. Conscious of her dignity, she hid her grief. She caused no scandal, made no public scenes. "She prudently feigns," wrote the perspicacious Dolfo to Gianfrancesco, "neither to see nor hear those actions of yours which must be hateful and injurious to her." It was Gianfrancesco himself who brought the injurious action to public notice. He had a mistress, Teodora, last name unknown, with whom he comforted himself, after his dismissal by Venice, without attempting to hide the connection. When a great tournament was held in Brescia in 1497 in honor of the queen of Cyprus, and Gianfrancesco was one of the participants, not Isabella but Teodora appeared at his side as the "Lady of the Joust," richly attired and acting as the official hostess.

Isabella's brother Ippolito was there, as was Galeazzo di San Severino. The scandal was titillating enough for Sanuto to record it in detail in the Diaries.

The insult to Isabella was gross, because tournaments, horse races, and similar sporting events in which princes participated were state occasions, watched by a large public. Five years before the Brescia tournament Gianfrancesco rode in a race at Florence. Then his love for Isabella was at its height, and after having won, he immediately dispatched a special rider with the news. Isabella rejoiced:

> Last night around the twenty-first hour Alberto, the courier, arrived with the news of the race in Florence, that is that your horse outdistanced the others by a considerable length. I cannot express to you how much joy this gave me. I was straining for news of you with open ears, while my heart kept wishing that it be good news. I was at dinner, but I decided to run out to meet Alberto, just to get the news a little sooner. . . . [June 26, 1492]

Now her husband's infidelity had been brought to public notice. Yet Isabella did nothing. Perhaps she tried to come to terms with the notion that monogamy was for women, not for men. Perhaps she understood Gianfrancesco's need for assuaging the hurt of his dismissal. That she did not regard his straying indifferently, that she was aware of a breaking away of a portion of that love which for a short time had belonged to her intact, wells to the surface in a later letter.

Nine years after the Brescia incident she was once again pregnant, he was away, and she wrote him a long "domestic" letter, in the middle of which both her grief and her anger break through:

> Your letter apologizing for not having written before has filled me with confusion, for it is I who ought rather to have begged your pardon for my delay, not you, when I know you have hardly time to eat! But, since you are so kind as to make excuses to me, you will also be so good as to forgive my delays, which were caused by Federico's illness and my reluctance to give you any news which would make you anxious. Now, thank God, he is perfectly well, and I can the more gladly discharge my duty. The hat for which you ask shall be made as soon as the hat-maker arrives, and shall be as fine and gallant as possible. If you will say how soon you require it, I will try and have a coat made to match, if there is time; but please tell me this at once. Thank you for wishing me to see your entry into Bologna. It will no doubt be a magnificent sight. I am very well, and, if you desire it, will come gladly. I think even a bomb would have some trouble to make me miscarry. Your Highness must not say that it is my fault if I quarrel with you, because, as long as you show any

love for me, no one else can make me believe the contrary. But no interpreter is needed to make me aware that Your Excellency has loved me little for some time past. Since this, however, is a disagreeable subject, I will cut it short, and say no more.

She follows this by referring to a disagreement they must have had concerning the naming of their youngest son, now a year old:

I am sorry Your Highness objects to my calling our boy Ercole. I would not have done this if I had thought you would dislike it. But Your Highness knows that when you were at Sacchetta you said he was very like my father, of blessed memory; and I said that, this being the case, you were wrong not to call him Ercole. You laughed, and said no more; but if you had told me your opinion, I should not have made this mistake. Only let me have another boy, and you may call him Alvise, or whatever you like, and leave the other to be Ercole for me. But I am sure that, if I had a thousand sons, I shall never care as much for any of them as I do for Federico. . . . I will not weary you any more with words of little importance, but commend myself a thousand times over to Your Highness. —By the hand of ISABELLA, who longs to see you. [Mantua, Oct. 5, 1506]

No doubt she wanted "Ercole" to underscore the Este heritage. No doubt he did *not* want it—for the same reason. Two weeks later she wrote to him:

Your letter, giving me an account of your fortunate progress, has given me great pleasure, both as showing me that you are in good health, and telling me of all the honor and glory you are gaining. I thank you exceedingly, and must tell you in return that I and Federico, Alvise [she now calls Ercole "Alvise," but the name "Ercole" remained], and all the girls are well. Alvise's nurse has had an attack of fever, so I have given him Livia's nurse, until she has recovered, which will not, I hope, be long now. As soon as the felt hat, which is being made after Bernardus del Armaria's directions, is finished, I will have it covered with velvet and embroidered with such taste that it shall be the finest and most gallant thing in the world. Please see that the pearls which I lent to the Duchess of Urbino are soon restored to you. . . . The Vicar of Serravalle writes to say that part of the Castle wall toward the Po has fallen down, of which danger, he says, he warned Your Excellency and the Inspectors some time ago. I sent orders to the said officers to provide for its repair. . . .

In her next letter, written on November 1, she again warned her husband to behave more diplomatically, as she had done often before. She has heard that the doge said:

"Look at those letters which we have received, informing us that the Marquis of Mantua every day speaks against this Signory, not in public, where he uses honorable expressions, but in private, and not only does he himself act thus, but his servants follow his example, which is most injurious to the State." It is plain that they nourish hatred against Your Excellency, and every day they say that they receive similar information. Messer Carlo [a Venetian friend] promised to behave with great circumspection, and advises Your Excellency to say some good words to the Signory's ambassador now in attendance on His Holiness, so that he may report them, and not leave the Senate under so unfavorable an impression. Whatever turn affairs may take, he begs you to be careful not to let anyone know that this warning has come from him. . . . Federico continues to gain strength.

It is plain that she is trying to hold on to the concept of "being married"; news of the children, a desire for more children, willingness to change the name "Ercole" to "Alvise," the "gallant hat," report of an accident, a warning—all these matters, important or unimportant, she imparts to him, spinning the threads which bind a husband and wife together. It did not work. He was even then far removed emotionally, embroiled in another affair.

Yet the failure did not destroy Isabella. On the contrary. Her defense of herself took a very different course from that of Beatrice. She determined to turn herself into an independent personality, a woman, not merely a wife, in fact into a human being dealing on equal terms with the favored sex. More than equal terms, she was to better the instruction. She was to outshine her husband in fame, outrank him in statesmanship, surpass him in family ambition, and excel him in that effort which was considered so important a privilege of Renaissance potentates, the accumulation and fostering of artistic wealth. Gradually she shed her outer humility, though she still observed the traditional amenities; for some years her letters to Gianfrancesco still are flecked with "Your dutiful wife," "By the hand of Isabella who longs to see you," "I rejoice in your wellbeing"; but these were little more than courtesies. It is true that even at the height of her love she was flattered by the attentions other men paid her, that she was attracted by Lodovico and may have been attracted by Louis XII more than policy required. Nevertheless, her deep love, the love which originally burgeoned in the young girl of sixteen, belonged to her husband. Yet now that love was shadowed by humiliation and the hurt of being rejected. For a little more than two years after she wrote the letters quoted here, they still lived together as man and wife; yet aside from occasionally sleeping together, they were apart much of the time, he in pursuit of glory, she as the determined collector of inanimate objects and of nimble minds. Not only did Isabella collect poets, painters, and philosophers; she exercised a catalytic magic on them. They gathered round and gave of their best and they admired her, not because—or not chiefly because—she was the Marchesa of Mantua, but because she was Isabella, listening Isabella, who would smile, understand, and challenge, and would draw from them the aphorism worth preserving. Her palace became a granary of thought. Ariosto wrote, using considerable poetic hyperbole:

> Sponsor of shining works and studies,
> I know not what to praise more highly—
> her graciousness, her beauty, her wisdom
> or her modesty—such is liberal and
> magnanimous Isabella.

VII

The Collector

No "supersubtle Venetian" is required to deduce that Isabella's love for works of art, whether they were created from paint or bronze, gold or marble, tapestry or cloth, wood or earthenware, received a heady stimulus from her first visit to Milan. She had been prepared for that experience from childhood on, when she gazed at the frescoes in the Ferrara Palace or when she was permitted to hold some fragile jewel in her small hand. She grew up with art. It was as expected an ingredient of her life inside the house as were the trees outdoors. Not only her eyes, but her ears too, were busy as she overheard discussions in which the virtues and defects of a new *Adoration of the Magi* were as hotly argued as the virtues and defects of a new pope, and the finding of an antique head of Hercules seemed as noteworthy an event as the finding of a remedy for herpes. What she had seen in Ferrara could not compare with the wealth she was to see in Milan and Pavia. What her father spent for the beautification of his city was frugal compared to the sums Lodovico Il Moro poured out to make his city into "a second Athens."

She was to become the most successful woman collector in a man's world, and she achieved this by turning herself into an adroit, charming, and often obstinately persistent bargain hunter. She went after dealers, using all her feminine wiles: now pleadingly, then imperiously, she pursued the artists of her time.

Sometimes she gave the artists great freedom—and sometimes she dictated to them with an almost offensive bossiness, telling them minutely what to paint or having a detailed "program" for a picture drawn up, as if she were the Muse. Sometimes she would show no end of patience with the usual artistic dilatoriness, the broken promises and evasions. Sometimes she would use her position to hold a high-and-mighty threat over the artist's head, though her banter was worse than her bite, and she could be as tolerant as a mother. She waited five years, without ever a word of reproach, for a painting for which Perugino had signed a contract. Ercole Fedeli, a famous Jewish goldsmith, took four years to make her a pair of silver bracelets. When they were finally delivered, Isabella allowed that they were so exquisite that "one must forgive him." (One may obtain an idea of his art from the decorated sword he fashioned for Gianfrancesco, now in the Louvre.) To Anichino, a famous jeweler in Venice, she sent a turquoise asking him to engrave it with a figure of victory. Months passed; nothing happened. She sent Brognolo to inquire. Anichino, reported Brognolo, "is a very capricious and eccentric fellow—you have to keep after him if you mean to get work out of him." When the jewel finally came, Isabella loved it so much that she sent Anichino another gem, to be engraved with a figure of Orpheus. It proved disappointing, but she said nothing to the artist. "I know," she wrote to Brognolo, "that he is the greatest master in Italy; too bad he is not always in the right mood."

After Lodovico's fall in 1499, Leonardo da Vinci left Milan and stopped at Mantua on his way to Venice. His visit was brief, yet long enough for him to sketch Isabella's portrait. It is one of the most famous portraits of the Renaissance. The pose, says Kenneth Clark, "must have influenced Venetian portraiture for the next ten years . . . in its ease and breadth [it] anticipates the Mona Lisa." But all it is is a sketch,* intended as the basis for a painting Leonardo never even began. There is some evidence as well in the outline of the face and in the robe of redrawing by a pupil's hand. Yet, however imperfectly preserved, Isabella's whole being blooms into full life; we seem to "see" her mind as we see her face. Leonardo pictures her at the apex of her beauty—she was twenty-five—without jewels or other adornment except a small band which encircles the rich mass of blond hair, combed straight back. She wears a simple dress low enough to bring into play her fine shoulders and to hint at her bosom. Her mien is serious, the expression of her eyes aware and awake, the profile elegant and like that of a goddess, though brought down to the human level by the suggestion, just a bare suggestion, of a double chin.

Leonardo seems to have made two versions of this sketch. One he

* Several contemporary copies exist, one of them in the Uffizi.

left in Mantua, and Gianfrancesco promptly gave it away. Leonardo took the other to Venice and showed it to Lorenzo da Pavia. The two artists must have been talking of Isabella. Lorenzo wrote: "Leonardo Vinci is in Venice, and has shown me a portrait of Your Highness, which is exactly like you, and is so well done that it is not possible for it to be better" (March 13, 1500).

Leonardo's visit to Mantua was probably the first occasion on which Isabella met him personally, though undoubtedly Lodovico had discussed him with her—how could he not, Leonardo being the artistic cynosure of the Sforza circle?—and we know that Isabella had seen some of his work, including the portrait of Cecilia Gallerani, in Milan.

A year after Beatrice's death, Isabella sent a courier to Cecilia with this message:

Having today seen some fine portraits by the hand of Giovanni Bellini, we began to discuss the works of Leonardo, and wished we could compare them with these paintings. And since we remember that he painted your likeness, we beg you to be so good as to send us your portrait by this messenger whom we have dispatched on horseback, so that we may not only be able to compare the works of the two masters, but may also have the pleasure of seeing your face again. The picture shall be returned to you afterward, with our most grateful thanks for your kindness, assuring you of our own readiness to oblige you to the utmost of our power, etc. [April 26, 1498]

Cecilia sent the picture and replied:

Most Illustrious and Excellent Madonna and very dear Lady,
I have read Your Highness's letter, and since you wish to see my portrait I send it without delay, and would send it with even greater pleasure if it were more like me. But Your Highness must not think this proceeds from any defect in the Maestro himself, for indeed I do not believe there is another painter equal to him in the world, but merely because the portrait was painted when I was still at so young and imperfect an age. Since then I have changed altogether, so much so that if you saw the picture and myself together, you would never dream it could be meant for me! All the same, Your Highness will, I hope, accept this proof of my good will, and believe that I am ready and anxious to gratify your wishes, not only in respect to the portrait, but in any other way that I can, since I am ever Your Highness's most devoted servant and commend myself to you a thousand times.

Milan, April 29, 1498

Evidently Isabella loved not only this portrait but the drawing of herself. From then on, she begged, implored, entreated, insisted, teased, and tried to browbeat him either to finish her portrait or to let her have a picture "by his hand on a subject of his own choice." When Leonardo moved from Venice to Florence, Isabella wrote to Fra Pietro da Novellara, a cultured friar at the Church of Santa Croce (Isabella had connections almost everywhere):

Most Reverend Father in God, —If Leonardo, the Florentine painter, is now in Florence, we beg you will inform us what kind of life he is leading, that is to say if he has begun any work, as we have been told, and what this work is, and if you think that he will remain for the present in Florence. Your Reverence might find out if he would undertake to paint a picture for our studio. If he consents, we would leave the subject and the time to him; but if he declines, you might at least induce him to paint us a little picture of the Madonna, so sweet and holy as his own nature. Will you also beg him to send us another drawing of our portrait, since our illustrious lord has given away the one which he left here? For all of which we shall be no less grateful to you than to Leonardo.

Mantua, March 27, 1501

The friar's answer was negative:

Most illustrious and excellent Lady, —I have just received Your Excellency's letter, and will obey your orders with the utmost speed and diligence. But, from what I hear, Leonardo's manner of life is very changeable and uncertain, so that he seems to live for the day only. Since he has been in Florence, he has made only one sketch—a cartoon of a child Christ, about a year old, almost jumping out of his mother's arms to seize hold of a lamb. . . . He has done nothing else, excepting that two of his apprentices are painting portraits to which he sometimes adds a few touches. He is working hard at geometry, and is quite tired of painting. I only write this that Your Excellency may know that I have received your letters. I will do your commission, and let you know the result very soon, and may God keep you in His grace. —Your obedient servant, Fr. Petrus Novellara.

Florence, April 3, 1501

Novellara went to see Leonardo, pleading for Isabella. Leonardo promised. "As soon as he has finished a little picture . . . he will do your portrait." Nothing came of this. Isabella wrote again, entrusting the letter to the Ferrarese envoy, who called twice on Leonardo and was put off by Leonardo's saying, "I have already begun—be patient."

Two years later Isabella, whom no rebuff could arrest, tried again. This time she applied to one Angelo del Tovaglia, a highly respected wealthy art dealer in Florence who knew Leonardo—and at the same time she wrote Leonardo directly.

To Tovaglia:

Since we desire exceedingly to have some work by the hand of Leonardo Vinci, whom we know both by reputation and by personal experience to be a most excellent painter, we have asked him, in the enclosed letter, to paint us a youthful Christ of about twelve years old. Do not scruple to present this letter to him, adding whatever words may seem to you most suitable, so as to persuade him to serve us; and let him know that he shall be well rewarded. If he excuses himself and says that he has not time, owing to the work which he has begun for that most excellent Signory, you can tell him that this will be a means of recreation and pleasure when he is tired of historical painting, and that for the rest he can take his own time, and work at leisure.

Mantua, May 14, 1504

To Leonardo, who was deeply immersed in the project of painting the *Battle of Anghiari:*

To Master Leonardo Vinci, the painter. Hearing that you are settled at Florence, we have begun to hope that our cherished desire to obtain a work by your hand may be at length realized. When you were in this city, and drew our portrait in carbon, you promised us that you would some day paint it in colors. But because this would be almost impossible, since you are unable to come here, we beg you to keep your promise by converting our portrait into another figure, which would be still more acceptable to us; that is to say, a youthful Christ of about twelve years, which would be the age He had attained when He disputed with the doctors in the temple, executed with all that sweetness and charm of atmosphere which is the peculiar excellence of your art. If you will consent to gratify this our great desire, remember that apart from the payment, which you shall fix yourself, we shall remain so deeply obliged to you that our sole desire will be to do what you wish, and from this time forth we are ready to do your service and pleasure, hoping to receive an answer in the affirmative.

Mantua, May 14, 1504

Leonardo himself is to determine the fee, she will be deeply grateful, she places herself at his service—it is one of the most pleading letters Isabella wrote. She was cognizant of Leonardo's worth, and in turn Leonardo was cognizant of Isabella's fervor. No doubt he honestly meant to please her. It was the polyhedral shape of his genius which prevented him from standing still before his easel. Isabella's portrait of the "youthful Christ" had to give way to a study of the flux of water or the invention of an armored tank. A thousand thoughts, a hundred questions, tore at him to drag him from the orderly process of completion. "Tell me if anything was ever done," Leonardo used to jot in his notebooks, again and again like a leitmotif, and though a man like Tovaglia did not know this—Leonardo keeping the notebooks secret—he had a pretty good idea of what was going to happen. He replied to Isabella's letter:

I received the letter of Your Highness, together with the one for Leonardo da Vinci, to whom I presented it, and at the same time tried to persuade and induce him, with powerful reasons, to oblige Your Excellency by painting the little figure of Christ, according to your request. He has promised me without fail to paint it in such times and hours as he can snatch from the work on which he is engaged for this Signory. I will not fail to entreat Leonardo, and also Perugino, as to the other subject. Both make liberal promises, and seem to have the greatest wish to serve Your Highness. Nevertheless, I think it will be a race between them which is the slower! I hardly know which of the two is likely to win, but expect Leonardo will be the conqueror. All the same, I will do my utmost.

Florence, May 27, 1504

Two years later, Isabella came to Florence and expressed her longing to Leonardo's uncle. He thought he could help, he tried—but it was no use. Isabella never got her picture.

She had begun working on her studio the year after she married and commissioned a local painter, Luca Liombeni, to undertake a part of its decoration. From Ferrara she admonished him in November 1491:

Since we have learned, by experience, that you are as slow in finishing your work as you are in everything else, we send this to remind you that for once you must change your nature, and that if our *studiolo* is not finished on our return, we intend to put you into the dungeon of the Castello. And this, we assure you, is no jest on our part.

If it was no jest, it was half a jest; but it was sufficient to frighten the artist, who assured her he was proceeding rapidly. Isabella replied:

In answer to your letter, we are glad to hear that you are doing your utmost to finish our *studiolo*, so as not to be sent to prison. We enclose a list of the devices which we wish to have painted on the frieze, and hope that you will arrange them as you think best, and make them appear as beautiful and elegant as possible. You can paint whatever you like inside the cupboards, as long as it is not anything ugly, because if it is, you will have to paint it all over again at your own expense, and be sent to pass the winter in the dungeon, where you can, if you like, spend a night for your pleasure now, to see if the accommodation there is to your taste! Perhaps this may make you more anxious to please us in the future. On our part, we will not let you want for money, and have told Cusatro to give you all the gold that you require. [November 12, 1491]

Mantegna, on the other hand, not only awed her, but she understood his prickly nature. No doubt it was she who influenced Gianfrancesco to grant him a gift of land as a recognition—the official decree reads—for his "admirable works and for the *Triumph of Caesar* he is now painting for us in pictures which seem almost to live and breathe." It is generally agreed that one of the "admirable works" so acknowledged is *The Death of the Madonna,* a work exceptionally tranquil for so turbulent an artist. Mary is at rest, while the saints perform the service of the dead in solemn ceremony, using the traditional appurtenances of candles, a palm leaf, a vessel containing oil, a censer, and a Bible. According to this picture, Mary died in Mantua, for in its center, and almost dominating it, we see the lake of Mantua, the long San Giorgio bridge, the churches and houses and fields that lie beyond it, and the wide sky above. It is the view which Isabella saw from her study.

Isabella's admiration was genuine. She did not pose, nor pretend to like what she did not understand. The enthusiasm which leaps from her letters—whether she is talking about a tiny turquoise or the symbol-laden decoration of an entire ceiling—is one of the most likable traits of her personality.

Along with zest, a related, but darker, passion grew in her which was gradually to drag her from the realm of free delight to that state of which a proverb of her country and her time said, "More wealth, more avarice." Her collector's mania, the greed to possess, the need to accumulate, and what one of her friends laughingly called the "Antiquity Insanity" increased with the years. She never let up; on the contrary, the more she stuffed into her Mantuan lair the more she wanted, and that desire obsessed her to the last of her life. To surround oneself with objets d'art, to hoard ancient treasures as well as those on which the varnish had hardly dried, was an urge which permeated her times. Not only the potentate or the prince, not only the cardinal or the captain, even the schoolmaster and the weaver collected. A work of art was prized not only for its beauty but as a symbol of order and of form become real and visible. It was something permanent, something to hold on to, and as such it possessed a moral connotation. Art not only stimulated the mind; it assuaged and improved the troubled soul. A clear painting on the wall, a nicely carved chair underneath, a bit of tapestry on the chair—they were as comforting as a cup of tea was to be to the English. Everything needed to be beautified, from the soup ladle to the arrow.

The collecting craze was nourished as well by motives less spiritual. Collections, then as now, were status symbols and bids for earthly immortality. They represented palpable security against the instability of the ducat and the impalpable hope of not being altogether forgotten. But to Isabella collecting represented something more: a balm for disappointment. As her marriage began to corrode, as Gianfrancesco drifted away from her, she turned increasingly toward the possession of inanimate objects as compensation for the lover she could not hold. Acquiring art became a sublimation, more exciting to her than her children and more absorbing, at least at certain periods, than the task of governing Mantua. Her collecting fever rose as her husband's love cooled.

She literally built the *studiolo* from the ground up: for the floor she designed colored tiles incorporating symbolic representations— for example, a dog with a muzzle denoting caution—and heraldic devices. Then she asked Giovanni Sforza, Lord of Pesaro, to have them executed, Pesaro being one of the centers of the majolica industry. Giovanni himself supervised the making of the tiles, sent them to Mantua in thirteen large crates, and then absolutely refused to take any money for them, "regretting only that they were not made of gold, to prove his affection for the house of Gonzaga".*

The *grotta*, built later, shone in blue and gold, its ceiling carved in wood and decorated with two of her favorite motifs: one was a series of musical notes and pauses. She used it everywhere, on cups, plates, utensils, dresses, tapestries. We do not know the precise meaning of this ubiquitous device; it must have had for her a more than musical meaning and may have denoted the harmony of life or an admonition for "silence." The other motif was several lotus leaves held by a ribbon. The lotus leaf symbolized the unknown future. Another of her devices was the numeral XXVII, *Ventisette*, perhaps a pun on *vinti siete*—"you are conquered."

---

* A few of these tiles are still to be found in the museums of London, Paris, Berlin, and Milan. The tile showing the leashed and muzzled dog is in the Metropolitan Museum.

For eighteen years Isabella worked to perfect both rooms, and in that labor she found surcease. She quickly learned of the death of anyone who possessed works of art, and almost before the funeral oration was spoken, she wanted to know if there were any bargains to be obtained from the heirs. Even her dwarfs and jesters were on the lookout on her behalf.

Occasionally, even she laughed at her own cupidity. Niccolò da Correggio had been sent to Paris by Lodovico on a diplomatic mission. Isabella charged him to buy works of French art for her; hardly had he returned when she besieged him. What had he brought back? She wanted everything at once: "Since I am of an essentially greedy and impatient nature, I hold those things the most precious which I can obtain the soonest."

One of her most devoted artistic guides was Cristoforo Romano. The gentle sculptor came to Mantua in 1497, after working in the Certosa of Pavia and at other tasks for Lodovico. In Mantua he carved the doorway for Isabella's study, and he cut her likeness in a superb medallion, a masterpiece of that finicky art. On the obverse appear the sign of Sagittarius and a female figure with a serpent, probably representing Hygeia, goddess of health. Isabella asked Niccolò da Correggio to compose a fitting motto for the medallion: she wanted "something unique," and his first four suggestions did not please her. She accepted the fifth try: *Benemerentum ergo,* which means something like "For those who merit it"; it hardly seems "unique," but Isabella was overjoyed and had many copies cast as gifts.

As the years passed, Romano, suffering from a disease which was to kill him in his forties, did less and less work and was advised by his doctors to seek "a change of air." Wherever he went he looked for treasures which might please Isabella, to whom he was utterly devoted. And so was she to him. In the summer of 1505 he was in Bologna and he called on Cristoforo Foppa, the great goldsmith, whose nickname was Caradosso, who had made Beatrice's jewels and of whom Cellini was jealous. Romano reported to Isabella that Caradosso showed him a bowl made of forty-nine pieces of crystal and mounted on a silver and enamel stand. It was beautiful, it was wonderful, he had *never* seen anything like it, but Caradosso was asking an exorbitant price for it and had already refused an offer of 300 ducats ($6,000) from Bishop Lodovico Gonzaga. She must on no account let him, Caradosso, know that she, another Gonzaga, was interested "till the bargain is concluded"; otherwise "the cunning old man will clap on another 50 ducats." Eventually Romano offered 400 ducats and told him who the intended purchaser was. Caradosso did not accept the offer and said that he would take the bowl to Mantua himself so that Isabella could see that it was a work for which "one need not grudge an extra 50 ducats or so." Romano told Isabella that Caradosso "has also finished the most perfectly beautiful inkstand of this age or of any other. He asks 1,000 ducats, and if you had to give 10,000 I should advise you not to let it go, because it is unique." What happened finally was that Caradosso did go to Mantua, and that Isabella did not buy the bowl—she said it was too large, but one may guess that she thought it too expensive—and did buy the inkstand, presumably for 1,000 ducats.

Later that year Pope Julius II invited Romano to come to Rome. He wrote Isabella and asked, should he go? She was all for it. She was ill at the moment, but not too ill to send him introductions, letters to friends, good wishes, and reminders:

We are very glad to hear that you are on your way to Rome, where we would rather see you than in any other place, and we hope that you will serve us as well there as you did at Milan, and will especially endeavor to find us some rare antiques from the recent excavations, with which we may adorn our studio. First of all you might see the sons of Zampeluna, who has lately died, and has, we hear, left many fine things which may suit us. And if you have need of any help in obtaining these antiques, you might present yourself as our servant to the Cardinal di S. Prassede, who, out of his unrelenting love for us, will give you the help of his authority. You can also confer with Brognolo, who is at present in Rome. Let us know when you have made any bargain, and we will send the money. I knew you would be grieved to hear of our illness, because of the love you bear us, and if you offered prayers and vows to God for our health, they came from a faithful and understanding soul, and were well-pleasing to us. We are now recovering, by God's grace, and are regaining strength every day. Go in peace, with our best wishes for your health.

Rome was no longer a shopper's paradise. The interest in collecting had become so great as to turn the city into a seller's market. Prices rose, good antiques had become rare, and Julius II made it quite clear that he was to be given first choice on everything. Nevertheless, Brognolo managed to find for Isabella a thrilling treasure, nothing less than a Greek marble Amor, sleeping on a lion's skin.

The experts, including Romano and Michelangelo,* said it was a Praxiteles; more probably it was a good Roman copy; at any rate Michelangelo was reputed to have pronounced it one of the finest little statues he had seen.

As to the "Praxiteles" Amor, and as to general conditions in Rome, Romano reported to Isabella:

Illustrious Lady mine, —This morning I presented your letter with much pleasure to the Cardinal di S. Prassede, delivering it with my own hands, and he spoke very warmly of you, and made me all manner of offers in your name, for which I thanked him sincerely. Only he is so old that he will hardly be able to do much more for us. Thank God I am keeping well, and live happy under the shadow of Your Excellency's protection, which follows me all over the world. Yesterday I kissed the feet of His Holiness and saluted him in your name, which pleased him greatly. He sends you his best thanks and will attend to your wishes, of which I informed him; but, as he was engaged with these Cardinals, I could not say anything more to him. Since then I have been spending my time in revisiting the remains of ancient Rome. So many fine things have been discovered since I was here last that I am dumfounded at the sight. Here many people take interest in these matters, so that it has become very difficult to get the best things, unless you are the first to see them and ready to pay well, as they soon fetch large prices. I must go and see a bronze relief worked in silver, which I hear is very fine, and which, it seems to me, Your Highness might like. I will strike the bargain if I can, because it would be an ornament worthy of any place. And I will keep my eyes open, and have already told the excavators to let me know, before anyone else, if they find a really good antique, and I will lose no opportunity of serving you. But, if Your Excellency comes to Rome this carnival, I am sure many fine presents will be given you, and here your coming is awaited with the utmost eagerness. . . .

I repeat that the Amor which Brognolo has secured for you is a most rare and excellent thing, and I swear, by the God I adore, that if it had been bought for anyone but Your Highness it should never have left Rome. In old days, when I was a boy, I used all my power and skill to prevent such things going to the Cardinal of Aragon and Lorenzo dei Medici, because it grieved me then, as it still grieves me today, to see Rome stripped of all its treasures. And there are few such marbles left here now. But for Your Excellency's sake I would do anything, and care for nothing else in the world as long as I am able to please you. —Your servant, ZOAN CRISTOFORO ROMANO.

* Michelangelo and Cristoforo Romano knew each other; with the architect Giuliano Sangallo they served on the commission Julius appointed to examine a sensational find, excavated near the Baths of Titus. The moment Sangallo saw this find, he exclaimed joyfully, "This is the Laocoon mentioned by Pliny." Julius bought it, awarding the finder an annuity of 600 ducats, for his lifetime and his son's. The Laocoon was then transported to the Vatican through streets which had been strewn with flowers. The people cheered. Such was the value at which classical statues were now being held.

The Amor was owned by one Alessandro Bonatto, a Mantuan priest living in Rome. He didn't want to sell. It needed the intervention of Cardinal S. Prassede, who persuaded the pope to grant Bonatto a "beneficiate" (meaning the income from a clerical community) which brought him 100 ducats a year for life. After trying to squeeze out an extra 50 ducats, Bonatto finally consented. The transaction took half a year, lots of correspondence and bickering; but in the spring of 1506 Isabella was able to write, "Imagine our satisfaction! You know how long and with what *appetito* we have attempted to possess it. Now that we have it we think our desire worth while. Its beauty lives up to the judgment of the experts and the reputation which preceded it." (The statue is lost.)

Even before this transaction Isabella had tried to purchase antiquities in Rome. The problem was how to get them out of Rome. The pope had placed a strict embargo on exports, threatening excommunication. It didn't faze her. Six years before the Amor transaction she had wanted an inlaid marble tabletop and written to Jacopo d'Atri:* "We need to be clever about sending it [the tabletop] out of Rome, because of those conservation-guardians. Speak to one of our friends, the Cardinals, like Borgia or S. Prassede, about the possibility of one of our mules transporting it, covered up."

She smuggled it out, hidden on the back of one of the mules which had been sent from Mantua carrying fish to the papal court. Later she wanted a whole Roman column. That could hardly be hidden. "Should there be any trouble getting it out of Rome, apply to Illustrious Madama Lucrezia [Borgia], our sister-in-law." In short, she was not shy in using all her connections or inventing subterfuges.

Sensibly she relied on the advice not only of professionals but of knowledgeable and experienced collectors, such as her banker in Venice, Taddeo Albano, or Cristoforo Chigi of the famous banking family in Rome, whom she asked "to keep his eyes open for objects that might please me, you who know so well the value of what is being offered." Her mistakes were usually prompted by her ea-

* He was no less a person than Mantuan ambassador to the French court. Isabella did not hesitate to use him for her personal "errands," any more than she hesitated to use Giorgio Brognolo, Mantuan envoy in Venice, or any other official.

gerness for a bargain; it was inevitable that that kind of bargain should occasionally turn out to be no bargain.

There was that head of Plato. It was offered to her by one of the Bellini family, Niccolò Bellini, of whom almost nothing is known and who may have been the black-sheep brother of Giovanni and Gentile. Niccolò offered Isabella an "antique marble head of Plato," owned, he said, by a Venetian matron; he was calling Isabella's attention to it merely as an act of friendship, having no financial interest in the matter. As it turned out, the Venetian matron did not exist: the head was owned by the Bellinis and it was they who wished to sell it. A likeness of the venerated philosopher—that was indeed something to grace any collection! The price was more than reasonable, 15 ducats. Isabella instructed Taddeo Albano and Lorenzo da Pavia to have a look at it. Well, the marble was cracked; the tip of the nose had been repaired with wax, and a bit of one ear was missing. Besides, they weren't sure that the head really represented Plato, though they had no doubt that it was an authentic antique. They were in a quandary. They were hesitant about spending Isabella's money; on the other hand, they did not wish to incur her anger by letting a possibly important antique slip through their fingers. They decided to buy it on approval: if Isabella did not like it, Niccolò was to refund the money within thirty days. Isabella, not knowing that the Bellinis were the real owners, had expressed her willingness to accept the statue sight unseen, should her experts, including Niccolò and Giovanni Bellini, deem it of undoubted antiquity. The "Plato" was shipped to Mantua. Isabella kept it, though Lorenzo now strongly advised against its purchase. She wanted it, it was an antique, it was inexpensive—that was all there was to it.

Why such stubbornness? Why did she ignore the expert advice she usually heeded? We may conjecture that her *appetito* overwhelmed her better judgment at a moment when she was particularly short of money, which was often her situation, since her expenditures bore no relation to Gonzaga's income. In the second year of her marriage, the Albano bank noted that Gonzaga owed them no fewer than 8,000 ducats ($160,000), and in 1494 one Antonio Galimbeni wrote her: "Every day the merchants are on my neck. I have to fob them off with words and promise that Your Excellency will pay soon." These dry periods, however, were relieved by periods in which money flowed freely into Mantua's court. And if it wasn't enough and if the shopping fever was in her, she would borrow, undeterred by her banker's gray-bearded admonition that the interest rate was *very* high. "We have more spirit," she wrote, "than to let the loss of 8 or 10 percent keep us from the things we covet."

The time of the "Plato" bust was an exceptionally dry period. The previous autumn (October 1511) she had to refuse to look at "a satyr of beautiful marble . . . and a head of Ariadne." She didn't even want to have them sent on approval, lest she be tempted. She was forced to economize because they were building a new palace in Mantua, the Palazzo di Porto. In other words, Isabella had not bought any works of art in some time, she longed to buy *something*—and she couldn't resist the "Plato" bargain.*

When she was in funds, she could be ruthless. In late March 1515 she wrote to Count Lorenzo Strozzi in Milan that she had heard that an acquaintance of hers, Galeazzo da Pesaro, was mortally ill and might die any moment. "God forbid!" However—"However, he has an excellent collection of antiquities, his heirs may want to sell, and I want to make sure of getting first choice of the best things." Three days later she wrote to her brother-in-law, Giovanni Gonzaga: one sentence regretting Galeazzo's death, one page discussing how to get his possessions. On April 8 she wrote to Giovanni that she was mistaken: Galeazzo did not die after all and please, not to utter a syllable about her letter to anybody. On April 11 she informs Giovanni that Galeazzo has taken a turn for the worse and he should get ready to go to his house and be prepared to bid "before the things are disbursed or hidden." Galeazzo died, and on April 21 Isabella wrote Giovanni again. After a few conventional words of sympathy—"I greatly regret his death, but there is no remedy, one needs to be patient and pray to God to give him peace"—she urges Giovanni once more to go and buy immediately, acting "as if he had first rights to the objects." She got the pieces she wanted, and in May of that year she invited the sculptor Antico to come and appraise them.

In Venice around the turn of the fifteenth century lived Michele Vianello, who was a well-known collector. Lorenzo da Pavia gave

* The "Plato" episode has been excellently researched and described by Clifford M. Brown of Carleton University, Ottawa, Canada (*The Art Bulletin*, Vol. LI, 1969). He gives the original text of the letters which passed back and forth, some of them very amusing. I am indebted to him as well for the facts about the art auction in Venice in 1506.

him a letter of introduction to Isabella when Michele visited Mantua in 1500: "The bearer of this letter is my great friend Michele Vianello, in whose house I have often been entertained and in which there are more beautiful objects than are possessed by any other Venetian."

Two years later Isabella visited Vianello in Venice and convinced herself that he was indeed the possessor of some fine works of art, among them one or two musical instruments made by Lorenzo da Pavia, a beautiful agate vase, a picture by Antonello da Messina, and two pictures attributed to "Janes da Brugia"—that is, Jan van Eyck. One was a self-portrait, the other *The Submersion of Pharaoh in the Red Sea*. The collection included a renowned painting by Giovanni Bellini: *Christ at Emmaus.**

Four years after that visit, Vianello died, on May 4. Exactly a week later Isabella wrote Albano: *Get busy!* The plague of 1506 was raging in Mantua, everybody was scared, her heart was torn for the suffering people, she watched in fear for her own health, money was in short supply—and yet, and yet, she couldn't let the opportunity slip by.

> We have felt greatly discomforted by the death of Messer Michele Vianello, for he was a virtuous man and our special friend. And because we recall having seen among the other beautiful objects in his house an agate vase and a painting of the "Submersion of Pharaoh," that we would have desired to own, we ask that you speak with Vianello's heirs together with Lorenzo da Pavia and find out if they are willing to sell them to us at an honest price. Should you have need of the authority of a nobleman, use the services of Messer Pietro Bembo.

So the famous poet Pietro Bembo was to be enlisted. Leaving nothing to chance, Isabella wrote to him as well.

Two days later, a messenger rode into Sacchetta, where Isabella had gone seeking refuge from the plague, to inform her that Vianello had left debts to the extent of 2,000 ducats and his creditors had decided to sell the collection at public auction. Lorenzo da Pavia wrote:

* In the early nineteenth century this was owned by Prince Andrei Rasoumovsky of Beethoven fame. It hung in his Vienna palace and was consumed by the fire which razed the palace in 1816. The painting enjoyed such fame as to be copied by several Renaissance artists. A small fine copy is in Berlin, a poor one in Philadelphia, a free and better copy in Baltimore.

The painting of the Pharaoh, more valuable than the agate vase, will have fewer bidders. I have learned that the creditors wish to sell the collection at auction with the following stipulation: that if within eight days of the sale they are able to find someone who will pay more than the sum for which it had been sold, then the object will go to him. But if none is found to offer more, then the object will go to the first bidder.*

Isabella's hope of buying the works quietly from the heirs thereby evaporated. She had to compete. Lorenzo, scrupulously honest as always, advised her not to bid on the organ made by him, because it was in bad condition. (It fetched 300 ducats at the auction—a high price.) He was going to help her get the vase and the Van Eyck Pharaoh for around 100 each. The auction took place, and on May 25 she was informed that she had got the vase for 105 ducats but had lost the picture:

It was not possible to obtain the "Submersion of Pharaoh" because prior to the arrival of your messenger the said picture was put up for auction and was sold and awarded to the Doge's brother Andrea Loredano for 115 ducats. Not having had a response from Your Excellency, Lorenzo da Pavia and I did not think it wise to bid beyond 100.

Taddeo Albano

Of course, the one thing she now wanted, the one thing she had most keenly desired all along, was that picture. She *had* to have it. She was not going to leave matters as they stood. She deliberated—then she wrote a letter. A special diplomatic courier rode posthaste to Venice bearing her letter to Andrea Loredano:

Understanding Your Magnificence to be of noble heart and to have given many proofs and demonstrations of friendship to our delegates, we have taken the courage, because of our desire, to entreat you to cede us this picture. We are willing to pay you both the 115 ducats together with such profit as you desire. You would in this way not only gain financially, but we would remain always in your debt, prompt to gratify your needs in any way possible. You can advise Taddeo Albano and Lorenzo da Pavia of your deliberations, for they speak in our name.

Loredano's answer was unexpected, to say the least. He said that he was willing to cede the picture, at exactly the price he paid for it, without a ducat of profit for himself, just to please the charming

* The eight days were later prolonged to thirty. Such a conditional auction would of course be impossible today.

Isabella. It was too good to be true, but it *was* true, as Lorenzo and Taddeo found when they called on him to take possession of the picture:

And in addition to the painting Messer Andrea [Loredano] showed us a head which was a portrait of he who made the Pharaoh, which cost two ducats. He also brought out certain pieces of porcelain which were seventeen in number and which cost twenty ducats and also two large porcelain vases and a flask of porcelain and other objects included in this dinner service. Then he said: "Come now, you have already taken the Pharaoh so take these other things as well." We did not think to refuse such items all the more as it was good stuff that could not have been better.

What was Loredano's motive? Was it pure generosity? Was it really Isabella's charm which wrought the sacrifice? Not very likely. It was far more likely that the whole affair was a cleverly engineered diplomatic move, made with the doge's knowledge and consent. Loredano had bought the collection away from Isabella with the intention of letting Isabella have it later and thereby placing her under an obligation. The Venetian Republic at that time was desirous of strengthening its alliance with Mantua, and the brother of the doge would hardly have acted as a private individual toward the wife of another head of state.

But the mystery does not end here. First—what was that self-portrait which was worth only two measly ducats? The crate in which the "Pharaoh" was shipped cost as much. Second—what happened to the van Eyck? It is never mentioned again, not in Isabella's correspondence, not in the various inventories, not in any contemporary reports, though van Eyck was a highly regarded artist. Did it turn out not to be a van Eyck? At any rate, none of the objects bought at the Venice auction can be traced, except the agate vase, which is probably the one in the museum of Braunschweig. A strange and sad dispersal!

With what extraordinary devotion men of high intellectual or artistic standing served Isabella! With all the polite and lumbering salutations which weigh down their letters, with all the reticence due a member of a reigning house, the affection they felt for this busy and eager young woman rises between the lines. Not only did they admire her, but they often talked to her as to one who understood the artist's struggle, almost as if she herself were wearing the smock of the painter or the apron of the woodcarver. When they found and recommended some antique faun, and she loved the find, both she and the finder shared the joy.

Her long friendship with Lorenzo da Pavia and his devotion to her furnish a testimony to her engaging ways. Here was a man who was one of the great craftsmen of his time, wooed by the high and mighty, the rich knocking at his door and begging him to fill their orders at whatever price he set. Lorenzo made the most precious musical instruments in Europe. He set himself a standard of craftsmanship which forced him to use only the finest materials—"ebony and ivory are good companions"—and to work much too slowly to satisfy the demand. An idealist, more of an artist than an artisan, interested in all the arts and indeed in all the intellectual efforts of his time, friend of men such as Leonardo and the Bellinis, he was the Renaissance man at his best. Isabella's correspondence with Lorenzo covers a span of twenty years: of the 182 letters which survive from this period—1495 to 1515—95 were written to Lorenzo. It began with this letter:

Honored Sir: We remember that when we were in Pavia we saw a very beautiful and flawless clavichord which you made for the illustrious Duchess of Milan, our sister. We now wish to own an instrument of such perfection, and hold the view that there is nobody in all Italy who could satisfy us better than you. We therefore ask you to make us a clavichord of such beauty and excellence as would be consonant with your talents and the confidence that we repose in you. We make only one condition: it must be light to the touch. Our hands are weak and we cannot play well if we have to press the keys hard. You will, we are sure, understand our wish and requirement. As to its form, make the instrument according to your usual style. And—the quicker you can finish it the more shall we be pleased. As to the payment—we will take care that you will be well satisfied. We recommend ourselves to your good graces.

[March 12, 1495]

Lorenzo replied that he would be delighted—but he couldn't undertake the work right away. He was too busy; there were commissions ahead of hers: a viola for her sister and a clavichord for the Milanese nobleman Antonio Visconti. Undeterred, Isabella immediately wrote Visconti. Would he do her a special favor? Would he allow Lorenzo to make *her* clavichord first and let his wait? Visconti, who probably did not want to offend Lodovico's sister-in-law, said of course. Thereupon Isabella wrote Lorenzo to ask if she could have her clavichord within three months. Certainly not—it

would take him at least four months. After a while, it appeared that
he needed more time for the "finishing touches," say six months.
The six months stretched into seven, eight, then ten. On Christmas
day Lorenzo himself appeared in Mantua, having personally carried the clavichord from Venice. He unwrapped it; Isabella thought
it a masterpiece. He was delighted at her delight. Before Lorenzo
left that Christmas, she had ordered a lute from him. The making
of this instrument, too, proved a long-drawn-out task. "I cannot
find any ebony that is black enough and fine enough to suit me," he
wrote Isabella. "I had hoped to make this lute the most beautiful
thing in Italy."

From then on the correspondence is all admiration on Isabella's
part, all dedication on his. He furnished or obtained for her mirrors,
a prie-dieu, an ivory Christ child, chess sets, rosaries, decorated
shears, several ornamental staffs—*bacchette*—which were used as
symbols of command both by her and by Gianfrancesco and were
elaborately carved, an ornate bed, watches, "portable pens," ingre-
dients for making perfume, bottles for holding perfume, special
varnish which Mantegna needed, goblets, drinking glasses made in
Murano to his design, ivory crucifixes, vases, many decorative
boxes, a chest his brother had brought from Damascus, a Syrian
cat, and even false hair which was "fine and pretty but too heavy
for me to wear," not to mention those other musical instruments he
made for her in the course of years, such as a spinetta, decorated
with intricate carving and ivory inlays.* Many a time he writes, "I
put everything else aside to execute your work." Many a time she
writes that what he chose was "beautiful beyond compare." She
never haggled with Lorenzo. He never asked for more money than
she gave him. She almost always accepted his suggestions. When in
1502 she wanted to make some changes in the palace and he recommended an architect, she sent a rider to Venice to take the architect
as it were by the hand and at once bring him bodily to Mantua.

Through Lorenzo da Pavia Isabella made the acquaintance of a
young man, Sabbà da Castiglione (a cousin of Baldassare Castiglione), who had joined the Knights Templars, a religious-military
order. Sabbà was assigned to the island of Rhodes, and before leaving on his long journey he visited Mantua, where he quite fell in

---

* The Metropolitan Museum owns a spinetta, made in Venice (though at a
later date, 1540) for Isabella's daughter Leonora.

love with Isabella. He promised her that he would try to find Greek
antiquities for her; Rhodes ought to be a fertile field in which to
plow up some treasures.

He arrived in Rhodes to find more marble, more statues, more
sculptures, lying about than he had dreamed of. Yes he could see
them everywhere; one bumped one's shin against them in the garden of his superior, the grand master of the Order. Yet neither the
grand master nor anybody else cared two straws for these me-
mentos of the past; they were exposed to wind, rain, and hail, and
some were falling to pieces. Sabbà grieved "as if the bones of my
father would lie unburied." He had found a magnificent marble
torso in Lindos, and an especially well-preserved statue of a faun,
and he had written a sonnet for Isabella and hung it around the
statue. But the other Knights—"of whom the less said the better"—
regarded his antiquarian interest with suspicion. Was he a heretic,
a heathen worshiper of false idols? It wouldn't take much and
"they'd consign me to a stake of green wood and reduce me to smoke
and ashes." He needed help in order to collect those wonderful
Greek pieces. Could Isabella apply to the nephew of the grand
master, Monseigneur de Chaumont, the viceroy of Milan?

Isabella did precisely what he wanted, Chaumont wrote the letter, though it took eighteen months before it reached Rhodes, and
Sabbà was then given permission to roam the island to his heart's
content.

He visited Delos, "the home of Apollo and Diana," and observed
"with a heavy heart the broken walls, the ruined columns, the statues strewn all over the fields"; but since there were no shipping fa-
cilities, he could send Isabella nothing except two coins which he
accompanied by a sonnet, so that she "could say at least that she
owned among her antiquities something from Delos." Later he conceived a more ambitious plan: to dismount and ship the great tomb
of Halicarnassus* to Mantua. He had managed to obtain from there
"a sea creature who embraces a nymph with a lustful gesture" and
a vase which unluckily the grand master laid claim to; "he wanted
to use it as a wine cooler." Sabbà didn't dare to oppose his superior
because "the least contradiction makes him as difficult to handle as
a prickly broom." Sabbà discussed the Halicarnassus plan with an
engineer and a sea captain. They agreed it was possible, but before

* Now in the British Museum.

Sabbà could get there he was forced to retreat because a Turkish fleet of twenty galleys was sighted. Shortly after, he received permission to return from his three-year exile. He probably never saw Isabella again.

2

Another artist who delighted Isabella was called "Antico," his real name being Pier-Jacopo Alari Bonacolsi. He sold his sculptures as genuine, dug-up-last-week antiques, convincingly besmirched with earth and covered with an ancient patina. He happened to be a genius in his own right, and his creations may be counted among the finest small works of that gifted age. A faker—and a great artist!

And when he was not imitating some ancient head of Apollo, he was totally honest. Isabella consulted him on various artistic questions, he repaired antiques for her, he advised her expertly on her purchases, and, more important, he sculpted several masterpieces for her, among them an *Andromache*, a *Mercury*, and a *Hercules and Antaeus*, inspired by a genuine antique piece which is in the Pitti Palace in Florence. This *Hercules* is a miraculous combination of powerful action beneath a smooth surface. Antico wrote Isabella that he thought it "the most beautiful antiquity I made for you." Isabella valued and liked him: once she sent him "one of our garments of inlaid satin, to show our gratitude, not as payment. Give it to your wife as a gift. We have heard that you love her more than you love yourself."

There was hardly a famous painter in Italy whom Isabella did not approach. For her *camerino* she wanted a series of allegorical pictures, populated by classic deities, and showing, in effect, virtue triumphant. These sermons in oil could be studied and unriddled by the guests who didn't take virtue all that seriously; they taught moral lessons, using Roman or Greek mythology as their texts, while paying due attention to the sexual beauty of idealized men and women. Such pictures told a story, as other paintings related events in the life of Christ or the adventures of Saint Anthony. They were "program music," the program written by poets and then given to the painter. Isabella herself tried her prentice hand at writing fantasies to be interpreted by the artist's brush. The more symbolism the painting contained, the more arcane its story was, the better. As with certain modern paintings, the onlooker stood there and asked, "What does it mean?" Then there was somebody around who could explain that that old woman in rags represented "Inertia" while the creature without arms she is dragging along is "Otium." Isabella called her painted charades *"istorie"* (stories) and sometimes *"fantasie"* or a *"poesia."* She wanted Giovanni Bellini to create such a picture. Easier wanted than done.* In 1501, when Bellini was about seventy years old, she approached him through her friend Michele Vianello to ask if he would do a "story" picture for her.

March 5, 1501. Michele Vianello to Isabella. Bellini is willing. However, he is overwhelmed with work. (That was the truth: besides working on the doge's palace, he was completing a *Baptism* for the convent of Vicenza and a *Saint Dominic* for Alfonso d'Este.) He wants eighteen months to do Isabella's *istoria* and 150 ducats. Vianello thinks that with a little bargaining Bellini will do it for a hundred.

March 10, 1501. Isabella to Vianello. Yes, 100 ducats is all she'll pay. And she wants the picture in one year. Never mind how busy Bellini is; he'll find time.

March 28, 1501. Isabella to Vianello. What is happening? She repeats "100 ducats, one year." She has heard nothing further. Vianello is to send a messenger with the latest facts. She is impatient.

April 1, 1501. Vianello to Isabella. Everything in order. Vianello has been to see Bellini once or twice: he agrees to the 100 ducats and one year. He insists on an advance of 25 ducats. He'll begin work after the Easter holiday.

April 4, 1501. Isabella to Vianello. Agreed. She'll send the 25 ducats so that Bellini will begin work "with a better spirit."

June 23, 1501. Isabella to Vianello. 25 ducats sent by her messenger Cipriano. (It took Isabella more than two months before she parted with the money!)

June 25, 1501. Vianello to Isabella. On the day Cipriano (her messenger) arrived with the 25 ducats, Bellini was in his country

* The dealings between Isabella and Bellini have been fully described by Jennifer M. Fletcher of the Courtauld Institute (*The Burlington Magazine*, December 1971). I give here the gist of her researches.

villa. He is expected back in five days. He has told Vianello that he really wants to work for Isabella, but he doesn't like the text or idea of the "story" he has been given. Isabella is a good judge of painting, and it is inevitable that his picture will be compared to "that work" Mantegna did for her.

("That work" was Mantegna's *Parnassus* [see below]. Mantegna was Bellini's brother-in-law, and influenced Bellini's style; yet there doesn't seem to have been much love lost between the two men.) He, Bellini, "wants to excel," and Vianello is sure that if Isabella insists on the theme he has been given, he won't be able to do anything satisfactory. Vianello suggests that Isabella permit Bellini to select his own story. What is her opinion? (Vianello implies that Bellini does not want to "compete" with Mantegna.)

June 28, 1501. Isabella to Vianello. All right, she'll concede. Bellini can invent his own: "some antique story or fable of fine import."

July 26, 1501. Isabella to Lorenzo da Pavia. (A month has elapsed, and she now turns to another of her aides.) Please ask Vianello to put pressure on Bellini.

August 3, 1501. Lorenzo to Isabella. Bellini is busy working on the doge's palace and on the picture for her brother, "very beautiful."

August 27, 1501. Lorenzo to Isabella. Bellini says he'll do the picture but he hasn't even started. Why don't you approach Perugino instead?

(Nothing—for four months.)

December 20, 1501. Isabella to Vianello. Go and see Bellini and find out if he has started the picture. He ought by this time to have done quite a lot of work on it! If so, encourage him to finish it. If not, make him send back the 25 ducats. She wants her *camerino* finished!

January 4, 1502. Vianello to Isabella. He has talked with Bellini, who told him that if she were willing to wait until September, he would positively paint the work. He has not only been busy but ill. If she doesn't want to wait, he'll return the money and Vianello will bring it to Ferrara. (Isabella plans to go there for Alfonso's wedding.)

January 15, 1502. Isabella to Vianello. She is willing to wait.

A seven-month break in the correspondence may be explained by Isabella's visit to Venice in March. It is reasonable to assume that she saw Bellini personally. It is clear that he had not begun the painting.

August 10, 1502. Isabella to Vianello. She wants her money back.

August 31, 1502. Lorenzo to Isabella. He and Vianello have prodded Bellini as much as they could—without the least result. Lorenzo is sure that Bellini will never do it. He *says* he will paint *istorie,* but he never does. He is not the man for it. Lorenzo has asked a poet friend to write a very simple story (enclosed) but even that won't suit Bellini. Vianello is trying to get her money back.

September 7, 1502. Isabella to Lorenzo. Pay 23 of the 25 ducats to one Andrea del Fiore (evidently to buy certain antiques) and for 2 buy some aromatic gum.

September 10, 1502. Lorenzo to Isabella. They are running into difficulties getting the money back. Bellini still pretends he will eventually paint "a fantasy." Vianello asks for an official letter from Isabella authorizing him to collect the money.

October 15, 1502. Vianello to Isabella. Bellini had been away. He has now returned and Vianello has been to see him. He proposes to paint a Nativity for Isabella, if she wishes on the same canvas that was cut for the other picture. The price, 100 ducats.

October 20, 1502. Isabella to Vianello. She is pleased to accept a Nativity in lieu of the *istoria.* It shouldn't be the same size, however, as she would hang it in a bedroom. She is sending the correct measurements with Baptista Scalona, her husband's secretary. But surely it isn't fair that Bellini should charge the same price for a Nativity as for an *istoria,* which would have required more figures. How about 40 or 50 ducats, more or less, according to Vianello's opinion of the merits of the painting? If Bellini would once again be inclined to change his mind and paint one of his Madonnas, she wouldn't be very happy. But a Nativity she could use; she hasn't yet got one. Scalona knows her wishes.

November 3, 1502. Vianello to Isabella. Scalona has given him the measurements. He went to see Bellini to tell him that she wanted a Saint John the Baptist in the painting. Bellini said he would be happy to oblige her, but Saint John seemed out of place in a Nativity. But if she liked, he would paint an infant Christ, the Baptist, a background landscape with other "free but appropriate inventions." Fifty ducats—all right, plus whatever Isabella would want to give in addition after she has seen and judged the work. Vianello has ordered the panel.

November 12, 1502. Isabella to Vianello. Bellini has changed his mind. He wants to paint a Madonna and Child with Saint John. She agrees but would like to include Saint Jerome. Please—she wants the picture *quickly*.

November 22, 1502. Isabella to Vianello. Let Bellini paint what he wants as long as it is beautiful and worthy of his fame. Panel or canvas, Nativity or Madonna—he must be encouraged to paint it in his own way.

(Another long hiatus follows; half a year goes by. But Isabella won't give up.)

June 7, 1503. Lorenzo to Isabella. Bellini hasn't begun. All he does is talk. Would Isabella write Bellini another letter?

October 6, 1503. Lorenzo to Isabella. The picture, says Bellini, will be ready in six weeks.

(During the autumn and winter no sign of the picture appeared. There were a few communications back and forth, unimportant ones, Lorenzo reporting that Bellini claims he cannot paint during the winter, Isabella thanking Lorenzo for all the trouble he has taken, and so on. At last, in April of 1504, Isabella's anger overflowed: on the tenth of that month she wrote two letters. One was addressed to Alvise Marcello, who had been the Venetian ambassador to Mantua and therefore had an official status.)

April 10, 1504. Isabella to Alvise Marcello. He must summon Bellini and demand her 25 ducats back. Bellini has no right to keep the money. Marcello is not to accept excuses or any offers for a painting. She doesn't want any paintings from Bellini, not anymore. If necessary, Marcello is to lay the matter before the doge.

April 10, 1504. Isabella to Lorenzo. She can't stand any more of Bellini's crookedness. She wants to escape from the clutches of this ungrateful man. She wants her money. If Marcello is unable to get it, he must appeal to the doge.

April 21, 1504. Lorenzo to Isabella. Marcello and he have been to see Bellini. They failed to get the money. "God knows how often I have solicited him. No, not solicited—importuned him. All I get is a 'We will do it,' followed by a flood of words."

May 4, 1504. Lorenzo to Isabella. He has been to see Bellini again, who is all apologies but begs Isabella to wait another month. The picture is three parts finished and he needs the money. He says he is hard up.

(Bellini hard up? Improbable. He was still working for the Venetian government.)

July 2, 1504. Bellini to Isabella. On bended knees he asks her pardon for the delay. It was due to pressure of work, not to neglect. If the painting doesn't satisfy her great wisdom and experience, put it down to the limitation of his talent.

(This letter is the only autograph of Giovanni Bellini extant.)

July 6, 1504. Lorenzo to Isabella. He has seen the painting. It is beautiful, much better than he had anticipated. Bellini has exerted himself, perhaps out of respect for Mantegna. Though his imagination is nowhere near that of Mantegna, he (Lorenzo) advises her to accept the picture. If she doesn't want it, he has found a buyer who does, so that she need not lose any money. He thinks Isabella ought to own a work by Bellini, one which is among the finest in Italy, and surely the chances are that she'll never obtain another, as Bellini is getting very old. If she wishes, Bellini will make her a beautiful frame for it.

July 9, 1504. Isabella to Lorenzo. You may make the final payment of 25 ducats, sent by Scalona. She gives careful instructions how the picture should be crated and transported so as not to damage it.

July 9, 1504. Isabella to Bellini. She hopes the picture will prove to be commensurate with his reputation. Then she will forgive him the trouble he has caused her. If she can be of any assistance to him, she would be glad to oblige.

July 16, 1504. Lorenzo to Isabella. There is a little misunderstanding about the final settlement: Bellini got only 24 ducats in advance, not 25; Vianello had spent one ducat on a panel. Would she now like a beautiful gilded and carved frame? What does she think of the painting? He would have preferred the figures to be bigger. Mantegna is unsurpassed in "invention," but Bellini wonderful in his colors. The painting is smoothly and subtly finished; everyone who has seen it thinks it is superb.

August 13, 1504. Lorenzo to Isabella. He is delighted she likes the painting. To him the figures seem too small. Yes, the painting is beautiful, but one should have asked Bellini to make two or three preliminary sketches from which to choose. Then he (Lorenzo) could have made a few suggestions. Bellini never allowed him to see the work in progress. The panel is in bad condition. He thinks astonishingly bad—but then he is hard to please and is often dissatisfied with his own work.

October 19, 1505. Isabella to Bellini (more than a year after she received the painting). The painting is as dear to her as any picture she possesses.

After all that, after more than three years of aggravation, what happened to Isabella's painting? It is lost, though the art historians Hans and E. Tietze-Conrat believe it to be the *Allendale Nativity* in Washington, generally attributed to Giorgione. What speaks against this theory is, first, the size of the *Allendale,* it being larger than the correspondence implies; and, second, the fact that it contains four major figures, in addition to angels' heads, the baby, and a minor figure. Would Bellini, who usually got 50 ducats for a single figure, have painted so rich a canvas for so small a sum? It is possible, since he might have wished to calm the infuriated Isabella, but it is not likely.

There remained a last scene to be played, perhaps the most astonishing of all. Isabella at once, and as it were hardly pausing for breath, returned to her campaign to procure a "story" picture from Bellini. Brushing aside all her disappointments, she asked Pietro Bembo to invent a theme for Bellini to paint. A theme by Bembo: that seems to have impressed the old painter, and it is possible that the result—which Isabella never got—was *The Feast of the Gods,* one of the glorious possessions of the National Gallery in Washington.

Was Bellini's behavior exceptional? Not all that exceptional. Was he especially difficult? Not all that difficult. The artists of the High Renaissance do not fit the notion of the man in the hovel, undervalued, underpaid, and begging patronage of some callous nobleman or church dignitary. Prevailingly—there were of course exceptions—they were highly esteemed, respectfully considered, and reasonably well paid, most of them bombarded by more work than they could handle, some of them revered, a few idolized. Michael Levey writes in *High Renaissance:*

Leonardo may be the most familiar example, but Bellini, Raphael and Titian also led several princes to stand—with increasing impatience—in Canossa-like situations outside their studios. But genius could seldom be swayed, still less hurried, and for all the secret or not so secret annoyance the patron had felt, when the object eventually reached him he usually wrote in hectically fulsome gratitude to the artist, praising his genius and confessing himself the artist's servant.

That is not to say that the artist had as yet dusted off for himself a position of privilege where he sat and contemplated with disdain the goings on of everyday life, safe in a high and carpeted aerie which only the reverential dared approach. He did not as yet consciously create to "express his soul." The artist still had to please the purchaser, portraits had to be good likenesses of the portrayed, pictures had to be done to given measurements, their contents were often mutually agreed on—and Leonardo did, or tried to do, practically everything Lodovico wanted done, while Julius II tried to lord it over Michelangelo. In short, the artist still had to worry about his relationship with his customer. The full development of the creed that art is a sacred rite whose mystery can be disclosed only to a few chosen souls and that its practitioner is a sibyl in a trance, not to be disturbed by common considerations—that creed had to wait for the Romanticism of the nineteenth century. Yet the roots were planted in the late Renaissance. Sympathy with and understanding of artistic idiosyncrasy grew—Isabella's "one must forgive him." Bellini's Madonnas had no difficulty finding purchasers. It was Isabella who had the difficulty.

She had better luck with Mantegna. Not only was he officially a Gonzaga employee but he worked within walking distance of the Palace and he must often have come over to discuss ideas with Isabella.

Mantegna painted three, or at least two and a half, "story pictures" for her studio. The first of these is known as the *Parnassus*. It can't be Parnassus because Apollo is absent, the central figures being Mars and an enticing nude Venus, with Mars obviously having eyes only for her. They are standing on a flowered hilltop, paying no attention to the jealous gesture of Vulcan, seen on the left in his foul stithy. Below him Orpheus plays his lyre, presumably for a love song. A little Amor mocks Vulcan. On the right a placid Mercury leans on Pegasus. In the lower center the nine Muses perform a dance which seems to range from an allegro vivace to an andante. The central Muse, who is pregnant, has been thought to be a portrait of Isabella; a drawing of this Muse is preserved in Berlin;

Berenson called it "masterly in modelling and in movement of line." The whole *Parnassus* is masterly and joyous, though what it means, whether it is based on a passage in the *Odyssey* or is meant as a tribute to Isabella and Gianfrancesco after Fornovo, is not clear.

Seven years later, Mantegna painted a second mythological story, *Minerva Chases the Vices from the Garden of Virtue*. One suspects that Isabella devised the content of this elaborate allegory, with not altogether happy results. It is a crowded canvas sinking under a weight of symbolic figures, though one figure at the extreme left marked *Mater Virtutum* (Mother of Virtue) is amazing: it is a partly human tree, or a woman imprisoned in and part of a tree, which lifts its branches as if they were arms in supplication toward the Virtues in heaven.

The third work in this series, *The Myth of Comus*, which Mantegna did not complete—it was finished after his death by Lorenzo Costa—is even more indecipherable. Comus was the god of joy, and the painting may refer to his sanction of the union of Bacchus and Ariadne—but who can tell?

Even so Isabella's thirst for allegorical pictures remained unslaked: from Perugino she ordered a *Triumph of Chastity*, and the "program" for this, written by the humanist Paride da Ceresara, on Isabella's wish, has been preserved: it is an essay in pedantry and it could not possibly have suited Perugino's purpose. After paying a substantial advance, Isabella had to write more than fifty letters to Perugino before she got her picture. What she got was a second-rate work, and her disappointment can be read between the lines with which she acknowledged its receipt:

Honored and most esteemed friend: The picture arrived intact. It pleases us, because it is well drawn and nicely colored. But had you painted it with more dedication, it would have done you greater honor and given us greater satisfaction, since it will have to be compared to Mantegna's paintings, which are punctiliously executed. We had hoped to have it painted in oil, a technique which suits you better and which is more beautiful. Nevertheless, as we said, we are satisfied and recommend ourselves to your pleasure.

Mantua, June 30, 1505

Much later, when Isabella was fifty-two years old, she harped once more on the didactic mode, ordering two paintings from Correggio, a *Triumph of the Virtues* and an *Allegory of the Vices*. The vices are better than the virtues, and both paintings are set in charming landscapes, but both works are forced. The masters of the Renaissance did not always turn out masterpieces.

3

Toward the end of his relationship with Isabella, that is in the last year or two of his life, Andrea Mantegna experienced the adversities which strike harder at the gifted personality than they do at the mediocre. Though we know little enough about Mantegna, we can guess that he wrapped a deeply feeling heart in a cloak of monk's cloth, that he was difficult with himself and toward others, that at one moment he could be gentle and at the next break out in wild rages, that he was both generous and avaricious, unsociable but avid of praise, a court painter and a hermit. He had long enjoyed great celebrity: as early as 1483 Lorenzo the Magnificent had called on him in his studio, where "he saw with great pleasure some paintings by his hand—with many antiques in which Andrea seemed to take great delight." At first he must have been suspicious of Isabella: she was advised to assure him that she considered him "not only a great artist but a fine man." Over the years she and the stern genius had come to understand each other.

Mantegna's son, Francesco, who painted in imitation of his father's style, was entrusted with the decoration of Gianfrancesco's favorite country villa, Marmirolo. Something happened, we do not know what, Francesco committed some transgression,* and the marchese banished him from Mantua. The father appealed to Isabella, and she wrote to her husband:

M. Andrea Mantegna came to recommend his son to me, looking all tearful and agitated, and with so sunken a face that he seemed to me more dead than alive. The sight filled me with so much compassion that I could not refuse to beg Your Excellency to restore his son to him with your usual goodness, for, gravely as he has sinned against you, the long service, incomparable excellence, and rare merits of M. Andrea claim this favor on behalf of his rebellious son. If we wish him to live and to finish our work Your Excellency must gratify him, or

* Francesco seems to have inherited his father's unbridled temper, though not his genius. In 1509 a tale went the rounds that he tried to murder his sister-in-law. Elisabetta Montefeltro interceded in his behalf because of the "love we bore [Mantegna] in life."

else we shall soon lose him, and he will die, rather of grief than of old age; so I recommend him with all my heart to your good graces. —Your wife, ISABELLA, with her own hand. [April 1, 1505]

Gianfrancesco, however, would not forgive. Andrea fell ill, presumably of grief, he worked little, and he seems to have suffered financial difficulties. He told Isabella in a long letter that he had bought a house for 340 ducats ($6,800), payable in three installments. Now, in 1505, times were terribly hard, the plague was threatening, his creditors were pressing him, he had other debts, he was unable to sell anything, and would Isabella help him out by buying from him an antique bust of Faustina (the wife of Marcus Aurelius)? The price was 100 ducats. "If I must part with it, I would rather you have it than any other lord or lady in the world."

It is possible that Mantegna had not received his stipend, Gianfrancesco himself being in financial straits. It is also possible that Mantegna was exaggerating his poverty in his despondent mood. It is certain that the house—which has been preserved—must have cost more than 340 ducats, being large and stately. It is probable that Isabella could not at once raise the 100 ducats. But it is strange that she did not answer Mantegna's letter at once. The plague, it is true, had by then reached Mantua, and Isabella and her children had fled to Sacchetta, but all the same, could she not have sent a comforting word to the old man? When, after a few months, the plague abated, she did dispatch a young courtier, one Calandra, to Mantegna. Obviously she wanted that statue—but she really couldn't afford the 100 ducats. Could she get it cheaper? Calandra reported:

This morning, I visited Mantegna in Your Excellency's name, and found him full of complaints on his sufferings and needs, which have compelled him to mortgage his property for 60 ducats, besides having many other debts. But he still refuses to reduce the price of his Faustina, and hopes to get it. I pointed out that this was hardly the time for any one to lay out so large a sum, and it comes to this: he would rather keep the marble than let it go for less than 100 ducats, but if great want should compel him to lower the price, he will let Your Highness know. This he promised me faithfully. But if he finds a purchaser who will give 100 ducats, since you cannot give that, he will let it go without writing to you again. I do not see that he has any hope of selling it at this price, unless it is to Monsignore the Bishop [Louis Gonzaga, Bishop of Mantua, and uncle of Gianfrancesco], who is fond of these things and spends freely. But I think he hoped to excite the jealousy of Your Excellency by the thought of another customer; I feel bound to tell you this. Afterward he begged me to entreat Your Highness to advance some money to supply his needs, that he might be able to work better at his picture of the god Comus. . . . I must tell you that he is hurt at your not having answered his letter, and he said with a smile that perhaps it was out of shame because you could not help him in his present necessities. And, indeed, it seemed to me that he quite understood my excuses. As to your reply to his letter, I told him that Your Excellency did him quite as much honor by sending her servant in person as by writing to him, and that, if you did not show him the courtesy and liberality which his talents deserved, you had no reason to be ashamed, since the state of the country was a more than sufficient excuse. I have written this to Your Highness, because it seems to me that a letter from you would console him, if you would write without taking any notice of his resentment. If you are not satisfied with what I have done in the matter, I beg you to forgive me, for I have done what I could, and I kiss your hands humbly. —Your faithful servant, JO. JAC. CALANDRA.

Mantua, July 15, 1506

Isabella then ordered the Faustina to be shipped across the lake to Sacchetta so that she could inspect it. She wrote to Mantegna saying that she wanted it "even if it was not worth 100 ducats." At the moment she had no cash, but she would assume Mantegna's debt for that sum and pay his creditor as soon as possible. She wanted to give him "ease and peace of mind."

It was done. The Faustina was hers. (It is still in the Palace in Mantua—but the statue's identification as Faustina has been questioned.)

Six weeks later, on September 13, 1506, Mantegna died, seventy-five years old. In his house were found several works with which he could not part, among them the *Dead Christ* and an ecstatic Saint Sebastian, inscribed with the words, "Nothing but the Divine is permanent—all else is smoke."

Lorenzo da Pavia wrote Isabella:

I am much grieved to hear of the death of our Andrea Mantegna. For indeed we have lost a most excellent man and a second Apelles, but I believe that the Lord God will employ him to make some beautiful work. As for me, I can never hope to see again a finer draftsman and more original artist. Farewell. —Your servant, LORENZO DA PAVIA in Venecia. [October 16, 1506]

To which Isabella answered:

Lorenzo, —We were sure that you would grieve over the death of M. Andrea Mantegna, for, as you say, a great light has gone out.

To succeed Mantegna, Isabella summoned Lorenzo Costa, who painted for her *The Muses at the Court of Isabella d'Este*, again a poetic allegory, densely populated, in the center of which a richly clad female figure—probably Isabella herself—is being crowned by Amor. Costa was kept busy decorating and painting, and he was generously treated, given a house and a yearly salary and remaining in Gonzaga employ until his death in 1535. Though Costa was a meek and mild man, he, too, had to be "humored," and Isabella knew this. She answered an inquiry by the Archdeacon Gabbionetta in Rome:

We have commissioned Costa, our painter, to do a portrait of Ercole [her son] . . . but even he has his bizarre side like most really talented men. We have understood that he is not much involved [in this portrait] and of necessity we must wait till he becomes inspired; then we think he will do it perfectly. However, since this might take much too long, we were thinking of Francesco da Verona [Bonsignori], who is a good portraitist as well, or somebody else who will work more quickly. [March 16, 1514]

Isabella amassed as well an extraordinary collection of glass goblets, majolica dishes, ornamental cups and plates. A few of these are still to be found in the museums of the world, usually passed over by the visitor like strangers' children in a boarding school: the collection in Chatsworth in England has a stunningly beautiful fruit dish by Giulio Romano; the Correr in Venice contains seventeen plates; majolica dishes are in the British Museum, in Bologna, in Berlin. Most of these are painted with mythological scenes, Apollo slaying the Python, Daphne turning into the laurel tree, Orpheus taming the beasts; some of them bear Isabella's musical design or her motto, *Nec spe nec metu,* "neither hope nor fear," or the number XXVII. A masterpiece of the majolican art, made in Casteldurante and painted by Nicola Pellipario in 1519, is in the Victoria and Albert, its subject Phaedra and Hippolytus. The story was one of Isabella's favorites, and the plate bears all three of her devices.

4

The reader who has bought this book—or borrowed it—owes a measure of thanks to a fanatic Venetian printer by the name of Aldo Manuzio, who latinized his name and became famous as Aldus Manutius. His shop was known as the Aldine Press.

He was not the first to put printed books into circulation. J. A.

Symonds states that by the end of the fifteenth century 4,987 books had been printed in Italy. But Manutius was the first to approach his task with the sternness of a good editor, the practical sense of an industrialist, and the enthusiasm of a proselytizer. His first plan was to collect and collate all the available texts of Greek literature, to have the most convincing version prepared from these texts, and to print that version in handy neat books which could be sold at a reasonable price. It was a tremendous challenge: paper and parchment were scarce, the manuscripts were scattered all over Europe in monasteries, universities, and courts, and the texts were stiff with errors. Type fonts had to be designed, new inks produced, typesetters instructed, printers trained. There was opposition to the idea; some people thought that printed books were mechanical vulgarizations of what ought to be works of art, handcrafted and exclusive. Elisabetta of Urbino hated them.

Manutius chose Venice as his headquarters because Venice gave refuge to many Greek scholars who could be employed as editors and proofreaders. He gathered them in his home, housed and fed them, gave them work, talked Greek with them, wrote learned prefaces to his editions, and worked day and night, never observing a holiday. Over the door of his study he placed an inscription: "Whoever you are, you are earnestly requested by Aldus to state your business briefly and to take your departure promptly." He wrote: "Those who cultivate letters must be supplied with the books necessary for their purpose. Until this is done I shall not rest." He did not rest but neglected his family and his health and emerged victorious from a hundred difficulties, strikes, wars, pestilence, and the high price of the manuscripts he needed. When he expanded his enterprise to include Italian and Latin classics, he had a calligrapher design a graceful cursive script now known to us as *italic*. He also began the custom of stamping a book with the publisher's insignia, known as the colophon. His was a dolphin and an anchor.

Isabella was fire and flame for the Aldine editions. She wanted all the books, every single one, though she wanted them printed on durable parchment. Lorenzo da Pavia, the ever-ready, reported:

Most illustrious Madonna, —I saw by your last letter that you wished me to send you the three books, i.e., Virgil, Petrarch, and Ovid, in parchment, and so I went at once to the house of Maestro Aldo, who prints these books in a small form and in the finest italic type that you ever saw. It is he who printed the first Greek books, and he is a very dear friend of mine. At present only Virgil is to be had in parchment, so I send it you herewith. The Petrarch is not yet finished, but they tell me it will be ready in about ten days. As yet they have printed only about fifteen copies on this paper, and have already bound them. This has been owing to the dearth of parchment, as they have great difficulty in obtaining the small amount required for the Virgils as well as for the Petrarchs. But Your Highness shall have Petrarch, which is not yet bound. Aldo has promised me to choose a copy for you leaf by leaf, so that yours shall be the finest of all, and the said Maestro will do this all the more gladly because he has been helped in his work by Pietro Bembo, who is most devoted to Your Highness. He it is who has had these poems printed from a manuscript which Petrarch wrote with his own hand, and which I have also held in my hand. It belongs to a Paduan, and is so precious that they have printed the book letter by letter, after the original, with the greatest possible care. As soon as it is finished I will send it to you, as they wish yours to be the first available, and hold this to be of good omen, and feel sure the work will obtain a great success since Your Excellency will have had the first copy. After the Petrarch, Dante will be printed, in the same shape and type, and after Dante, Ovid, which I think they will begin toward the end of September, but the Dante in about twenty days; and I beg you to seek for some goatskin paper, which should be clear and very white and fine and even, not thick in one place and thin in another, because formerly I have seen beautiful paper in Mantua. The great difficulty is to find good paper for the Dante and Ovid. . . . Nothing in the world pleases me more than to obey your orders, remembering the kindness which you have always shown me. The Virgil and Petrarch, they say, will cost no less than 3 ducats apiece. —Your servant, LORENZO DA PAVIA.

Venice, July 26, 1501

Two years later, Aldus asked Isabella to do him a favor she must have hated. A man he knew, Federico Ceresara, a Mantuan subject, had killed his brother in a fit of rage and been forthwith condemned to prison. He had now served two years and his mother was desolate. It is not clear what Aldus's interest in this criminal was; he may have been one of his assistants. At any rate, Aldus now asked Isabella to plead with her husband to get Ceresara pardoned. It was a lot to ask, but Isabella granted the request and succeeded in persuading Gianfrancesco to free the man. Aldus, deeply grateful, wrote Isabella a long letter of homage (in Latin) and sent with it several of his new publications. That, however, was not the end. In the summer of 1506 Aldus and Ceresara were returning from Milan, where Aldus had been examining certain Virgilian manuscripts. Arrived at the Mantuan frontier, they were arrested. Ceresara managed to slip by the sentries and cross a river to safety. He left his horse and a bag containing manuscripts. Aldus was held fast. He was furious. What was the meaning of all this? He learned that two thieves had escaped from prison, and the guards took him and his companion for the missing criminals. The descriptions tallied. "But I am Aldus Manuzio, printer of Venice, well known to the Marquis and the Marchesa!" "Indeed," said the soldiers, and slapped him into a dungeon. He wrote a letter to Gianfrancesco saying that "he ought rather to have been protected on Mantuan territory than mishandled, since he was engaged in bringing new glory to the Mantuan poet, Virgil." Yet it took four days before the mistaken identity was corrected. Gianfrancesco apologized.

Isabella did not invariably consent to pay the special prices Aldus charged her for her special editions, while he continued to produce books at popular prices. Before the incident of the false arrest, he sent her four Latin books, printed on fine vellum, priced varyingly from "6 ducats, or at least 4—to 3 ducats, or at least 2½." She sent them all back:

M. Aldo, —The four volumes on vellum which you have sent us are pronounced, by every one who has seen them, to be twice as expensive as they ought to be. We have given them back to your messenger, who does not deny the truth of this, but excuses you, saying that your partners will not take less. All the same, when you print any more, at a fair price, and on finer paper, with more careful corrections, we shall be glad to see them, and hope still to be served by you. [June 30, 1506]

He was still served by her, with pleasure on both sides. In the inventory of Isabella's library the words "a stampa d'Aldo" appear quite often. Aldo himself died in 1515, poor but happy in having achieved his purpose. His sons carried on.

5

A hundred poets were weaving rhymes as if language needed to be as finely worked as one of Isabella's necklaces. In perfecting form they neglected content, in cultivating the artificial flowers of metaphor they failed to embed the roots of vital thought. The prize went to cleverness; there was glory in prankishness. One hears with astonishment of a poem which was a praise of women when read normally; read backward it could be interpreted as a condemnation. Poetry was a game, to be played in a bower.

One thinks of the Italian High Renaissance as being in all arts admirable. In point of fact they marched at an unequal pace, the pictorial arts striding ahead in magic boots, while literary achievement limped in the rear. The great age of Italian literature had long been over. Nothing the sixteenth century produced could reach the peaks Dante, Petrarch, and Boccaccio had scaled. Lodovico Ariosto came closest to greatness with his *Orlando Furioso,* but the others—Trissino, Bembo, Equicola, Bandello—were literary hummingbirds.

Isabella gathered these hummingbirds around her in such great numbers that for a considerable time Mantua was considered "the Court of the Muses." In good weather her friends would sit in the garden overlooking the lake, clinking wine glasses and bons mots. She called the assembly her "Academy of Saint Peter" in imitation of the academies established for the purpose of classical studies in Rome and Florence. Matteo Bandello, who was proud to be called "the Boccaccio of Lombardy," would appear with his manuscript and try out a novella or two, the most lascivious of which he would tell behind Isabella's back. Or so he has us believe. He was relating "Various Spicy Episodes from the Lewd and Villainous Life of an Archdeacon of Mantua" when one heard the bark of a little dog signaling Isabella's arrival, whereupon "he broke off, the gathering rose, and everybody made his way to the loggetta of the garden where she was." At another time he told the history of pretty "Lucrezia of Vicenza, enamored of Bernardino Losco, who went to bed with him and two of his brothers." But at still other times he would unhesitatingly unroll his yarns to Isabella. She was certainly not a prude.

The Mantua Academy, let us repeat, was not a solemn school of otherworldly philosophers seeking the answer to the question: "What is life?" Isabella and her circle were as aware of the daily events around them, and observed the second hand on the clock of history with as much curiosity as Sanuto or any other diarist. Isabella got especially excited about the new geographical discoveries without in the least understanding their import. Early in 1493 a friend in Ferrara wrote her:

I hear that a man named Columbus lately discovered an island for the King of Spain, on which are men of our height but of copper-colored skin, with noses like apes. The chiefs wear a plate of gold in their nostrils which covers the mouth, the women have faces as big as wheels, and all go naked, men and women alike. Twelve men and four women have been brought back to the King of Spain, but they are so weak that two of them fell ill of some sickness which the doctors do not understand, and they had no pulse and are dead. The others have been clothed, and if they see anyone who is richly clad they stroke him with their hands and kiss his hands to show how much they admire him. They seem intelligent, and are very tame and gentle. No one can understand their language. They eat of everything at table, but are not given wine. In their own country they eat the roots of trees and some big kind of nut which is like pepper but yields good food, and on this they live.

Columbus's discoveries were published in 1493 under the title *De insulis inventis;* the book was translated into several languages and even put into verse by Giuliano Dati. In 1499 Gianfrancesco sent Isabella some letters written by Portuguese sailors "who have sailed to unknown parts of the world where no one has ever been"— perhaps on Vasco da Gama's expedition. He sent these reports "so that you can participate in the pleasure of their fascination."

6

One other "collection" of Isabella's needs to be discussed; it is not the least interesting. She surrounded herself with a group of court ladies, her "damsels," as appetizing a bevy of flower maidens as could be met in Klingsor's garden, light-hearted, frivolous, but not stupid. None of them could be accused of taking morality too ponderously. That these Francescas, Aldas, Angelas, Adrianas, twittered gaily was of secondary importance to Isabella; what was important was that they acted as adroit *charmeuses* to the personalities who came to the court, that they knew how to put a travel-weary ambassador into a good humor, to please a prince, captivate a cardinal, and induce a viceroy to talk, while he gazed at those pretty eyes which gazed at him with such deep interest. Isabella, herself not highly sexed, knew the value of sex. She used it as an instrument of government. The damsels were not, of course, ordinary trollops. They came from good families, and quite a few of them went on to produce good families: when they got married Isabella treated them generously, sometimes supplied a dowry, and often underwrote the elaborate wedding. The personnel changed, but the idea remained the same, and the more Isabella concerned herself with the state, and the more the state was threatened, the more she used the houris of her paradise for espionage. For many years the group was in charge of a friend of Isabella's, Beatrice dé Contrari, whom she had known as a girl in Ferrara. In the early days of Isabella's marriage, Beatrice had had wit enough to turn away with a quip a proposition from Gianfrancesco; Isabella was in Milan, Beatrice was sick in bed, and Gianfrancesco visited her. Beatrice wrote to Isabella:

> He [Gianfrancesco] was out of sorts because Your Excellency is away and said as long as you are not here he wanted to go to bed with me. I replied that this would be no bargain for him, since Your Excellency is beautiful, young, and very lovable, while I am nothing but an old bag of bones.

Perhaps the incident gave Isabella the first inkling of her husband's sexual inclinations (they were but two years married), or perhaps the whole thing was just a joke. At any rate, the "bag of bones" lived on merrily with the court attendants in the perfumed garden.

One of the dainty damsels, whose history happens to be partially preserved, was called Leonora Brognina, "la bella Brognina." She must indeed have been a razzle-dazzle girl, for several of the panjandrums visiting Mantua vied truculently for her favors. The two favored rivals were Ramon de Cardona, viceroy of Naples, and Matthias Lang, the worldly and powerful Bishop of Gurk whom Emperor Maximilian appointed as his negotiator. Lang appeared in Mantua to confer with Isabella. He knew no Italian and so the two conversed in fluent Latin. But for the others he needed an interpreter, and this interpreter, Girolamo Cassola, left a record of what went on:

> We had a great time. The conversation [with Brognina] was so risqué that we all laughed until our stomachs ached. The sole subject was lovemaking, how to do it from the front and from the behind. Then we sang a song which suggested various actions such as "doing with the hand," and I told the Marchesa that the Bishop of Gurk asked her to act out the actions which the song suggested. . . . All very indecent, but quite pleasant. . . .

During the carnival, January 1513, they all went to Milan—one chronicler noted that the marchesa came "with her own girls, or rather with her own handmaidens of Venus"—and Isabella herself reported that "Monsignor Gurk would throw himself on the floor, forgetting the dignity of his office, and would make love with her

[Brognina] whenever he wished." This did not prevent the beautiful Brognina from becoming the mistress of the viceroy. She liked him better—or perhaps she thought him more important.

Isabella was then supposed to have become fed up with Brognina's erotic escapades, fond though she was of the girl and useful though Brognina proved herself to be, and she was supposed to have decided to dismiss her. Letters from Isabella, recently found, indicate the contrary.

Isabella to Lucrezia Borgia:

Something happened today as unexpected and strange as anything I have experienced in a long time. Leonora Brognina and Leonora Prospero [another of her damsels] suddenly fled to a nunnery, without knowing any of the nuns there, entered the sacristy, found some habits there, put them on, and would have cut off their hair had a pair of scissors been handy. I was dumfounded; when I heard the news I burst into tears. I couldn't talk to them without choking with weeping. I sent my secretary—and my major-domo—to see them and to persuade them to return to me so that at least we could talk matters over. . . . At the same time my Illustrious Consort and my son Federico offered every possible argument to them. . . . My husband went in person to talk to them . . . but neither praises nor threats could induce them to leave. There was nothing to be done. . . . [May 24, 1513]

Isabella now had to inform the lovelorn Viceroy Cardona that la Brognina was gone forever. Cardona apparently believed that his mistress had been badly treated by Isabella; he could account for the girl's flight in no other way. This suspicion represented danger to Isabella; she could hardly afford the enmity of so powerful a man as the viceroy, who seems to have gone mad with longing. In several long letters Isabella had to reassure him.

Isabella to Cardona:

I understood from the answer Your Excellency wrote me about the disappearance of Brognina to the nunnery that you harbor the suspicion that it was due to some "contempt" on my part. It therefore seems proper to clarify what is in Your Excellency's mind, as it seems proper to clarify my position. I have tried everything possible, persuasion, threats, and other means, to call her back from her sudden leap, or at least to search for the cause which prompted her. I could bring nothing to the surface. She insisted she became a nun through "divine inspiration." Finally I sent for her mother. I thought the girl would have confided more to her mother than to anyone else. Yet though I spoke with her mother several times quite alone, closeted in my room, and though I charged her specifically to find out whether [the girl] had conceived this fantasy because she believed herself mistreated, the mother could get no other answer except that she had thought about taking such a step for many months, that she was guided by divine command and inspiration, and that she was never going to leave her abode. The mother, hearing this, declared herself convinced and gave the girl her consent and blessing. Your Excellency may be sure that she did not flee because of mistreatment or accusation, being loved by Me, being treated with respect and sweetness, and being favored and fondled by the entire court. She was indeed the most beautiful and gracious of them all. For that reason I feel her leaving me as a great privation. I have to bear it—I cannot fight against the divine will. She could not be better taken care of than where she is. The nuns lead a fine life: in the winter they wear furs, when the weather is hot they sleep under sheets, they wear linen shirts, they undress at night, they eat meat three times a week. The nunnery is full of ladies from noble families, very discreet. . . . [June 9, 1513]

Isabella to Cardona:

Your Excellency speaks truly: only the ugly ones ought to lock themselves up in a nunnery; the pretty and the gay ones ought to stay where they can be seen. My experience appears to be the contrary; the flower of my female court has gone that way. . . . [June 21, 1513]

The alternation between licentiousness and ruefulness, the exchange of the joyous life for the monastic existence, the swing from gaiety to claustral repentance—that shift was characteristic of the age of Savonarola. La Brognina was but one small example of the sinner turned saint, and a very imperfect example at that.

Two years later, her fame had reached the ears of François I, the newly crowned king of France, and he thought it might make a divertissement, for all to chuckle over, if Brognina could be abducted from the nunnery, thus playing a trick on Cardona and the Spaniards, whom he disdained. He had one of his scribes forge a papal order, gave it to the Bishop of Nice, and sent him off with a detachment of French soldiers. The men appeared in the middle of the night and carried Brognina away, screaming and kicking, thus neatly anticipating the second act of *Rigoletto*. Suddenly near Brescia the French, with the girl in tow, came upon a troop of Spanish soldiers whose protection Brognina implored. The Spaniards drew their swords, chased the French, and freed Brognina, who returned to the cloister. The bishop, having botched the job, fled and hid for days in a little boat on the lake near Mantua, fearing the punishment both of the king and of Cardona. Everybody thought it an excellent lark. Everybody except Brognina, who after some months could not bear her separation from Cardona, by whom she had had a child, left the cloister, and rejoined him as his mistress. Years later, after Cardona's death, she asked Isabella to take her back. Isabella took her back.

7

Isabella provided no exception to the observation that the collector becomes the servant of his collection. Like Henry James's Mrs. Gereth in *The Spoils of Poynton*, she held tight her "sunny harvest of taste and curiosity," and like that lady she was proud of "her personal gift, the genius, the passion, the patience of the collector— a patience, an almost infernal cunning, that had enabled her to do it all with a limited command of money."

Like most collectors, too, she never tired of showing the results of her patience and cunning to sympathetic admirers. Two years before her death, she received a welcome visitor; it was Pietro Bembo, who hadn't seen her for thirty years. The old poet, humanist, philosopher, was the last survivor of the group which had once helped make Isabella's circle lively. For five or six days Isabella dragged him through the vast Palace and showed him her possessions, new and old, the soft Correggio paintings and the tiny Murano glasses, the Greek marble torsos from Rhodes and the Michelangelo Cupid, the Roman coins and the gold bracelets, Lorenzo da Pavia's lutes and viols, the manuscripts and the Aldine books, the atlases and the alabaster vases, Caradosso's inkstand and Sperandio's medallions. Bembo described this visit in a long letter. He enjoyed every strenuous moment of it: she was still the Isabella he had known as a young girl.

VIII

Isabella and Lucrezia

She is the teasing mystery of the Renaissance. What was she, a Thaïs, a Spanish Messalina, or a Helen abducted? For centuries her name denoted "poisoner"; later she was absolved of that specific crime, still later to be judged free of all malefaction. She is the heroine of a play by Victor Hugo and an opera by Donizetti, the central character of a dozen romances, the subject of a half-dozen biographies, welcomed by historians to help them spice a dry recital of combats and conflicts—yet not during her lifetime and not during all the years since has agreement been reached as to her true nature. "Modest, lovable and decorous," "Voluptuary and treacherous and conceited," "Totally manipulated by men," "A schemer who exercised her physical attraction on men to obtain all she wanted," "Secretive and underhanded," "Open and all too trusting," "One of God's masterpieces," "A female devil"—these are quotations from contemporary judgments of Lucrezia Borgia.

On one characteristic the accounts tally: she radiated sexual attraction. To her natural endowment—blond hair so heavy and long as to give her headaches, swimming "innocent" eyes which changed color with the light, a full high bosom, a "skin of honey," a grace which made her seem to "walk on air"—was added a careful training in the erotic role. From girlhood on, she had been taught that woman's place was in the bed. Her father, Alexander VI, loved her even more than he loved her brother Cesare, and in turn Cesare loved his sister with a fire all too burning: she was probably the only being whom he did love.

Before Alexander became pope, he had promised his eleven-year-old daughter to a Spanish nobleman in marriage, but as soon as he was elected he felt that such a marriage was not good enough, that Lucrezia could be of greater help in forming Borgia alliances. Accordingly, at the age of thirteen she married Giovanni Sforza, Lord of Pesaro and nephew of Lodovico Il Moro. Lucrezia was not happy in provincial Pesaro, far from glittering Rome, and after four years of an uncertain marriage Alexander annulled it. On what grounds? On the only possible legal ground, which was that Giovanni was impotent. The pope appointed a committee, headed by two cardinals, in the presence of whom Giovanni was to perform the sexual act. Giovanni, though he denied his impotence, indignantly refused to submit himself to such a trial, and accused Alexander of incest with his daughter. Lucrezia swore that she was still a virgin. The truth, of course, never came to light, but under pressure Giovanni signed a statement that the marriage had not been consummated, returned Lucrezia's dowry, and agreed to the annulment. Battista Scalona reported to Isabella with veiled but unmistakable malice: "The Lord of Pesaro has quit Rome in despair . . . leaving his wife under the apostolic mantle." That was in 1497. Everybody understood what was meant by "the apostolic mantle." Eight years later Giovanni's third wife gave birth to a son; there was no evidence that the child was not his own.

Lucrezia was free again, to be used for further plans. Those plans called for an alliance with Naples and its house of Aragon. In August 1498 Lucrezia was married in the Vatican to Alfonso of Aragon, the bastard son of King Alfonso II. She was eighteen, he seventeen. The two young people were happy for a time—Lucrezia seems to have been sincerely in love with her handsome husband—until the political climate changed again, Alexander formed a pact with Louis XII of France, the archenemy of Naples, and Alfonso precipitously left his wife and fled home. Lucrezia wept. Her father could not bear to see her tears and awarded her the regency of Spoleto, where Alfonso could join her in quiet reunion. Later he persuaded the young couple to return to Rome. There Lucrezia gave birth to a son, named Rodrigo after her father.

Not for long did they remain untroubled. Cesare conceived an almost insane loathing for Alfonso, and Alfonso returned the sentiment. The satirists of Rome were sure of the reason: Cesare was jealous, being himself in love with his sister. Both father and brother—the rumormongers whispered—had visited Lucrezia's bed, and they called her "the Pope's daughter, wife, and daughter-in-law." These charges were almost certainly calumnies—which does not preclude the possibility that Cesare, violently possessive, could have hated anybody Lucrezia loved. Though nothing was proved, it cannot have been a mere accident that on the night of July 15, 1500, as Alfonso was leaving Saint Peter's, a band of assassins attacked him. Bleeding horribly, he yet managed to escape. He reached home, Lucrezia nursed him, and Alexander sent sixteen guards to protect him. Not yet recovered, Alfonso one day saw Cesare walking in a garden below the window. Alfonso seized a bow and shot. The arrow narrowly missed Cesare, who called his soldiers and sent them up to Alfonso's room. They smothered him to death. Lucrezia may have witnessed the scene.

The widow retired to a castle, signed her letters "the most miserable of princesses," and waited, knowing that only for a short interval would either her father or her brother allow her the repose of grief.

The time had indeed come for the boldest Borgia moves. Cesare was readying his second campaign. It would be most advantageous, thought Alexander, to bring powerful Ferrara under the papal scepter, to have the Este domain ruled by a son-in-law; such a relative would entail as well a bridge to Mantua, where he knew another Este, Isabella, to be the real power. Cesare agreed: the two territories would serve him well as bases from which to attack Bologna.

However, there were difficulties in the way. Old Duke Ercole was proud enough of his ancestry to pronounce his own name with bated breath. Indeed, the Estes were one of the oldest and noblest families of Italy; for centuries their ancestors had looked out from their palace on the Cathedral Square of Ferrara, secure in their possession. A connection with a girl illegitimately born, twice married, thrice beset by lurid rumors—that was hardly Ercole's idea of progress. Was the clear Este blood to be polluted by a Spanish strain? Isabella, too, hated the idea. This creature who, "if one husband does not please her asks for another," was surely not good enough for her beloved brother. Alfonso, the intended bridegroom, between whom and his father not much love was lost, frowned and set his face against a bride he did not know. "If you want whores," he said to Ercole, "you can find them in the town brothels. No need to bring them into the palace."

It did not matter. The pope wanted it, Cesare wanted it. Resistance was futile, or possible only if one dared armed combat. One did not dare. Alexander left no doubt as to his intentions: "Tell the

Duke [Ercole] to treat my daughter kindly, and we will exert ourselves in his behalf," he told the Cardinal of Modena. The best Ercole could do was to prolong negotiations, squeezing out increasingly favorable terms which in the end included a fortune in jewels and a dowry in gold equivalent to $4 million.

While the haggling was going on for a good part of the year 1501, Alexander and Cesare gave a party at the Vatican to which not only prominent cardinals and noblemen were invited but at which Lucrezia was present. What happened at the party proved so scandalous that some historians doubt that the event took place at all.* The facts were reported by Johann Burchard, who did not invent, nor was capable of inventing, fanciful stories. His version was seconded by a contemporary Perugian historian, Francesco Matarazzo. Sanuto too mentioned the evening.

On Sunday evening, October 30th, Don Cesare Borgia gave a supper in his apartment in the apostolic palace, with fifty decent prostitutes or courtesans in attendance, who after the meal danced with the servants and others there, first fully dressed and then naked. Following the supper too, lampstands holding lighted candles were placed on the floor and chestnuts strewn about, which the prostitutes, naked and on their hands and knees, had to pick up as they crawled in and out amongst the lampstands. The pope, Don Cesare and Donna Lucrezia were all present to watch. Finally, prizes were offered—silken doublets, pairs of shoes, hats and other garments—for those men who were most successful with the prostitutes. This performance was carried out in the Sala Reale and those who attended said that in fact the prizes were presented to those who won the contest.**

The puzzle lies not in Alexander's giving such a party; the puzzle lies in his having his daughter present.

At the time a representative of Ferrara stationed in Rome was commanded to send Ercole and Alfonso a report on Lucrezia. This man, Joannes Lucas, either fell completely under her spell or was well and truly bribed. He sent a catalog of praise, calling her "intelligent and lovely" and "modest, lovable and decorous"; "she is very beautiful." One sentence is significant: "In short, her character is such that it is impossible to suspect anything 'sinister' of her. . . ." So somebody was suspecting, and it sounds as if Signor Lucas was protesting too much.

* Yet the conservative and unprejudiced Mandell Creighton in his *History of the Papacy during the Reformation* asserts the truth of it.
** Translated by Geoffrey Parker.

Lucrezia began to make her preparations for the journey to Ferrara. It was to be, her father had determined, the most luxurious procession ever to be lavished on a bride, her clothes, her jewelry, the size of the cavalcade, the choice of horses, the linen, the lace, the armor and gold chains of the knights, the costumes and boots and caps of her ladies-in-waiting, all of such wealth as to leave open-mouthed astonishment in her wake.

Isabella was to be the official hostess at the wedding, Ercole being a widower, and she did not intend to be outdone by this dubious bride. By no means: whatever it cost or by whatever means she could, she determined to best Lucrezia in splendor, if only for the sake of the historians who would describe this affair in enjoyable detail. The first thing Isabella did was to send a spy to Rome to find out the details of Lucrezia's trousseau. He is known to us only as "il prete" (the priest), but we have his letters to Isabella: "I will follow the most excellent Lady Lucrezia as a shadow follows a body: where the eyes fail to reach I will penetrate with my nose." He did just that, even visiting Lucrezia's Roman dressmakers. From Niccolò da Correggio, Isabella received descriptions of Lucrezia's bearing, behavior, conversation. She knew that she could hardly compete with Lucrezia in beauty; well, then she would excel in taste, in wit, in the way she dressed, the way she rode to horse.

On the sixth of January 1502 Lucrezia and her knights and ladies left Rome. Alexander watched the procession from Rome's highest hill, following his daughter with a father's glance as long as he could. Slowly and with frequent ceremonial stops, they traveled north. Il prete wrote Isabella that Lucrezia not only changed her costume and jewelry every day, but had the accouterments of the horses changed as frequently. In Gubbio the procession was joined by Elisabetta of Urbino, clad entirely in black as a compliment to Spanish custom. Isabella in the meantime had journeyed to Ferrara to oversee the preparations for the reception. After twenty-seven days, that is on the first of February, the two women met in Malalbergo on the Po, from where they were to proceed by ship. Lucrezia was clad in dark red velvet, the sleeves of her gown worked through with gold threads in the Castilian fashion. Her gown indicated that though she was now an Italian bride, she was still a Spanish woman. Around her neck hung a chain of huge pearls. Isabella wore a gown of green velvet decorated with her favorite musical motif; she was weighed down by a load of gold chains and earrings, a cap of gold and diamonds on her head. They greeted each other with "gay fury," as a contemporary account has it. As they traveled up the Po, Lucrezia, Isabella, and Elisabetta sitting high on the ship, a troupe of Spanish clowns entertained them. Isabella had tipped them secretly and generously to sing her praises.

They alighted near Ferrara, and there the representatives of the court were assembled: seventy-five mounted archers in red and white uniforms; twelve court ladies who were to be added to Lucrezia's train, all wearing gowns the same color as Lucrezia's; the state coach drawn by four white horses which was to convey Lucrezia, and some twenty other carriages, covered with brown velvet, drawn by matching horses. They spent the night at Casale, about two miles from the city, where Lucrezia's ladies shivered in the cold and huddled as close to the fireplaces as they could, while she retired to write her father the daily letter she was to send him for some time to come, using the Valencian dialect in which they communicated. The next morning Ercole, Alfonso, and the ambassadors and dignitaries rode out to conduct her to the city. She kissed Ercole's hand; he kissed her lips. In the afternoon the princes and the diplomats assembled, and, preceded by trumpeters, Lucrezia entered Ferrara, while two rope-walkers dropped down from a high tower to deliver a welcoming poem to the bride. She was acclaimed by the people, partly because she was beautiful, partly because many of them knew that she had brought peace from the Borgias. At the river bridge her horse shied at the noise of the cannons and stumbled. She was thrown, shaken, but at once picked herself up, laughed, and proceeded on a mule. This redoubled the popular enthusiasm.

Gianfrancesco was absent. He thought he had better stay in Mantua. Isabella wrote him long, chatty letters, mostly assuring him that the Ferrara-Mantua contingent was in wealth and pomp a match for Lucrezia's suite: none of the Spaniards, she writes, "had necklaces equal to those worn by our own gentlemen"—which was certainly an overstatement—and Alfonso's "gray velvet suit covered in scales of beaten gold was worth 6,000 ducats" ($120,000)—which was probably an overstatement. At any rate, the theme of money runs all through the wedding. One of Isabella's ladies wrote Gianfrancesco:

The bride is not extraordinarily beautiful, but she has a sweet face. Although there are many ladies in her suite—including the most illustrious and most beautiful Duchess of Urbino, who demonstrates that she is indeed the sister of Your Excellency—our Lady is adjudged the most beautiful of all. . . . No doubt about it, and so much so that had the bride foreseen this she would have made her entry by torchlight.

That was so much melted butter.

A little later the same lady wrote:

> My lady [Isabella] was dressed in a rich blouse embroidered with gold. Around her neck she wore a necklace of huge pearls, an enormous diamond in the middle, around her waist a string of rubies of great value. . . . On my honor I say to Your Excellency that when she passed through the rooms the eyes of every single person followed her. Surrounded by her damsels, she was a star whose bright rays obscured all the others. . . .

It was not only a wedding, it was carnival time, and the guests were entertained by the greatest possible variety of diversions. Moors performed torch dances, clowns sweated and rolled and slapped one another to make a quantity of barren spectators laugh, a knight fought with a mechanical dragon to free a virgin, a tourney was staged in the Cathedral Square, Tromboncino sang his songs with tears in his eyes, a Mantuan musician played on three lutes, ballet dancers dressed as satyrs chased wild beasts over the stage, a golden ball melted away and revealed four maids singing a quartet, the ambassadors read laudatory addresses, the company danced until five in the morning, meals were endless and so were the theatrical performances. Duke Ercole had five Plautus comedies performed, each with elaborate scenery, each uncut.

Isabella was in rotten humor. She made no effort to hide it, either. During the performance of the *Miles Gloriosus,* she began talking with her neighbors at the top of her voice, ordered sweetmeats to be brought, and distributed them with much commotion. She would not allow her damsels to attend the performance of *Casina,* a play of pimps and whores, judging it "lascivious and immoral," although she had sat calmly through tales more lascivious than that of Plautus. She was always up early, "the first to be dressed," as she wrote Gianfrancesco, while "Madonna Lucrezia chooses to spend all hours dressing, so that she may outshine the Duchess of Urbino and myself in the eyes of the world." Isabella received ambassadors and delegates in her room, sang and recited poetry on every possible occasion, and in short did everything in her power to assert her intellectual superiority. When the Venetian delegates addressed the assembled ladies in an artful oration, Isabella replied with an impromptu speech which was "so charming and elegant" that the entire audience rose to its feet. She must have savored that triumph. Nevertheless, she complained to her husband:

I will not deny that Your Excellency, in my eyes, enjoys far greater pleasure in being able to see my little son every day, than I find in these fetes. If they were the finest in the world, they would not please me without Your Excellency and our little boy. But I will not believe that he has forgotten me already. If he does not remember me out of affection, he must remember me if only because he is kissed so often! So I hope Your Excellency will be sure to kiss him a few more times for love of me! Don Alfonso and the bride slept together last night, but we did not pay them the usual morning visit, because, to say the truth, this is a very cold wedding! I hope that my person and suite compare favorably with those of others who are here, and we shall at least carry off the prize of the card-playing, since Spagnoli* has already robbed the Jew of 500 gold pieces. Today we are to dance till four o'clock, and then see another comedy. —Your wife, ISABELLA. [February 3, 1502]

It was true. Alfonso had slept with Lucrezia before the wedding "without benefit of ceremony," as Isabella wrote in another letter, adding, "I have been told he walked three miles" in the bedroom.

What was Lucrezia's reaction to the animosity which pervaded the wedding feast? She knew very well what Isabella's sentiments were, though Isabella addressed her as "loving sister." Lucrezia smiled the calm smile of the woman who knows she is desirable. She said little and remained aloof. What need had she of the literary conceits and erudite witticisms Isabella was giving forth? It was obvious that she would conquer. It was obvious that she had conquered already, Alfonso being enraptured by her. Ercole wrote to his ambassador in Rome that it appeared that the two were "well satisfied with each other." The cold man smiled.

All the same, Lucrezia must have been happy when Isabella and Elisabetta came to say goodbye. She said she was heartbroken to see them go. Isabella summed up the spectacular wedding: she called it "a dull affair."

* Battista Spagnoli, a Carmelite priest and a poet and orator, attached to Isabella's suite.

2

Pausing only briefly in Mantua, Isabella and Elisabetta went to Venice. Isabella needed a little change of scenery after her duel with Lucrezia, and Elisabetta had never been to Venice and wanted her friend to show her around. They planned to go as tourists, incognito, and took with them a suite of only five people. They spent one miserable night at a filthy inn near the city—"I have spirit enough to put up with such trifling inconveniences," Isabella wrote her husband—and then, arrived at the Grand Canal, lodged themselves in the Palazzo Trevisan, which housed the Urbino Embassy. Of course they remained as incognito as a star on the stage. At once friends, government representatives, art dealers, church officials, began to call—including the banker Albani, who worried about collecting his money. Isabella was short of funds, having spent great sums for the Ferrara wedding. She now pawned some of her jewelry, the need to impress Lucrezia having passed.

As soon as the doge heard who was in town, he sent over gifts: there arrived four large chests of fish, eight marzipan cakes, twenty-nine boxes of sweetmeats, four pots of ginger, four vials of syrup of violets, twenty pounds of wax candles. Since neither Isabella nor Elisabetta was in danger of not getting enough to eat, she promptly sent the whole offering to Mantua, telling Gianfrancesco to do as he liked with it. Presumably he ate the fish and little Federico gobbled the sweetmeats. The doge extended an invitation for Isabella to appear before the Senate. Isabella refused: she was in Venice as a tourist and had not brought the proper clothes for an official function. Before so weighty an argument the Senate of the Republic of Venice had to yield. As a tourist, then, and indefatigable sightseer, she piloted Elisabetta around from early morning until late at night, from San Marco "to the Treasury, to the Great Hall of the Council, to the Armory, after which we went on foot along the Merceria as far as the Rialto, where we took a boat and came home to dinner." More sightseeing after dinner, several social calls, including one on the old queen of Cyprus living in retirement on a little island, "and so the day ends and if Your Excellency considers all we have seen and done, you will judge us to be the most intrepid women in the world." She was happy: "I thank Your Excellency for allowing me to come here, and am enjoying Venice much more than I did the last time, finding the city far more beautiful. The Duchess thinks it is more marvelous than Rome . . . and is lost in admiration."

She was happy. Yet in spite of excursions, in spite of the compliments and attentions bestowed on her, in spite of the secret satisfaction she felt in her rivalry with Lucrezia, in spite of her joy at being with her beloved friend, worry, doubt, foreboding lay at the base of her mind. It was as if the fingers of a hand were closing to make a fist. Trouble could be descried, though as yet only its direction was clear, its impact not yet felt. She was under no illusion that either Lucrezia's becoming an Este or her own flattery of Cesare, or Cesare's assurances that he loved Isabella like a sister, could guarantee her evading a fate like that of Elisabetta and her husband. She knew that Cesare had told Guidobaldo Montefeltro that he "loved him like a brother" a few hours before he invaded Urbino. Whatever drops of gallantry might have remained in Cesare's blood had by now evaporated. He had become, according to one observer, "the most arrogant man I have ever met," his successes feeding his violence; at one meeting in the Vatican, when a cardinal disagreed with him, he drew his dagger and threatened his opponent, and when the pope severely reproved him, he bade his father hold his peace or "he would do the same to him." Isabella had been quickly apprised of the incident, and her worries were not allayed by the behavior of her own father. Lucrezia had surrounded herself with her Spanish entourage and would have nothing to do with the Ferrarese ladies-in-waiting who had been assigned to her service. The Spaniards were spies, Ercole declared, shifty foreigners, untrustworthy, and he began to ship them back to Rome, one by one.

What Ercole really wanted was to reduce expenses. He thought it unnecessary for Lucrezia to be served by so extravagant a retinue, and he refused to give her the 12,000 ducats of allowance which she said she needed to live decently. Ten thousand was all he would grant, and these only after heaving a great sigh. Lucrezia appealed to her father. Alexander VI pointed out, not unreasonably, that his daughter had brought 200,000 ducats into the Este coffer and that "that mean old merchant of an Ercole d'Este" had better accede to her wishes. Lucrezia on her part paid no attention to Ercole, whose hand she had respectfully kissed, but ordered fresh velvets, brocades, jewels, and trinkets from Venice. Alfonso stayed away from these squabbles and visited his wife at night, his days being occupied with government business or with conferences with painters, armorers, and architects.

After her visit to Venice Isabella returned to Mantua. She decided to stay away from her new sister-in-law, and except for one brief visit in April 1503 during which the two women were exquisitely polite with each other, she did not visit her parental home for a long time. Lucrezia, on the other hand, attempted a more friendly approach. A relative visiting Lucrezia a few months after the marriage wrote Isabella:

> She made me sit down, and asked with charming sweetness after Your Excellency, begging to hear about your clothes, and especially about your headdresses. Afterward, in speaking of her Spanish robes, she said if she had anything that you would care to see or possess, she would gladly oblige you, being most anxious to please Your Excellency. And she expressed a wish that you would write to her sometimes and be more familiar in your intercourse with her, and asked repeatedly if the betrothal of Duke Valentino's daughter with your son had been arranged. . . . Her manners and gestures were most natural and quite charming, and she looked very pretty, but has grown rather thinner, although she is not ill.

But Lucrezia *was* ill, that summer of 1503. It began with a fever and continued with a pregnancy which seemed to her physicians dangerous. They were right: after a terrible labor she gave birth to a dead child. Cesare appeared in the middle of the night, having precipitously left his commander's post to comfort his sister, and while the doctors applied leeches to her beautiful body, he held her foot and tried to distract her by telling her risqué stories. Then he remained with her, the two alone behind closed doors. Not even Alfonso was admitted. The pope, ignoring as usual the ways of God, let it be known that "should the Duchess die, the Estes might have even greater reason to mourn her than the Borgias."

Isabella now recognized that her own security, as well as the security of her family and her state, depended on that gravely ill young creature who lay in the Ferrara Palace. Isabella realized that as long as Alexander was alive she had to accept his daughter; as long as Cesare was powerful she could not offend his sister. She knew she had to act politically. She did so; publicly and loudly she prayed for her sister-in-law's recovery. She announced—and made sure that both Alexander and Cesare heard of it—that she would commission the "most splendid possible altarpiece to the Madonna" if Lucrezia got well again.

The altarpiece was never ordered, but Lucrezia recovered all the same. Slowly she got back not only her health but her daylight smile. Alfonso, by nature stern, morose, and pessimistic, who had shown himself genuinely concerned and tender while she lay in her dark room, delighted in her regained lightness; as husband and lover he doted on her. There was now no fur expensive enough, no necklace costly enough, which she could not have if she desired it. Presently she accepted Ferrara as her home.

In Ferrara lived Ercole Strozzi, the scion of a rich family, whose father had been a poet and one of Italy's eminent Latinists. He himself was a poet—he was to write a long poem, "The Hunt," and dedicate it to Lucrezia—and a man who wore his wealth lightly. He too became devoted to Lucrezia and ran all kinds of errands for her. When she decided secretly to pawn some of her jewels and turn the cash over to Cesare, who was in need of streams of money for his armies, it was Strozzi who arranged the matter in Venice. While Alfonso absented himself on business, his interest being above all the improvement and modernization of artillery weapons, Lucrezia stayed at home. Strozzi entertained her. And in Strozzi's house she met Pietro Bembo.

3

In the summer of 1503 the French were holding Milan, but in Naples the Spaniards had won a major victory, decimating Louis XII's army of occupation. Cesare was now overlord of virtually all central Italy, but not content, he was planning a new series of conquests. He wanted to subdue Florence and Bologna. Ferrara was allied to him, willy-nilly, Mantua neutral and falsely friendly, balancing on a high wire.

Louis XII knew that the situation in Naples represented an even graver defeat than the possible loss of that one kingdom, important though it was. He saw the struggle as nothing less than the battle for "world" power, the hegemony of the European world going either to France or to a Spain freshly nourished by the gold of the newly discovered continent. He sent his best troops south and managed to persuade Gianfrancesco to lead them. "Persuade" meant paying him enough to lure him into decision. Not trusting Gianfrancesco entirely, Louis put La Trémoille at his side: the two were to divide the command.

Isabella was left alone in Mantua. Every day she heard of mysterious deaths, men disappearing without a trace. "No one any longer dies from natural causes," read a report from one of her ambassadors. Pestilence followed war, flowing north from Rome as punctually as the tide, and the plague carts made their appearance to haul off the corpses. Difficult as was the course she had to steer, she saw it clearly: Mantua was not to be stranded on the shoals of the Venetian Republic, which would dearly have hauled it in as a prize catch; nor was it to be hacked to bits by Cesare's stiletto.

Gathering her councillors around her, she steered with finesse. Not one angry word, not one truculent statement, escaped her palace. Whatever armed strength Mantua may have possessed was carefully hidden. She knew sword-rattling would be useless. Publicly she was everybody's best friend. To the doge went a picture by Mantegna; to Cesare she sent a pair of hunting dogs of a particularly rare breed. To all who could help her went ingratiating letters, stuffed with flattery. Yet not for a moment did she fool herself into believing that her state would be allowed to stay at rest. It was merely a question of a postponement in the hope of a miracle. If she looked into the future, she saw the hordes sweeping down on her, led by the man she hated, his face covered with a mask— Cesare now wore a mask habitually, his face being disfigured by syphilis—the hunting dogs at his side.

Lucrezia, however, feared not the heat of politics that humid summer. Pietro Bembo, then thirty-two years old, tall, noble, and ascetic-looking, had fallen in love with her. It was a love pitched to a high poetic frenzy, and it is difficult for us now to assay how much was due to the natural attraction of a man toward a beautiful woman, how much was a poet's tribute to his lady, and how much derived from the titillation secrecy created. Secretive they had to be, Lucrezia writing him over the signature "FF," Bembo addressing her sometimes as "angel" in the masculine form, Strozzi acting as cautious go-between. Some of Lucrezia's letters to Bembo are preserved, but we cannot be sure that these seething phrases represented more than the grandiloquent dalliance beloved by the Renaissance mind. We cannot be sure that Lucrezia and Bembo were lovers physically.* It seems improbable that Lucrezia would take such a chance only a year after her marriage and with a very satisfactory husband at her side.

Isabella seems to have suspected something. In January of that year she had invited Bembo and Strozzi to visit Mantua and take part in her Academy. Bembo refused. Later that year Isabella told Elisabetta in a passing reference that she now understood "why the famous poet was held fast in Ferrara." Whatever she knew or guessed, she never breathed a syllable to her brother. At any rate, it all lasted less than a year. At the end of 1503 Bembo went to Venice, then to Urbino, then to Rome. He and Lucrezia corresponded now and then, but they never saw each other again.

4

The miracle happened. It was no miracle. On August 5, 1503, Alexander VI, Cesare, and a few friends dined in the open air at the villa of a cardinal. A week later both Alexander and Cesare fell violently ill with a high fever. Of course they had been poisoned, said the know-it-alls of Rome. Cesare had ordered poisoned food to be given to the host so that he could appropriate the cardinal's wealth; by mistake, he and his father had swallowed the poison. The statement by the doctors that it was a malarial infection, malaria being rampant that summer in Rome, was disbelieved. Alexander died on August 18. The people of Rome broke out in jubilation, mobs chased the Spaniards from the city, a hundred of their houses were burned, many others ransacked; and a story made the rounds that a devil, a little one, very black with a long tail, had appeared to carry Alexander's soul to hell. Even the least credulous could not believe that this man, so strong and healthy, full of the juice of life, had died a natural death. With only half-concealed relish Gianfrancesco, from his camp, wrote the details to Isabella:

Most Illustrious and Beloved Wife—In order that you may hear the latest details which have reached us of the Pope's death, we write to inform you how, in his last illness, he began to speak and act in a way which made those about

* For a contrary opinion see Joan Haslip, who writes that "there can be little doubt" that they were lovers.

him think that he was wandering, although he retained perfect possession of his faculties. His words were: "I will come, you are right, only wait a little longer," and those who were in his secrets afterward revealed that in the conclave held after the death of Innocent III, he had made a compact with the devil and had bought the papal tiara at the price of his soul. One article of the compact was that he should sit in the papal chair for twelve years, which he actually did, as well as four more days. There are others who say that seven devils were in the room at the moment when he gave up the ghost. And when he was dead, his blood began to boil, and his mouth foamed as if he were a burning caldron, and this lasted as long as he was above ground. His corpse swelled to such a size that it lost the very shape of a human body, and there was no difference between its breadth and length. He was carried to the grave with little honor, his body being dragged from the bed to the sepulcher by a porter, who fastened a cord to his feet, because no one would touch him, and his funeral was so miserable that the wife of the lame dwarf at Mantua had a more honorable burial than this Pope. And every day the most shameful inscriptions are written over his grave for his last epitaph. . . . We hear that the enemy are at Genazzano and are advancing against us. Monseigneur Tremoglia [La Trémoille] is ill and has been forced to retire, so we are left in command of the camp. *Bene valeat. Conjux Marchio Mantuae. Ex Insula.* [September 22, 1503]

The Borgia power was broken and everybody knew it. Everybody except Cesare. For many weeks he lay ill, then slowly recovered his health if not his strength. One by one the lords of the conquered territories, the Colonnas and the Orsinis, reentered their palaces, remounted their chairs of government, strutted with raised salutes before their people, who sometimes showed less than wholehearted enthusiasm for the change of masters—and before long renewed the petty quarrels which made a disunited Italy no match for the monarchical power of France, or Spain, or England. But among the first to be welcomed home, and welcomed sincerely, were Guidobaldo Montefeltro and the beloved Elisabetta. Isabella rejoiced when she read the report given by her seneschal, one Alessandro Picenardi:

I venture to give Your Highness an account of the entry of Her Excellency the Madonna [Elisabetta] into Urbino, but could not describe the disasters and discomfort that we suffered from bad weather, bad roads and bad hostelries between Venice and Urbino. When at length we were four miles from Urbino, the whole population poured out to meet her, chanting Te Deums, with olive boughs in their hands and crying "Gonzaga and Montefeltro!" And when we reached Urbino, a great number of gentlemen and citizens were at the gates, and came out to greet her with the greatest joy, kissing and clasping her hand with tears of tenderness, so that it was three hours before Her Excellency could reach the Piazza. Then she alighted from her horse in front of the Bishop's Palace and entered the church, where all the ladies of Urbino were assembled, bringing her an olive branch with golden leaves, and all with one voice called out Her Excellency's name and embraced her with great joy.

Cesare tried to regain his power. He tried desperately. Lucrezia begged her husband to help her brother. He wouldn't. She implored Isabella. Isabella kept silent. After several unsuccessful attempts to raise a sufficient force, Cesare was arrested, shipped to Spain, and imprisoned. Like Napoleon, he escaped, but he was killed in a skirmish on March 12, 1507. He had ceased to be a serious threat before he died, only thirty-one years old.

The death of the Borgia pope, inevitably bringing about the downfall of his son—six months after Alexander's death the Mantuan envoy wrote Isabella from Rome, "Of Valentino one hears no more"—marked the beginning of a new era. Isabella was still alone, Gianfrancesco was still in the field, Venice was still a dangerous neighbor, and she knew that there would be fresh problems to meet. Yet for some time to come, Ferrara had been saved and Mantua remained free. Isabella's letters during that winter, as she sat before the fireplace wrapped in her ermine coat, were full of confidence.

In Ferrara Ercole hastened to make it clear that he had always disliked the Borgia pope: his death "was in no way displeasing to us," he wrote to his ambassador in Milan in a document meant to be shown to the French king. "There never was a Pope from whom we received fewer favors than from this one, even after concluding an alliance with us." Cesare "was never frank with us." He was Spanish, while "we remained a good Frenchman."

What was now to be the fate of Alexander's daughter? What was going to happen to the girl who wept for her father and wept for her brother? Louis XII let it be known that in his opinion the Estes could well annul the marriage. Alfonso could now do better than to continue as the husband of a dead pope's illegitimate daughter. Would not a French princess be more advantageous? Alfonso answered with a resounding "No." None but Lucrezia did he want; he wouldn't dream of changing for any reason whatever, the more so because the people of Ferrara had taken the blond beauty into their hearts. Lucrezia was beloved by high and low, and her husband's eyes took on a glow when he rode out from the Castello, Lucrezia by his side, each time in a new and astonishing dress, while the men tore off their caps and swung them high.

Isabella had to accept the situation. She liked her sister-in-law no better than when they first met. Soon she was to have a good reason for hating her.

Isabella d'Este as a young woman, by Titian.

Beatrice d'Este, by Ambrogio da Predis.

Elisabetta Montefeltro, attributed to Raphael.

Gianfrancesco Gonzaga, by Andrea Mantegna.

Lodovico il Moro, by Bernardino dei Conti.
(Detail from *The Virgin Enthroned*)

Cesare Borgia, by Marco Palmezzano.

Hercules and Antaeus, by Antico.

Aerial view of the Ducal Palace, Mantua

IX

The Marriage Breaks Up

What a change was here! On October 31, 1503, thirty-eight cardinals immured themselves in the Vatican Palace to choose a new
pope. It was the second time they had met that year, because Pius
III, Alexander's successor, an old, weary man, had died after serving only a month. Now they had to choose a candidate who promised to be more durable. Each cardinal was assigned to a room in
which the windows were sealed and the doors locked. At mealtime
servants placed the food on special wooden plates and a senior
official cut the bread, carved the fowl, and held the wine to the
light to make sure that no message from the outside would be
smuggled in. Louis XII did everything possible, alternating induce-
ments with threats, to effect the election of his favorite Georges
d'Amboise. But there was Cardinal Giuliano della Rovere, who for
years had worked toward the high goal, had shrewdly escaped the
persecution of the Borgia pope, and now by promises, grants,
bribes, and by the argument that the choice of a Frenchman would
move the papacy back to Avignon, tried to swing the vote his way.
The cardinals argued all day, while Giuliano privately expanded his
commitments. Late in the evening, the cardinals met at the conclave table, a piece of paper and a quill before each one. Each
could write one name only on that paper, each took it to the altar,
on which a golden urn had been placed, and each solemnly
dropped in his vote. When the votes were counted, thirty-five of
the thirty-eight cardinals had voted for della Rovere. It was the
shortest conclave on record.

As pope he took the name of Julius II, in tribute to the Roman
Caesar.

He was sixty when he became pope and he reigned for a decade
(1503–1513). Near the end of his life Raphael painted his portrait.

Let us look once more at this profound psychological study: it shows a man worn with care and age, his back bent, his beard snow white, his habit simple and devoid of ornament except for the ceremonial rings on his emaciated fingers. Yet what he was is evident: the high forehead which shielded the forge of thought, the lips compressed in determination, the deep-sunk, wise, and stern eyes, the left hand clutching the arm of the chair with a force that age could not altogether extinguish. This was the warrior pope, the man who rode to battle with a curse on his lips, the administrator who cleaned up the sty that was Rome, the man who, for a time at least, chased the foreign invaders from Italy and very nearly succeeded in uniting the country, the patron who by his iron will forced the iron-willed Michelangelo to paint the Sistine Chapel ceiling and gave Raphael the opportunity to decorate the Stanze of the Vatican, and whose boldest idea, the tearing down of the venerated Saint Peter's in order to build on its site the world's most ornate Christian temple, was to be completed many years after he was dead. He was nervous and restless, violent, rude, and short-tempered, sharing some of Michelangelo's *terribilità;* he ignored his doctors' advice when ill, ignored the suave diplomats around him, said what he thought, and was capable of belaboring a lazy servant with a stick. Yet he could be just and generous, and his personal courage knew no limit.

Julius's purpose was essentially the same as Alexander's: the recapture of the papal states, most of which had broken off from the central authority as soon as the Borgias had fallen. Venice had taken advantage of the confusion and snatched Faenza, Ravenna, and Rimini, rich cities which had been tribute states of the Vatican. The local princes, the Orsini, Baglioni, Bentivogli, had flown home like pigeons, but Julius was to swoop down on them like an eagle.

The defections were intolerable, and Julius acted. But two important differences set him apart from Alexander, the first being that he did what he did for the glory of the church, not for the glory of his family. Julius was untouched by nepotism, though he had three daughters. He wanted little for himself, little except fame, fame as huge as the memorial tomb he planned when he had been in office only eighteen months and which Michelangelo was to execute. He wanted peace, Italy unified around the Vatican. That task, as he saw it, could not be delegated, and he himself took command, rode into the field, slept in the camps during icy nights, drove his horse through treacherous rivers, directed the firing of the cannon, and stumbled onward against the wind, swearing more eloquently than any of his sergeants. As is characteristic of most idealists, his idealistic courage was nourished by personal inclination: he loved being a soldier; he was bored in church. When he decided to fight Louis XII, he rose from a sickbed—he had been so seriously ill in Bologna that for a time he lay unconscious—and rode to battle saying, "Let's see who has the bigger balls, the King of France or I."

Earlier he had been allied to France, and, indeed, the forming and breaking of leagues during the Julian years was a dizzying dance of changing partners, with Julius extending his mailed hand now to Germany, now to Spain, now excommunicating Venice, now making friends with the doge's artillery if not his insolence.

In Naples the French under Gianfrancesco were defeated in the winter of 1503, Ferdinand of Aragon remained king, and Gianfrancesco resigned his post, being unable "any longer to endure the pride, quarrels, and disobedience of the French." He returned to Mantua. Both he and Isabella quickly understood that they had better get on the good side of Julius. Isabella was ready to go to Rome, but Julius let her know that he didn't have the money to entertain her adequately. He wanted to cut expenses, Alexander having left the cupboard fairly bare. She and Gianfrancesco thereupon entered into negotiations to marry their eldest daughter, Leonora, to a relative of the pope, Francesco Maria della Rovere, who was in line to rule Urbino after Guidobaldo's death. Julius was fond of Francesco, the marriage pleased him, Leonora's portrait was sent to Rome, he approved, and the quid pro quo was spelled out by him. The bride was to bring a dowry of 30,000 ducats, two-thirds of which was to be paid immediately, in return for which Gianfrancesco's brother Sigismondo Gonzaga was to be made a cardinal. (Where the Gonzagas raised this far from trifling sum at such a time remains a mystery.) The marriage was celebrated in March 1505 in the Vatican, without either the bride or the parents being present. In the same year Julius summoned Gianfrancesco to join his army. The warrior pope trusted him as little as did the other sovereigns, yet believed him to be "the most valiant and expert captain in Italy," and with his help Julius conquered Perugia and Bologna. Gianfrancesco reported home and Isabella answered:

I received Your Excellency's letter, describing your entrance into Perugia, and all the honors and favors and promises which you have received from His Holiness. May God in the highest be praised! And I thank your Excellency for informing me of this, since nothing can give me greater joy and satisfaction than to hear of your prosperity and exaltation. Let Your Signory boldly ask the Pope to come to Mantua, and we shall contrive to do him honor. I will have the corridor arranged, and the *camera dipinta* restored by Maestro Francesco [Bonsignori], because, as you will have heard, Messer Andrea [Mantegna] died immediately after your departure. Federico's cure has been pronounced complete by the doctor this morning. He dressed, and dined with good appetite, and is playing merrily in his room, so he is making a good recovery. I will not write more now, as Monsignore is sending this courier in great haste. Ercole and the girls are well.

But Julius did not go to Mantua, much to Isabella's chagrin, preferring to visit his relatives in Urbino. Elisabetta wrote her best friend all the details of this visit with unconcealed satisfaction.

Two years later, in the early spring, Louis XII once more came down to Italy with a large army, to reaffirm his hold on the north and to quell an insurrection which had broken out in Genoa. He, too, asked for and obtained Gianfrancesco's services. Genoa was besieged and conquered, and the victory was celebrated in Milan. Louis asked Gianfrancesco to invite his wife to this celebration: he meant the invitation to be a signal honor. Isabella, seemingly untroubled by memories of Lodovico or her dead sister, accepted joyfully. It was now her turn to write to Elisabetta:

Since Your Excellency went to Rome and Rome came to Urbino, I have never ventured to rival the grandeur of your court, nor to pretend that I have seen as many rare and excellent things as you have done, but have looked on in silence and not without hidden envy at Your Highness. But now that I have been to the first and noblest court in Christendom, I can boldly not only challenge you, but compel you to envy me. A few weeks ago, I was summoned by my illustrious lord to Milan to pay homage to His Most Christian Majesty, and arrived there on the vigil of Corpus Christi. After dinner, as I was about to go and pay my respects, I received a message from him, desiring me to go to the steps on the Piazza where the joust was being held. So I went there at the stated hour and found His Majesty, who came to meet me on the steps and received me with the greatest courtesy possible. All the Milanese ladies were present . . . as well as all the barony and nobility of France and the great lords of Italy. . . . His Majesty is always most courteous and respectful to all who presume to approach him, and above all to ladies, always rising from his seat and lifting his cap to show them honor. Three times he came to visit me in my lodgings. . . . We danced in an informal manner both before and after supper. His Majesty danced with me; the Cardinals Narbonne, San Severino, Ferrara, and Finale, who were present at the banquet, were constrained by him to dance, much to our amusement and diversion. I will not write about the public spectacles held on the Piazza, because I know that they will have been fully described by your ambassador. Certainly I have seen better-managed jousts, but I never saw, and do not think that, in all Christendom, it would be possible to see, a greater number and variety of people! Most of them were nobles—not only those of Milan, which must be the first or second largest city in the world, but the whole court of France and most of the courts of Italy were here assembled, so that Your Excellency will understand how proud and glorious a sight it was! . . . If Your Excellency could have seen the procession of Corpus Christi set out from the Duomo with little enough order—first the clergy, then an infinite number of Swiss guards with halberds on their shoulders, behind them the Gentlemen of the Guard, battle-axes in hand, and after them under a baldacchino borne by the chief lords came the Legate of France bearing the Body of Christ, followed by the king, with seven Cardinals and all the barony of France and Italy, and people of Milan and the neighboring towns—it would have seemed to you the finest spectacle which you had ever witnessed! . . . I might go on and describe all the separate visits which I received from Italian and French lords and Milanese ladies, as well as from the King and the Cardinals, but this and all the rest I will leave to Your Signory's imagination, lest I give you too much reason to envy me!

Elisabetta answered:

If I could, my dear lady, express in words or writing the pleasure and satisfaction which I take in reading your eagerly expected and much prized letters, it would take me all eternity! And I am sure that if you realized a small part of the happiness they give me, you would more often employ your secretary. . . . Although Your Excellency thinks that you have delivered yourself from the sin of envy in order to excite my jealousy by telling me all the great and magnificent things which you have seen at Milan, I must reply that I feel no envy whatever. What sight can be greater than that of Rome?

Isabella soon had another high card to play. Louis invited her to come to Paris and be the godmother of the child his queen, Anne of Burgundy, was expecting. How great an honor! Isabella hastened to report this news as well to her beloved friend:

The Most Christian King thinks that the Queen cannot bear a son unless I am present, and he has therefore begged me earnestly to stay with her for this event, in order that I may both honor the birth with my presence, and hold the infant at the sacred font. What greater honor could there be in this world than to be gossip and sponsor to a King of France! Oh, what splendor, pomp, and glory will be mine! I shall not only visit Paris, the most flourishing University and populous city of the universe, but the whole of France, Burgundy and Flanders, and may perhaps reach Sant' Iago of Galicia. O how many new lands and royal sights I shall see on this journey! . . . I do not know if after this you can claim to be my equal, and if it will be possible for me to accept your invitation to Urbino so easily! When I return to Italy I begin to wonder if this earth will be worthy to bear me, if carpets will not have to be spread under my feet, and a baldacchino sent to meet me wherever I go! But, joking apart, I really hope to start for France in a few days, and am busy making preparations. When I return we must think of meeting, for I am as anxious for this as Your Highness can be.

2

At the time of the French victories, when Isabella went to Milan, she was at the apex of her charm. She was admired and catered to, not because she was the wife of the famous soldier, but because she had developed into a fascinating woman who could be stern in matters concerning her state, and immediately after light-hearted in enjoying her vanities. She now set the fashion not only for Italy but for France, and to dress "à l'Isabelle" determined the Paris style. (François I sent her a doll "dressed like her both on top and underneath.") Her extreme décolletage, revealing the nipples of her breasts, first shocked the conservative French court but was presently imitated even by Queen Anne. In contrast with the rich embroidery of her dresses, she wore a severe cap, of which one man complained that it made "women look like boys." She paid great attention to the care of her hands, a friend sending her a special kind of wood "which is said to have a marvelous property for polishing the nails and the hands, as well as a recipe for washing the teeth used by the Queen of Naples." She concocted her own perfumes, which were much prized as gifts. (She sent some in silver vials to Elisabetta, to Pietro Bembo, to Anne of France, but apparently none to Lucrezia Borgia.)

Yet, as happened so often in her life, "when fortune brings up one blessing it pours out three evils." The quotation from Demetrius was well known in Isabella's time.

She could not go to France, as she so ardently desired. Gianfrancesco forbade it, alleging that money was too scarce to finance such an expedition properly. Isabella probably did not know the real reason: Gianfrancesco was conferring secretly with Julius—it was a top-secret affair—planning to go to war against Venice. If war came and Gianfrancesco had once more to take to the field, Isabella would have to stay in Mantua; the state could not be left without a head.

Trouble also arose between her and her brother Alfonso. Their father had died on January 25, 1505, while Alfonso was away from Ferrara, on a journey which took him to France, England, and Spain. As soon as the news of his father's illness reached him, he hurried back, arriving in Ferrara the day after Ercole's death. He was now the reigning duke, and he rode through his city clad in white during an exceptionally heavy snowstorm.

In November of that year, some months after Alfonso had become duke, a fierce quarrel broke out between his brother Ippolito, the cardinal, and his half-brother, one of Ercole's illegitimate children, named Giulio. Both were enamored of one of Lucrezia's maids of honor, Angela Borgia. Angela not only refused the cardinal, but told him that Giulio's eyes were worth more than Ippolito's whole person. Like the villain in one of the cruder Italian novelle, Ippolito hired a band of ruffians to attack Giulio and put out his eyes. They partially blinded him, and although Giulio later recovered his sight and a reconciliation appeared to have been effected, it was only a pretended one. He burned with a fierce resentment not only against Ippolito but against Alfonso. As a consequence, he entered into a conspiracy with still another brother, Ferrante, to kill both Alfonso and Ippolito. The plot was discovered. Ferrante was apprehended. Giulio of the beautiful eyes escaped to Mantua, and there Isabella sheltered him, pleading with Alfonso to save him. Alfonso resented her intervention and sent Niccolò da Correggio to Sacchetta, where Isabella was staying for the summer, to lay documentary proofs of Giulio's guilt before her. Reluctantly she gave him up, to be imprisoned along with Ferrante,* but she frowned on Alfonso's implacability. A shadow fell between brother and sister, and some time passed before it was lifted.

Then, in January 1508, Isabella's baby Livia died, and in April she learned that Elisabetta's husband, the gentle Guidobaldo, had succumbed to his long illness. As he lay on his deathbed, he turned to his weeping Elisabetta and said, "Is it not good to be freed from this terrible pain?" and then he quoted a passage of Virgil to her. Elisabetta did not want to continue living; life had no further

---

* Ferrante died in prison after thirty-four years and Giulio was not released until 1559, when Isabella had been dead for twenty years. Giulio was eighty-three years old when he tottered out of his cell, dressed in clothes of half a century before. The people of Ferrara stared at him as at a ghost. He lived on for two years.

meaning for her. Isabella felt her friend's grief all the more keenly because she could not go to Urbino to offer consolation. She sent her secretary Capilupo, who reported:

> I found this illustrious Madonna surrounded by her women in a room hung with black, with the windows all closed, and only one candle on the floor. She was sitting on a mattress spread on the floor, with a black veil over her face and a black vest up to her throat, and it was so dark I could hardly see, and had to be led up to her like a blind man by my cloak. She took my hand, and we both began to weep, and it was some time before her sobs and my own allowed me to speak. I gave her Your Excellency's letter, and expressed my sympathy in as few words as possible. . . .
>
> Today we spent more than three hours together, and I induced her to talk of other subjects, and even made her laugh, which no one had as yet succeeded in doing. I begged her to open the shutters, which no one had dared suggest, and I think that in two days' time she will consent to do this. She still eats her food on the floor. I complained of the black veil which displeased Your Highness; she excused herself for wearing it . . . but says that when Donna Leonora comes here as a bride, she will change it joyfully, and says that if this marriage proves as prosperous as she desires, she will no longer feel widowed, and that this will be the greatest joy that she can ever hope to know on earth. . . .

But the hurt Isabella was to feel more sharply even than the death of her child and far more than her disagreement with her brother or her sharing of Elisabetta's grief, slid toward her first in the smirks of one or two persons in the know and in her husband's behavior. She could no longer doubt what seemed utterly improbable, fantastic even.

Lucrezia and Gianfrancesco were having a passionate love affair. There was nothing platonic about their relationship, nothing poetic; no high-flown verses accompanied it—it was sex, impure and simple. That the affair was acutely dangerous—a man climbing into bed with his sister-in-law while the sister-in-law was married to a man of fierce, proud, and vengeful temperament—was obvious to both Lucrezia and Gianfrancesco. Their attraction for each other began, almost certainly, as early as 1504, two years after Lucrezia's marriage, though we do not know how soon after they were united in the bedroom. On July 10, 1504, Gianfrancesco wrote to Lucrezia, still openly, that he felt miserable because he was "deprived of the atmosphere of Ferrara which suits me so well and of the conversation of Your Excellency so very pleasing to me," and he excused himself for not sending "those sonnets I promised." Gianfrancesco was not in the habit of sending sonnets for their literary value.

From then on their love was wrapped in such secrecy that even after all this time and research all the details have not been uncovered. We know enough, however. We know that they used as their go-between Ercole Strozzi, the confidant of the Bembo episode. Why Strozzi should have lent himself once again to this perilous role we cannot even guess. It is inconceivable that Lucrezia bribed him; he was rich himself. He may have hated Alfonso—perhaps the most plausible explanation, since Alfonso disliked him. Perhaps he himself was in love with Lucrezia. At any rate, he would write on Lucrezia's behalf to Gianfrancesco (only rarely did Lucrezia write directly, and most of these letters have disappeared), addressing the letters to his brother, Guido Strozzi, living in Mantua. Guido would then take the letters directly to Gianfrancesco or transmit them through his brother-in-law Uberto Uberti or through a person known to us only by the initials J.A. Gianfrancesco answered by the same route. Pseudonyms were used; Lucrezia was "Barbara," Alfonso "Camillo," Isabella "Lena," and Strozzi signed himself "Zilio." An example: Strozzi to Gianfrancesco, March 23, 1508: "I gave her your letter and I burned the others. As to Madonna Barbara—I assure you that she loves you. It is true that your lukewarm attitude does not please her, but she approves of your keeping the secret, and she praises a thousand of your traits." She is "wholly yours and no flighty creature." Lucrezia to Gianfrancesco: "Of so many other matters I will speak to you in person, because I don't dare to write them." Lucrezia is reckless one day, cautious the next, and enraptured both days. As far as we can tell she seems to have been the dominant force in the relationship. Later the lovers wrote of themselves as "hawk" and "hawker" and Gianfrancesco begged for a letter "from her own hand, to console him."

Alfonso and Gianfrancesco were politically at odds, but Alfonso told Lucrezia that he would try to reconcile their differences. Strozzi to Gianfrancesco: "You must try your best to bring this about, because then you can come immediately to the place where she is." Wherever she was, there Gianfrancesco tried to be.

The affair went on; the letters passed to and fro. But the idyll changed when Alfonso in 1508 returned from another visit to France. On the morning of June 6, 1508, a laborer who arose early to go to work stumbled across a corpse lying on the ground. It was Ercole Strozzi, his body pierced by twenty-two dagger wounds.

Some of his hair had been pulled out and was lying beside his head. Who was the assassin? Rumor had it that it was a soldier of the duke and that although the soldier's identity was known he had been allowed to escape. Alfonso hardly bothered to investigate; the murder remained unsolved. The most likely supposition is that Alfonso had discovered something about the affair and not wishing to create a scandal, or cause a definite break between Lucrezia and himself, he wreaked his vengeance on the go-between. What is fairly certain, however, is that Isabella knew of the affair—knew and brooded and suffered. Blaming Lucrezia, she burned more hotly against her than against Gianfrancesco. The year after Strozzi's murder, Gianfrancesco's secretary reported to his master: "Today my illustrious lady [Isabella] greatly mocked the Duchess of Ferrara, because she [Lucrezia] has one Pietro Giorgio sleep in her anteroom, just to show that she is chaste and faithful to her husband."

Isabella cast about for a remedy. Characteristically, she would not accept repudiation without repeated attempts at conciliation. She proposed sending a Fra Anselmo to her husband as a sort of marriage counselor. Apparently Anselmo was to say nothing about Lucrezia (if he knew about it) but was to discuss the incident of the lady-in-waiting whose hair Isabella had pulled. Gianfrancesco answered angrily that he had "no need of friars or priests" and, using offense for defense, criticized Isabella for surrounding herself with damsels of loose morals, "some of whom even got themselves pregnant." He denied that the girl whose hair Isabella had pulled had ever "played the nymph" with him, and announced that on his return from Genoa he intended to talk things over with Isabella and establish order in the household. "Remember, I am the Marchese of Mantua, and no one else is." Nothing was said of Lucrezia.

Two months later Isabella answered in a mild mood, in a letter in her own hand.

Considering the sufferings and fears—which at present strike me as outweighing the good—I have come to the conclusion that I would really prefer being the wife of a physician who comes home at night and consumes his supper at his hearth in all tranquillity than to participate in honors which carry so much danger with them. I write this half in jest. Really, I wouldn't like to be married to a nobody. As a matter of fact, I wouldn't want to be married to anybody who is different from Your Excellency—at least in certain respects. As to certain other traits you have, well, I wouldn't mind if you changed them.

Most astonishingly and most unbelievably, Lucrezia, sick with love's despair and risking the danger, not only ignored the warning of Strozzi's fate but continued to pursue Gianfrancesco. Another Strozzi brother, Lorenzo, now entered on the scene to play the part of Pandarus. On August 21, 1508—less than three months after Ercole Strozzi's assassination—Lorenzo wrote Gianfrancesco Gonzaga a letter in which he transmitted an urgent invitation from Lucrezia to visit her in the town of Reggio. It is possible that this letter was a trap. The documents prove that Alfonso was in Reggio at this very time. The letter could have been written at Alfonso's instigation—significantly enough it was written and sent openly and without pseudonyms—because he wanted to lure Gianfrancesco to Reggio, confront him there, challenge or kill him. At any rate, Gianfrancesco seems to have suspected something: his secretary replied that illness prevented such a meeting. He refused as well to accept an invitation to come to the next carnival in Ferrara. But although the correspondence of the lovers became less frequent as both Ferrara and Mantua became embroiled with the pope and both Gianfrancesco and Alfonso had to face new problems, neither Lucrezia nor Gianfrancesco lost desire for each other. To Isabella Lucrezia stood as the blond temptress, a smile of triumph on her lips. And still another humiliation, a horrible one, was heaped on the wife.

When, along about the year 1509, Gianfrancesco began to show symptoms of illness and complain of pain, it took some time before his doctors diagnosed his condition: it was syphilis. Where he contracted the disease we do not know, but we may assume he was infected by one of the prostitutes who followed the soldiers. We know that the case was a severe one, leading slowly toward physical and mental disintegration. As a soldier he was still functioning competently the first year; as a man he had to renounce sexual relations both with Isabella and—what then grieved him more—with Lucrezia.

3

It galled Julius to think of Venice's defiance. How could he dream of a united Italy when its most powerful state, possessing the mastery of the seas, acted openly against the papacy and was not intimidated by excommunication? To cut the claws of the Lion of Saint Mark, Julius told Machiavelli, he would join with France, Maximilian, anyone. That is precisely what he did in 1508 when he formed the "League of Cambrai" with France, Germany, and Spain. Alfonso of Ferrara and Gianfrancesco were signatories to this treaty, with Gianfrancesco continuing to lead a part of the papal forces. Off they marched against Venice, and on May 14, 1509, they defeated the Republic in a great battle near Cremona. "In one day," Machiavelli wrote with some exaggeration, "the Venetians lost what they had acquired in eight hundred years."

The Venetians ceded the cities on the mainland to Julius. Yet stubbornly they kept on harassing the victors in surprise skirmishes. Gianfrancesco remained on the battlefield, while Mantua was overrun with licentious French soldiers whom Isabella found more irksome than the enemy. When Gianfrancesco sent her a brace of partridges as a gift, she replied that even the June heat could not make her thin and she therefore could not allow herself to eat such fattening food; but if she suffered as much from strain and worry as she had suffered from those rascally French soldiers, perhaps she *could* reduce her weight.

Worse was to follow.

About a month later, Gianfrancesco was sleeping in a farmhouse. A spy disclosed his whereabouts to a Venetian patrol, which at once surrounded the house. Gianfrancesco, awakened by the noise, jumped through the window and hid in a field of wheat. There he was found by four peasants, taken prisoner, and borne to a joyful doge, who greeted him sarcastically, "Welcome, Marchese of Mantua." He answered, not without dignity, "He to whom you are speaking is Gianfrancesco Gonzaga. The Marchese of Mantua is not here now—he is in Mantua." He was led through the streets of Venice, the people crying, "Hang the traitor!" and presently was immured in the tower of Torresella, which, to make a sure thing surer, was provided with new locks and bolts.

Julius, on hearing the news, flung his papal miter to the ground and cursed Saint Peter. Consternation raged in Mantua. Confusion spread among the members of the League. Lucrezia wept secretly. Louis XII, safely in Milan, scoffed at Gianfrancesco's carelessness.

But Isabella lost neither her head nor her resolution. Buoyed by her desire to show what leadership she was capable of, convinced that it was she, not he, who now had to become "the Marchese of

Mantua," she acted at once. The day after her husband's imprisonment, she arranged to have young Federico ride in procession through the city. A Gonzaga was still here: "It was a glorious sight," she wrote. She summoned all her councillors and officials. "The calls made on us give us no rest, but we are quite willing to assume all burdens, seeing around us so much faithfulness and good will," she wrote to Jacopo d'Atri. She sent an open letter to all vicars and mayors of the state: they were to assure the people that they need have no fear. The people were to continue calmly about their business. They were not to stop working. She would do her best to liberate the marchese and she would do "everything possible to keep the state safe."

We can read her detailed instructions to her officials: "Kindly remember," she wrote to an abbot, "that we discussed your improving the singing of the nuns. I find it shameful that the Women's College performs in a disorderly fashion. If they learned to sing, they would not only offer greater glory to God but please me better. . . . My ears are offended when I hear such discords."

To the vicar of Sacchetta ("vicar" was the title of a governor of a district or township):

Several times I have explained to you that I do not wish the office of the vicar and the judge separated. Now I tell you that at the first fresh complaint regarding the construction of the arsenal and the progress of the excavation, we will remove you from your post and give the office to a person who does not think these matters beneath his dignity or too much trouble. . . . We do not want to hear any further complaints nor be annoyed by the poor handling of these functions.

General Memorandum: "I wish to be informed of all instances of citizens performing their work with exceptional zeal and good results; whether these citizens be artisans, workmen, or farmers, I will reward their efforts in these parlous times. I must now be in charge of the welfare of Mantua."

To the Podesta Ostiglia, who reported that a painting of the Madonna was shedding tears: "We are of the opinion that the phenomenon has a natural cause, due to humidity. We would be obliged if you would find means to quiet the excited populace. I do not want to have to intervene in these senseless tumults."

To a judge: "Even if he is a peasant he is a man. If we had him in our house we would pity him as a man."

This is what she wrote publicly. Privately she wrote Elisabetta on February 10, 1510, that "being made of flesh and bone, I very often despair. I want to unburden myself of this unhappy business of governing. I am tempted to abandon the State." This was obviously written in a moment of depression. Most of the time she loved her task.

"Everything is referred to Isabella," wrote Mario Equicola; "not a leaf is allowed to stir without her knowledge and consent."

With a persistence and an energy which are all the more admirable considering the state of their marriage, she went about trying to free Gianfrancesco. She besieged virtually everyone of importance whom she knew. She wrote letters to the queen of France, the Dukes of Bourbon, Anjou, Savoia, to the reigning heads of Florence, Siena, Lucca, Monferrato, Saxony, Bavaria, Brandenburg, to Cardinals Medici, Volterra, Sanseverino, Aragona—and we don't know how many others. She pleaded through envoys sent at considerable expense to Emperor Maximilian, Louis XII, and most persistently to the pope. She sent Bishop Lang of Gurk an exquisitely worked silver vase, to Anne of France a painting of the Madonna by Costa, with which she parted most unwillingly. She laid it on thick; to Anne of France she wrote: "Believe, Madama, if I did not have the confidence I do have in His Majesty and in you I would kill myself with my own hands. That seems to me a better fate than living on without my lord. When I think of the place he is in I die a thousand deaths."

She wrote a letter to the Venetian Senate begging them to allow her husband, who was "very ill," at least the services of a doctor and a valet, and she assured them that "in his heart of hearts" he had never been an enemy of Venice. The senators probably grinned when they read that.

She sent Gianfrancesco a copy of her portrait and that of Leonora by Costa, and she dispatched his favorite tenor and lute player, but they were not allowed to visit the prison often enough to make their maintenance in Venice worthwhile and they returned to Mantua. No letters from Isabella to the prisoner are extant, while the few scribbled by him to her are almost indecipherable and reflect his desperate mood. Perhaps his best consolations in prison were the letters and gifts Lucrezia managed to smuggle to him, using Angela Borgia as her confidante. She imagined him as the victim of circumstances, as Knight Roland, on whom an evil spell had fallen. She prayed for him. It is extraordinary that none of the Estes knew her secret thoughts and deeds.

All of Isabella's zeal availed nothing. Gianfrancesco had offended the Republic too deeply, he was too valuable to the opposition for the Senate to consider clemency. For a time nothing happened, and then, after almost a year, Louis XII and the doge came forth with a plan for Gianfrancesco's liberation which shocked Isabella to the core. Gianfrancesco was to be freed provided he would undertake no military action against Venice or any of its allies—and, to ensure his keeping the pact, his first-born son, Federico, was to be delivered to Venice and kept there as a hostage. The son would pay for any transgression by the father.

Isabella was frantic. This was a pressure not to be borne. The being whom she loved most exposed to a Senate capable of any cruelty? The little boy in whom she centered her future hopes removed from her to become a threat card in the squeeze play of politics? The handsome son—and he *was* handsome—to be exposed to the corruption and temptations spread before him by a cynical Venetian society? Federico gone from his mother? Take away my state or even my life, she cried in one letter, it is the same to me as taking away my son. This letter was written to her agent in Rome. He was to entreat Julius, who must understand "that a mother's love may seem all too selfish."

Emperor Maximilian, though he admired Isabella, agreed with the Venetians' demand. Allied in the League with France and the pope, he had little choice, or else he was too weak to disagree. He did propose that Federico should be sent to him instead of being sent to Venice, but Isabella rightly did not trust Maximilian any more than she trusted the doge. She wrote to her envoy at the imperial court in the same distraught tone in which she had written to the pope:

As to the demand for our dearest first-born son Federico, besides being a cruel and almost inhuman thing for any one who knows the meaning of a mother's love, there are many reasons which render it difficult and impossible. Although we are quite sure that his person would be well cared for and protected by His Majesty, how could we wish him to run the risk of this long and difficult journey, considering the child's tender and delicate age? And you must know what comfort and solace, in his father's present unhappy condition, we find in the presence of this dear son, the hope and joy of all our people and subjects. To deprive us of him would be to deprive us of life itself, and of all we count good and precious. If you take Federico away you might as well take away our life and state. . . . Once for all, we will suffer any loss rather than part from our son, and this you may take to be our deliberate and unchanging resolution.

Gianfrancesco ordered her to send the boy. Ill and half-crazed in his cell, he wanted his freedom at any price. Nothing would happen to the boy, he was sure of it. Let her do as she was told. Isabella wrote him:

If in this matter Your Excellency were to despise me and deprive me of your love and grace, I would rather endure such contumely, I would rather lose our State, than deprive us of our children. I am hoping that in time your own prudence and kindness will make you understand that I have acted more lovingly toward you than you have to yourself.

Have patience! You can be sure that I and the Cardinal think continuously of your liberation and when the time comes we will not fail you, as we have not relaxed our efforts. As witnesses I cite the Pope, the Emperor, the King of France, and all the other reigning heads and potentates of Christendom. Yes, and the infidels as well. [She had written to the sultan for help.] If it were *really* the means of setting you free, I would not only send Federico but all the other children as well. [This was a refusal, of course.] I will do everything imaginable. Some day I hope I can make you understand. . . .

Pardon me if this letter is badly written and worse composed, but I do not know if I am alive or dead.

> Isabella
> who desires the best for Your Excellency,
> written with her own hand.

Mantua, May 14, 1510

Sanuto reports in his diaries Gianfrancesco's reaction to this letter. He broke out crying:

"That whore of my wife is the cause of it all." He wept and mourned greatly, saying, "Send me into battle alone, do what you like with me, I have lost in one blow my state, my honor and my freedom."

Later, notes Sanuto, he added threats: "If she does not obey, I'll cut her vocal cords."

When the pope heard the news, he exploded:

"That whore of a Marchesa doesn't want to give in. I won't excuse her any longer. When he comes out he'll castigate her. She is a whore. The Marchese is a prisoner not only of the Signoria but of a rebel wife."

Detail from *Parnassus*, by Andrea Mantegna. The apparently pregnant Muse in the center is believed to represent Isabella.

St. Catherine, detail of a fresco by Bernardino Pinturicchio. Believed to be a portrait of Lucrezia Borgia.

Pope Julius II, by Raphael.

Federico Gonzaga, Isabella's son, by Francesco Francia.

Pope Leo X, with Cardinals Giulio de' Medici (later Pope Clement VII) and Lodovico de' Rossi, by Raphael.

La Bella: Isabella's first-born, Leonora Gonzaga, in her youth, by Titian.

Federico Gonzaga, by Titian.

Leonora Gonzaga in her old age, by Titian.

Isabella, paying little attention to these epithets, if indeed she knew of them, kept on working. On one point she remained firm: no Federico. Even when Louis XII decided that to quiet her *he* would take Federico to his court, out of reach of the Venetians, she sent a diplomatically worded no to her French agent:

Tell His Christian Majesty that we do not deny that he [Federico] might be better off near his Majesty than in our care, insofar as the example of virtue and the acquisition of practical knowledge useful to men are concerned. Nor am I unmindful of the honor and benefits he would derive. Yet we feared—and now we are certain—that he might die, considering his tender age and his delicate constitution. He could not stand the voyage on horseback, nor the change of air, nor the different customs, being yet in the care and under the supervision of women. . . .

The father is not as linked to his children as the mother is. And Federico now is husband and son to me.

On July 1, 1510, she wrote her husband again trying to explain. He did not answer.

4

Gianfrancesco was freed not by Isabella's pleas but by a sudden change of policy. After being firmly allied with France against Venice, Julius decided that he had sufficiently brought Venice to its knees—literally, as the envoys of the doge kneeled before him in an endless ceremony before they received absolution—and that his real enemy was now Louis XII. The French were the villains, the French must be driven home, "Italy must be freed of the barbarians." Accordingly, he changed partners, linked arms with the doge, and proceeded to battle his friend of yesterday, "His Most Christian Majesty." For this enterprise Gianfrancesco could prove useful —let him be released! Venice agreed at once.

Gianfrancesco emerged from prison in July or August 1510, a dour, embittered, suspicious man. We have to be careful how we hold this eel, said Julius. He proposed to the Gonzagas a politer version of what Venice had demanded, that he "invite" their Federico to the Vatican; the boy, now ten years old, was to live near him, be well taken care of, receive the best of tutelage both spiritually and physically. Undoubtedly Julius did this partly to reassure Venice: they were nervous about Gianfrancesco.

An invitation from the pope, a chance for the boy to grow up at the very fulcrum of the world's power—that was an offer Isabella did not dare refuse. In her maternal heart grew a hatred of Julius—in an unguarded moment she went so far as to write to her brother Ippolito that "I hope God will soon ruin him and he will die"—but on her lips and through her pen she voiced her thanks and pretended to a satisfaction she did not feel. It was useless for her to resist. She knew that Julius would treat the boy well, but separation tasted bitter, all the more so because in having Gianfrancesco back she knew that she had received but a sorry bargain. She cried many a tear. She commissioned Francesco Francia to paint the boy's portrait.* Isabella was delighted with the result: "It couldn't be finer, or a better likeness. I marvel that Francia was able to produce so exceptional a work in so short a time. No doubt he wished to show us the perfection of his art." She sent Francia 30 gold ducats. She then wanted the hair slightly darkened—it was too blond. But Francia refused to touch the painting, nor would he paint another portrait "for all the gold in the world," though he was very grateful for the "too liberal payment." Later there was talk of Francia painting Isabella's portrait. She refused, because she found sitting still and posing "so tiresome that I never want to do it again" and because she did not want to offend Costa, her court painter.

Before Federico finally went to Rome, she gave the boy a bracelet to protect him on his journey: it contained the text of the Gospel of Saint John written in miniature and enclosed in a capsule. (The bracelet was soon lost.) A dozen times a day she kissed him goodbye, until she could delay no longer. She sent with him three excellent tutors, and she begged the famous Bernardo Bibbiena to see to it that Federico was treated with the same mixture of strictness and tolerance "which the magnificent Medici accorded their sons." She heaped letters on the tutors, instructing one of them, Matteo Ippoliti, not to use corporal punishment. She disapproved of beating a child: "It is not fitting for somebody who is stronger to lay hands on somebody who is weaker." She exhorted Federico as verbosely as a female Polonius: "You have every opportunity of acquiring knowledge and necessary experience in Rome; you can enjoy yourself and at the same time study literature, which is far more important for a prince than for private individuals." When she learned

* Now in New York's Metropolitan Museum.

that Federico had given one of his servants a gold embroidered cap, she rebuked Ippoliti for permitting his charge such an extravagance. If it had been his own cap and he had taken it off his head to present to some courtier as a sign of favor, well and good. But a servant? A child ought to learn the value of money.

The pope was as good as his word, or better. He took a great liking to the comely, confident child. One of the tutors wrote to Isabella that her son

is lodged in the finest rooms of this palace and takes his meals in a most beautiful Loggia overlooking the Campagna, which is rightly called the Belvedere. He spends all day walking about those halls and the garden of orange trees and pines, which affords him the greatest delight and amusement, but he does not neglect his singing, often sending for his master himself. . . .

As time went on, Julius looked on Federico as a son. He arranged for the boy to eat his meals with him, held serious talks with him, played backgammon with him, let him be present at Vatican meetings. Julius suggested to Raphael that he introduce the boy's portrait into the great fresco he was painting in the Stanze, the *School of Athens:* there on the left we see Federico, behind the philosopher in the Oriental robe.

For the first time in many months Isabella managed to breathe freely. She did not, however, stop the work she had begun while Gianfrancesco was still in prison, that of strengthening the Mantuan fortresses and adding to the city's protective wall. One could never tell where Julius's policy would lead next.

She was now regarded as a political figure of prime importance. She had earned general admiration for the way she had handled the Venetian affair, kept Mantua officially neutral, and avoided raising Julius's already high blood pressure. Emperor Maximilian declared that her actions were worthy of an "intelligent Prince of antiquity." He said that of all Italian women she was "the most interesting" and he "was half in love with her." Venice sent an envoy to her to apologize ceremoniously for any derogatory remarks the Senate may have uttered during her husband's captivity. They recognized "her prudence and wisdom of behavior." Let bygones be bygone.

But Isabella felt uneasy.

5

Ferrara, that is to say Isabella's brother Alfonso, sided with the French. Julius promptly proceeded in all-out warfare against Ferrara. He began by excommunicating Alfonso, calling him a "son of iniquity and a root of perdition." He then summoned Gianfrancesco to join him in the campaign. Isabella was informed: "The Pope intends to celebrate the carnival in Ferrara . . . then on to Parma and Piacenza, they all belong to the Church." Lucrezia wrote Gianfrancesco, "I will die from this grief." Gianfrancesco attempted reconciliation, the only answer to which was a choleric tantrum from Julius, who threatened to shove Federico into prison. Both Gonzagas now found themselves in an egregiously difficult position. At each of three doors, so to speak, a sharply pointed pike awaited them. Where were they to turn? How were they to solve the triple problems of keeping Mantua inviolate, of cooperating with the pope, Gianfrancesco's new employer, and of avoiding conflict with Alfonso? The third problem may have loomed largest: Gianfrancesco still enamored of Lucrezia Borgia, Isabella tied by blood to Alfonso.

Gianfrancesco behaved in the manner one has come to expect of him: pretending that his illness had worsened*—perhaps it was half the truth—he delayed going into the field as long as possible, and when he did go he pursued the papal cause half-heartedly, although he seems to have been convinced that Julius would win the war and make short work of Alfonso. An amazing letter is extant, dated January 23, 1511, to the Archdeacon of Gabbionetta, the pope's closest adviser, assuring him that if Alfonso were ever found in Mantuan territory he, Gianfrancesco, would at once hand his wife's brother over to the pope. But he asks for clemency for Lucrezia:

Give the safety of the Duchess formerly of Ferrara [the pope had declared Alfonso's title to be void] into our hands. She alone, among our several relatives, employed loving and loyal ways to help us when we were prisoner in Venice and we are bound to show our gratitude. Had the wisdom of Your Holi-

---

* Julius was suspicious and sent his private physician to examine Gianfrancesco. The evidence suggests that the physician was bribed to tell the pope that Gianfrancesco was "unable to move."

ness not aided us, we could have found no others who proved that they were as compassionate as this poor girl.

"This poor girl"—Gianfrancesco's love transpires through the phrase. Julius must have said or implied, "You can have her," because Gianfrancesco actually began to furnish a sumptuous apartment for her, near Mantua, choosing the furniture, tapestries, and paintings himself. He wrote Lucrezia about it. "Let us hope," Lucrezia answered, "that we will be able to enjoy it together."

Isabella, unaware of a proposal so humiliating to her, now began to emulate her husband in deceit. Duplicity is the daughter of diplomacy. She swore fealty to the pope and vowed that His Holiness could count on her in his great enterprise. Secretly she wrote to her daughter that she wished Julius would drop dead. She pawned some of her jewels to pay the soldiers Gianfrancesco was employing for Julius's war against Ferrara—and at the same time she made it possible for French reinforcements to join Alfonso by permitting them to march through Mantuan territory. Write me a letter—she directed the commander of one of her fortresses—stating that "these martial troops arrived so unexpectedly out of the nowhere that you didn't have time to consult my disposition, whether to grant them passage or not. And anyway, you couldn't do anything to prevent it." She was going to make sure that the pope got to see this letter, to prove how innocent was Isabella, Marchesa of Mantua. Secret letters passed between her and her brother daily, mostly in cipher, with false names and addresses, informing Alfonso of the pope's moves.

The pope was not so naïve as not to suspect her. Yet Isabella had a few powerful adherents at the Vatican (including Cardinal Francesco Alidosi, a man of dubious honesty whom Julius trusted nonetheless). She told her brother Cardinal Ippolito that Gianfrancesco had every intention of "playing dead," proceeding neither against Louis XII nor against Alfonso, nor for the pope. He would use big phrases, but it was all talk, no action. She was doing likewise. Louis XII must understand that her husband was forced to pretend to be the pope's man, because he held their son as hostage. The French were to occupy Mantua and seem to plunder it; secretly they agreed to pay for the damage. It was all make-believe. Ippolito thought that was a "very beautiful trick." In the Venetian Senate it was said that Gianfrancesco "had one foot in two shoes," that he was "totally influenced by his wife," and the doge exclaimed, "Have I not always said so?" but Julius ignored the matter and Isabella kept sending him gifts and flattering letters.

She handled her adversaries with cool disdain. One of them, Lodovico da Camposampiero, she hated passionately, suspecting him of having supplied her husband with prostitutes and young boys during a previous campaign. The pope sent Lodovico to Mantua, and Isabella learned that he was to supervise the building of a military bridge across the Po. She dispatched a courier to Alfonso. The man galloped through the night, using one of the swift Barbary horses. On receiving the message, Alfonso immediately hurried a detachment of soldiers to the spot; they chased Camposampiero away. He wrote a furious protest to the pope and one to Isabella, accusing her not only of interfering with him but of maligning him. Her answer was simple: "It is true that I have never had a good word to say about you, because there is nothing good to be said. I said nothing bad either, because that's not in my nature." Then she bribed somebody at the Vatican to filch Camposampiero's complaint to the pope, and she kept the document for years as insurance against Camposampiero. If he were ever to accuse her to a future pope, she could prove that he had been her enemy right along. She didn't have to use the letter: Camposampiero was stabbed to death in 1521 by an unknown assassin. Isabella rejoiced: "The miserable traitor has found just punishment."

Amid the muddy intrigues which surrounded him Julius remained firm as the Moses that Michelangelo planned for his tomb. To bend with the venal servitors around him, to treat in secret with the egocentric princes, to let his actions contradict his words—such was not his style. Whatever his faults, his aim was straight, his purpose lofty. Several times the old man seemed done for, his health ruined, his cause lost. Every time he rose and, reaffirming his will, once again stood steady against the rushing winds. In August 1511 he was so ill that preparations for the election of a successor were begun. One of Federico's tutors wrote Isabella:

As we all had given up hope . . . because His Holiness would take nothing to eat, Federico seized a cup of beef brew with the yolk of two eggs in it, carried it to the bed, and implored His Holiness to drink it, for the love of him and the Madonna of Loreto.

They said in Rome that Federico had saved his life. It was news which Isabella must have received with less than wholehearted joy.

For, no question, she hated him. It was whispered in Rome that Federico had become Julius's sexual playmate. That was probably untrue. Perhaps Isabella heard the rumors. Whether she did or didn't, she saw in the pope the man who had usurped the love of the child she loved and was in addition her brother's enemy. His plan to form an Italian nation was beyond her ken. Mantua was her fierce concern; large as was her viewpoint, it was still a parochial one. Julius and Isabella never met; she did not understand the great pope.

6

The historians tell us that the reason Julius found it so difficult to conquer Ferrara lay in Alfonso's defensive preparations, his armies of devoted soldiers, and his use of new artillery weapons, a subject to which he had devoted much study. That is true; yet Isabella's help, her secret spy service, was of greater value to Alfonso than has been acknowledged. She was as good as three regiments.

Yet, after a fierce struggle, after the siege of Mirandola (a fortress in the state of Ferrara) during which Julius was nearly killed, after the pope swore that he would not shave off his beard until the last Frenchman was expelled from Italian soil, Julius emerged victorious. His enemies—Spain and Germany as well as France—were exhausted. Ferrara was exhausted. Alfonso, humbled, asked for absolution.

The end of the war came early in 1513, when 18,000 Swiss hired by Julius routed the French at Novara. The great pope had achieved his great purpose: he had given Italy to the Italians, while reasserting the supremacy of the Church. But he himself, sinews and nerves, was used up. It was the end for him, too. In January he took to his bed; calmly he gave instructions for his funeral, summoned his cardinals, conferred with his treasurer. On February 20 he died. The people of Rome wept, and thousands came to kiss the feet of the dead man. Yet not all Italians mourned him. Isabella didn't. Alfonso d'Este didn't.

7

Before Julius died, he had come to suspect Gianfrancesco more and more, sufficiently for the once proud soldier to attempt to excuse himself by writing the pope as groveling a missive as guilt could dictate:

It is very possible that our consort, who by bonds of blood feels herself bound [to the Estes] and who is a woman who follows the dictates of her own head—as Your Holiness well knows—that this woman established secret connections with Ferrara by letter and by messengers. If she did so it was without guilt on our part. She could well have done so without our knowing about it.

He wrote in a similar vein to a political representative of the Peace Conclave, Lodovico Guerrieri: "We confess having a wife who acts on her own opinions. She has demonstrated that on a number of occasions."

Her husband, then, did not support the efforts of the wife who acted "on her own opinions." The cleft between them became wider.

After Julius died, Isabella went away from Mantua, going to Pavia and Parma and Piacenza and there conferring with various relatives and friends about future alliances. The conferences were not really necessary. Isabella invented their necessity. She wanted to get away from her husband.

Gianfrancesco, ill and in need of solace, wanted her back. His disease, treated with mercury, seemed to have abated. In January 1513 Capilupo, the old reliable secretary privy to all the secrets, wrote Isabella that "our Lord has not yet left his chamber, only occasionally his bed. He cannot speak fluently because the malady has attacked his mouth. Yet he hopes to be cured." But a month later Capilupo wrote:

When he showed me that his wounds were healed, he was full of joy over his daily progress and I perceived that he would very much like to resume marital relations with Your Excellency. He remarks, and it may be true, that you are behaving like a young girl, a regular "don't-touch-me" piece. Get ready, Madama, to satisfy our Signor and make up for lost time. . . . The Signor is younger than I, but I too can have my little pleasures, even if my "thing" is not in quite as good working order as his. . . .

In the same month Gianfrancesco himself wrote her that because of his sickness her presence in Mantua was now required "to govern our affairs. . . . We ask that you start on your way back after next Sunday." She made no move.

Capilupo reported that Gianfrancesco had told him that somebody in Milan had told Isabella that he, Gianfrancesco, had said nasty things about her. Absurd! Never, under any circumstances, would he hold his honor at so small a price as to malign his own wife. Isabella ought now to furnish him with proof that she still loved him and was willing to make peace. On her return she was to tell him who was the man who had spread such evil gossip. If she didn't, it would convince him that Isabella, become "too proud," no longer cared about him. Capilupo stuttered something in Isabella's defense, wrote the whole interview down, and sent it to Isabella. She did not react.

In March, Isabella still not having come home, Gianfrancesco ordered her to return. In a peremptorily worded letter he reminded her that "she owed him respect" as well as "duty." The people are beginning to talk. "Return at once!" Isabella answered the next day:

My illustrious Lord: I am pained, though not surprised, that Your Excellency was dissatisfied with my explanation. I would feel even keener pain were I to think that your anger resulted from real guilt on my part. Considering, however, that I have not given in to Your Highness's wish solely because I acted in the interests of one of my brothers and to please my nephew, the Duke of Milan—and this with your knowledge and consent—it seems to me that you have no cause to feel aggrieved with me. I lament my unlucky fate, which always renders my deeds, however good they may be, repellent to you. I do not believe that either my behavior or any of my doings during this voyage to Milan are such as to "make people talk." I know that I have made a thousand new friends for you, as well as for myself. I know I have done my duty as always. God knows I have never needed an instructor to set down rules to teach me behavior or attitudes. Whatever my shortcomings may be, God has at least granted me this grace. Your Excellency owes me as much gratitude as any husband owes a wife. Even if you honored and loved me with a greater love than ever a human being loved another, you could never repay my fidelity. This, my loyalty, may be the reason why you sometimes claim that I am haughty, but it is only because I am cognizant of how much I deserve from you—and how little I receive. Yes, sometimes I fall into a dark humor and I appear other than what I really am.

Yet even if I were sure that I could expect from you nothing but bad treatment, I would not cease to try to do good. The more you show me that you love me with but a scant love, the more will I prove my love through deeds. In truth, I was born for this love. I was given to you at so early an age that I can no longer remember having lived without your love. It seems to me that through my love I ought to have earned the freedom to decide to postpone my return two or three weeks for reasons cited above—without incurring your ill will and your anger and without your jumping to the conclusion that I do not want to see you again. Read the signature of this letter! If you truly still longed for me, you would make it possible for me to see you in Mantua more often than I actually do. I commend myself to Your Excellency and hope you will read this overlong letter with forbearance.

> She who loves you as well as herself
> Isabella, Marchesa of Mantua

Piacenza, March 12, 1513

"Read the signature!" Its forgiving tone softens the letter, which, in a sense, was another plea for reconciliation. It failed.

Gianfrancesco's answer was brief: though he had found in her letter neither the reasons nor conclusions he had hoped to find, he read the whole letter avidly, including that signature. If the signature had expressed the truth, nothing in the world could have prevented her from returning. Be that as it may—she had better return!

She finally did go home, to find Federico, now thirteen years old, a graceful and charming boy, but spoiled, petulant, and knowing beyond his years. She did not, and she could not, resume marital relations, and when Gianfrancesco's health worsened during the following winter she soon absented herself again, although at first only on inconsequential excursions to Lake Garda, Sermione, Milan, and so on. Her letters to her husband from these travels are lively and friendly, and nothing more. She kept up appearances. Overtly she remained Gonzaga's consort. But the marriage as a marriage was finished. She had to face that truth and she faced it.

X

A Spell of Peace

Peace once more, and a little peace entered Isabella's soul. As she wandered through the regions of her state, where the olive trees stood like old men with green hair, as she bathed her feet in the lake whose waves seemed to whisper welcome to so august an intruder, as she visited the vineyards and the fields which appeared to her "so well cultivated that they were all gardens," as she climbed a hill where she discovered a Roman grotto which so enchanted her that she dreamed, "If God restores your health and we are able to come here together to enjoy this place in peace, we ought to build a villa, not for the fame of the State, but for private pleasure and delightful conversation," as she rode among the drooping apple trees and the stalks of shining grapes, she began to think of her husband with pity. Shut into a heavily perfumed room, its walls adorned with pictures of the famous Gonzaga horses, he reclined on a couch near a fireplace—he was always cold now—his pet dwarf near him, three greyhounds at his feet; several falcons and hawks hung in cages. Three pages stood by, waving fans to chase the flies away. (That is how a visitor from Venice described the scene.) Isabella wrote him:

If I ever longed to see Your Excellency restored to health, I do so now, in order that you might be able to enjoy these delicious scenes. But your letter of today troubles me sadly, and makes me fear that the pills have not done you as much good as you had hoped. But you must not be disappointed at this, because medicine does not act upon us as quickly as we expect; and now the fine weather is coming, I feel sure that, with careful diet, your health will soon improve. God grant this!

Alfonso d'Este was once again in possession of Ferrara—and of his Lucrezia. The affair with Gianfrancesco was over, husband and

wife drew together, and for the rest of her short life Lucrezia
proved an ideal wife. He entrusted her with many decisions concerning matters of state, and she, having observed Isabella, proved
herself most capable and judicious. She, too, experienced her portion of sorrow: her son Alfonso of Aragon died in 1512, and although Isabella could not bring herself to write to her directly, she,
who knew what it was to lose a child, had enough humanity to ask
a Ferrarese nun to call on Lucrezia and tell her that "extreme sorrow was rendered all the more unbearable by expressions of condolence." That was why Isabella would not write. But—"Let her know
with whatever skill you have that when we heard the news we felt
as much grief as if one of our children had died. To comfort her
and counsel patience seems to me useless, knowing she will receive
plenty of that. Nothing helps except time. . . ." Later Isabella and
Gianfrancesco sent Fra Anselmo to Lucrezia. He told Isabella:

> Lucrezia said to me: "This [Anselmo's] visit is proof that the Marchese loves
> me. Nonetheless I think he has cooled toward me." I asked her why she
> thought so. She answered: "It seems to me that he has come to an under-
> standing with his wife. Neither he nor she has been to visit me in my tribula-
> tion over my son."

Lucrezia was to bear Alfonso four sons (one died when five years
old) and a daughter and found comfort in devoting herself to their
education. But another child, delivered on June 14, 1519, was stillborn, and ten days later Lucrezia herself was dead, not yet forty
years old. Alfonso mourned long and deeply. The wife whom he
had taken against his will had been, he said, "the dear partner of
his life." He fainted at her funeral. And the people of Ferrara worshiped Lucrezia's memory; they "declared her a saint." Isabella had
not forgiven her.

2

The next pope to be elected who was to give his name to an age
was a Medici, one of the three sons of Lorenzo the Magnificent,
who christened him mellifluously Giovanni Romolo Pomaso. When
he became Leo X he remained every inch a Medici. Art and literature were the wellspring of his nature, and the appreciation of the
beautiful, what he called "mankind's untouchable wealth," was his

religion. In his father's house he had grown up with the sculptors, painters, poets, and philosophers who took their ease in the Medici gardens. He had been taught poetry by Poliziano and Ficino and Greek by Chalcondyles, the great grammarian. He hoped to make Latin—which he spoke fluently—the universal language of cultivated men, and for this purpose he summoned to Rome, among others, Pietro Bembo, the most elegant Latin stylist. He was amiable, courteous, diplomatic, and a liberal, in both the spiritual and the monetary meaning. Artists, good and mediocre, could count on Leo's open purse; in fact he spent his own and the Church's funds so freely that when he died he left Rome in a financial panic. With these millions of ducats, he did make Rome the center of the civilized world, a citadel of thought and achievement, almost comparable to the Athens of Pericles.

Leo varied his learning, his sponsorship of contemporary art, his grammarian ambitions, his study of philosophy (he delved into Greek and Latin thought as vigorously as into Christian dogma), his collecting—he varied those epicurean interests with a love of horseplay, puerile diversions, monster hunts, and endless and thoroughly unhealthful banquets. Leo was fat and flabby, very myopic (in Raphael's portrait he is holding the lens, which he used constantly) and vain, especially of his hands, which he adorned with many rings. He suffered from an anal fistula which had frequently to be operated on and which was so painful that it was often agonizing for him just to lift his arm. Yet he never missed a spectacle or a festivity.

With such a man Isabella could come to an understanding; here was a fellow connoisseur who knew for what purpose money should be spent. She had known him briefly some years earlier when he stood as godfather to her son Ferrante. Now she couldn't wait to renew their acquaintance. She wanted to leave for Rome immediately, and she lost no time getting in touch again with Bernardo Bibbiena, "il bel Bernardo," poet and classical scholar, priest and pagan, art collector and gambler, and one of her very good friends. After sending Mario Equicola to Rome to kiss Leo's foot, she wrote to Bibbiena on the twenty-eighth of March, 1513, some two weeks after the election:

You will have already heard from Mario Equicola of the joy and delight with which this happy event has filled us, and really, since the day of our birth, we have never had any greater pleasure than this good news, which reached us immediately after we heard of the death of Pope Julius. For all of which we praise and thank our Lord God, hoping that, by the great goodness and wisdom of His Holiness, we may see the safety of the Duke our brother's state secured, that of our nephew the Duke of Milan established, as well as the honor and exaltation of our husband the Marchese and the peace of all Italy confirmed. On our own account we are satisfied that we shall enjoy the protection and perpetual favor of His Holiness, both because of the bond of our common sponsorship and of the love and regard we bore him as Cardinal dei Medici, not to speak of our intimate friendship with his brother, the Magnifico Giuliano. No less do we reckon on the favor and influence which you will retain with His Holiness, feeling no doubt that neither rank nor honors will change your nature, but that you will be as kind and affectionate to us as ever, even though we have made you lose 500 ducats!

She had long yearned to see the holy city, envied Elisabetta for having seen it, imagined it in her thoughts. Both Bibbiena and Pietro Bembo urged her to come, of course with Leo's consent. But Gianfrancesco was ill, and however adroitly Isabella put forth the argument that it was politically wise and indeed necessary to consolidate a relationship with the new pope, he put on a dark face and implored her to stay. His condition at one time became so bad that Isabella, who was on the way to Milan, had at once to turn around and go back to Mantua. Physician after physician, each with his own salve, medicine, *aurum potabile,* was consulted, to be forthwith dismissed. In the summer of 1514, however, Gianfrancesco's health showed signs of improvement. His eyes had given him much trouble; now he could see more clearly. Isabella advanced a new argument: she intended not only to go to Rome but to Naples, there to woo the widow of the king of Naples for her nephew, Massimiliano Sforza. If successful, it would constitute a clever political alliance. Gianfrancesco gave in. Very well, let her go. Isabella began preparations for the journey. In the autumn she left Mantua with all her damsels, a cavalcade of guards, a suitable selection of jewelry and robes, gifts for her friends, and her prized perfumes for Leo. As long as she was going away, she decided to make her absence as long as possible, and she traveled by a circuitous road, first visiting Milan, Pisa, and Genoa before turning south. It was evident that Mantua and her sick husband had become oppressive to her. On the journey she would breathe air more bracing.

No sooner had she gone than Gianfrancesco began to complain. Where was she? Why had she undertaken these side excursions?

What was the meaning of so slow a progress? Poor Capilupo—he had to invent excuses for her. He wrote Isabella in October:

For your information—every day I have to utter a thousand lies and I cover up what your ladies and gentlemen report here, whether inadvertently or stupidly. . . . Our Lord now believes that I have a secret understanding with Your Excellency for the purpose of deceiving him. . . . I had to admit to him that you are not yet on your way to Rome nor to Naples . . . with the result that our Lord now thinks I am a dissembler and privy to moves designed to trick him.

Isabella's answer to her husband was: "I am no longer a child and I ought to be allowed to stay away as long as I think necessary." To her son she wrote in a different vein:

My Federico: It seems to me a shame that while you were growing up in Rome I have never seen it. Therefore I have determined to visit it myself, just not to have to envy you. But because . . . I was told that you, out of love, desire my return, I will return as soon as possible. Be good and virtuous because all my happiness depends on you. I send you a thousand kisses, remember me to Our Lord, and give a kiss to your brother and sister from me.
Greetings to Mathe [Matteo Ippoliti], etc.

Your mother Isabella who loves you,
written with her own hand
Pisa, October 5, 1514

Isabella was met at Bolsena by a deputation from the pope. The meeting place was symbolic, since a miracle was reported to have taken place there in the thirteenth century. In the old castle the two groups met, Isabella surrounded by her staff. The papal delegation was headed by Leo's brother Giuliano, Bibbiena, and the singer "l'unico Aretino," who had become one of Leo's favorites. Aretino's conceit, never exactly small, had by now swelled to the point where he insisted on usurping the honor of being the official welcomer. Thereupon the others pointed to one damsel after another as being the marchesa. Discovering the trick, he sulked and withdrew, no doubt to everybody's satisfaction.

She finally reached Rome on October 18, having left home early in September. Like tens of thousands of visitors before her, like tens of thousands of visitors after her, she saw for the first time, as she traveled south on the Roman road, the Via Emilia, the shifting outlines of a field of stone, with the domes of the churches rising like huge haystacks above a yellow haze, pierced by the occasional gleam of an autumn sun. The old wall with its narrow portal slowed the progress of the riders, as if each visitor needed to be inspected before being judged worthy of entering. They made their way past marshes and unruly hedges, past mean huts and hovels pressed together, the horses' hoofs scattering dust on the people who came to gape. On they rode to the center, where poverty gave way to pomp in the great palaces of the cardinals. At one of the largest of these, the palace of the Cardinal of Aragon, the procession halted. There Isabella was housed with her retinue, the Vatican assuming the cost of her stay.

Isabella, to judge from her letters, lived in a state of euphoria. She was, in Berenson's phrase, the "Passionate Sightseer." She got up early every morning to ride to one marvel after another, one antique monument after another. She climbed the Capitoline Hill. She gazed from the top of the Belvedere at the dark Alban mountains and at the aqueduct which marked the end of the Campagna with calligraphic flourish. She walked through the jagged remains of the Baths of Titus, where Roman frescoes had been newly restored, she rummaged through the Golden House of Nero, and she said a prayer in the Pantheon, now converted into a church. She was almost forty, but her energy was that of a teenager. Above everything, she had to see her fill of the works of art, the Laocoon, the Apollo Belvedere, the Michelangelo *Pietà*, the gay new Villa Farnesina, a pleasure dome illuminated by Raphael's *Triumph of Galatea*. Only two years before her visit Michelangelo had finished the ceiling frescoes of the Sistine Chapel, to which all who had eyes to see and necks to crane made a pilgrimage. Perhaps Raphael himself took Isabella to see *The School of Athens*, that epic of painting he had completed five years earlier. He was now at the height of his fame and lived in a great house designed by Bramante. Yet he had not lost his *gentilezza*, his charming modest manner. Isabella asked him to paint a Madonna for her. Raphael said, "With pleasure"— and forgot all about it.

Tommaso Inghirami, the Vatican's head librarian, served as Isabella's guide and became one of her fervid admirers. Bibbiena, Bembo, and Castiglione called. "Such a stream of visitors wend their way to her house," wrote the Archdeacon of Gabbionetta to Gianfrancesco, "that she hasn't got a minute to herself." The pope was away hunting when Isabella arrived, but he sent her immediately a purse containing 500 ducats, with a message that "once these are used up there's more to come." Soon they *were* used up, and 1,000 more came from the Vatican. (Nevertheless Isabella spent so freely that she had to borrow 1,000 ducats from the banker Agostino Chigi, which she had difficulty in repaying later.)

Between the sightseeing, the visits, and the entertainments, Isabella was so joyously involved that she had no time to go to church on Sundays! She therefore sent three ducats to a Mother Superior to pray for her by proxy. Equicola wrote to Federico that his mother

... is always accompanied by a group of nobles from the court. When she rides more than 150 horses ride with her. She seems to be the Queen of Rome. Everybody admires her for her beauty and virtue, as well as for being your mother. . . .

She wrote almost no letters to Gianfrancesco (only one is extant), but she did write to Federico and to Capilupo, to whom she reported that Cardinal Riario had given a banquet in her honor "so sumptuous as to be fit for a queen. We remained at table more than four hours. Much conversation." Agostino Chigi also entertained her in the "nightingales' tongues" manner for which his feasts were famous.

Her first audience with Leo took place on October 29, 1514. She did report this to Gianfrancesco: "His Holiness took my hand and insisted that I not kneel. He made me sit down next to him, told me how glad he was to see me," and so on. It was not the only time she saw Leo. He entertained her on several occasions, discussed his acquisitions, caressed the new jewels he had bought in Venice with white plump hands, spoke lovingly of an antique statue of Antaeus and Hercules which had been found in fragments (and of which Isabella was to order a bronze copy from Antico some years later). But when Isabella wanted to talk politics, when she tried to sound him on the future of Mantua, he swerved the conversation to his plan for Saint Peter's. Leo did not disclose his intentions, partly because he himself was not certain *what* he intended. Sometimes she made him laugh and he forgot his fistula for a moment or two. Even the envious had to admit that she knew how to get along with Leo—"no master of ceremonies was needed." In fact, her behavior in Rome was declared "exemplary," quite in contrast to that of her damsels, who went to bed with the richest cardinals.

The most spectacular entertainment Leo offered her was the staging of *La Calandria,* the play Bibbiena had written some five years before, which had already been performed in Urbino. With Machiavelli's *Mandragola* (a wittier work), it represents the first thrust of Italian prose comedy. *La Calandria's* plot, like the plot of *The Comedy of Errors,* deals with twins, a theme which may have been an old story when Plautus used it in the *Menaechmi.* Bibbiena, unlike Shakespeare, makes the twins a boy and a girl, each of whom for good and insufficient reason assumes the disguise of the opposite sex. The device enabled Bibbiena to introduce double entendres in bedroom adventures, the comedy being nothing if not salacious. For the performance at the Vatican in November 1514 Baldassare Peruzzi, a Sienese painter, was commissioned to design the scenery, and Vasari in his *Lives* waxes rhapsodic in his praises of Peruzzi's scenery and describes the miracle of perspective he achieved. In the interludes ballets were performed, music was played and sung, the voices, viols, and flutes buttressed by the tones of a new organ which Lorenzo da Pavia had made for the pope. The play pleased, Isabella laughed, Leo laughed, and so the high dignitaries laughed with him.

It was time to proceed to Naples. Isabella and her suite did so, arriving on December 2. They were greeted by three thousand horsemen of the royal court, blinding the guest of honor with the colors of their uniforms and the jewels worn by their steeds, suffocating her with the heat of their bodies, deafening her with the noise of hoofbeats. The visitors were lodged in the Royal Palace, from where Isabella wrote to Capilupo: "Our four private rooms are so beautifully furnished and decorated that it is impossible to imagine it. Her Majesty has spared no expense to welcome my whole 'family' most sumptuously." The queen had ordered all Naples to be decorated with flowers and garlands; the Mantuans were "stunned." Feast followed feast. At one banquet a reproduction of the Mantua Palace made of spun sugar was served; a pastry cook's masterpiece, it was said to have cost "70 or 80 ducats." Yet Isabella missed the gay, free, and intellectual atmosphere of Rome and wearied of the stiff Spanish protocol which ringed the ceremonies. All that etiquette was too much for her; she coined a word denoting "exaggerations": *napolitanerie.*

Leo wanted her back for Christmas. Therefore she began at once to discuss the projected marriage of Massimiliano Sforza. The negotiations proved complicated, but Isabella obtained an agreement in principle—as it turned out later the marriage did not take place—and she was back in Rome on December 23. The solemn Christmas mass was to be celebrated in Saint Peter's, and Leo had ordered the construction of a special tribune from which the Mantuans could watch it in comfort. In point of fact, Isabella had no further business in Rome; she ought to have returned home; Gianfrancesco had sent word that he was waiting. But Leo wouldn't hear of it or, more probably, she used his authority as a pretext for staying longer—and he issued a papal *breve* that she was to remain at the Vatican for the carnival. Cardinal Bibbiena advised her by all means to obey the pope; it was hardly selfless advice, as he was enjoying a flaming love affair with Isabella Lavagrola, one of her prettiest damsels. Gianfrancesco was stymied; he did not dare protest against Leo's order.

Thus she didn't leave for home until the twenty-seventh of February, traveling by way of Siena and Florence. She spent only one day in Florence and used it to place several artistic commissions. She didn't have the money to pay for them; well—she would later. When she reached Mantua on March 18, she had been away more than six months. Gianfrancesco wisely did not reproach her; on the contrary, he welcomed her warmly, and Isabella wrote to her Roman friends that "all had gone better than expected." They in turn wrote her that she had left behind her a group of sad "malcontents" and the city now seemed as "empty and horrid as it had been brilliant and gay in her presence."

The evening of her arrival she wrote Bibbiena:

> I am in Mantua, but all my desire is to be in Rome. At least I feel some comfort in having satisfied and obeyed my illustrious Lord. How different are these little rooms, how different is the life I lead here from that I led in Rome, how strange it all appears to me, Your Excellency may imagine. My body is here, my spirit there. In spirit I am still walking and conversing with you and the other cardinals, and kissing the foot of His Holiness. With my fancies I try to deceive myself and pass the time with less boredom. . . .

She concludes by asking him to send her "a beautiful antique object" from Rome, as she had left without obtaining anything. Presently she sent gifts to Bibbiena, Bembo, and the others, including a quilt artfully worked in satin and stuffed with feathers. Bibbiena replied:

Your Excellency, in her kind and courteous letter, tells me that she has so much idle time on her hands that she is ready to make a present of it to the first comer, which seems a difficult thing to believe, knowing as I do that even if you had no other occupation than your own wise and charming thoughts, you could never be idle. In truth, like that old Roman (was it Scipio?) who was never less alone than when alone, Your Excellency may say you are never idle when you are most idle. I showed your letter to His Holiness, who read it very gladly, and with more praises of you than I can possibly express, saying that the affairs of your brother, the Duke, were already arranged according to your desire, and could not be altered. Toward this happy settlement His Holiness was from the first so naturally inclined that there has been little need of my intervention. But I will not deny that, besides his personal inclination, the great respect and affection with which His Holiness regards Your Excellency has considerably helped to bring about this fortunate result. I will obey Your Excellency with regard to the matter you mentioned to me in Rome, and will not breathe a syllable to anyone, but wait until you think the right moment has come. As for your illustrious son, I really believe he will turn out as well as you desire, thanks to your prudence and loving exhortations and to his own excellent nature. I am delighted to hear of Your Excellency's high credit and favor with your illustrious husband, which must give you the greatest satisfaction. I rejoice greatly over this, but beg you not to make too large demands on his favor, lest you should some day live to repent it.* I am also very glad to hear your husband is better, and pray that God may restore him completely to health, so that Your Excellency may be the better able to enjoy his affection. The feather quilt which Your Excellency sent me could not be more acceptable than it is, both on account of its rare delicacy and beauty, and still more because it comes from you. Certainly I have never slept better in my life, and I should not forswear myself were I to swear to Your Excellency that not a single night passes in which I do not remember you! His Holiness hopes that you will send him the one of which you speak in your letter, and really likes the idea of the gift extremely, so that Your Excellency may safely have it made and sent to Rome at once. The fact is, you may, I assure you, treat His Holiness with as much friendliness as you would your brother, since it is certain you are as dear to him as a sister or daughter. . . .

Even six months later she had not freed herself of the spell of Rome. Alone in her country place she wrote that she preferred "her complete solitude to the sparse and silly conversations of Mantua."

3

Leo was a pope of peace, but a long peace was not vouchsafed him. Louis XII died in 1515, and on his deathbed he cried revenge,

* Bibbiena seems to have known what the situation was.

bloody revenge for the Italian defeat and the loss of that pride of cities, Milan. His young son-in-law, now King François I, listened eagerly, and in the very year of his succession he organized an army of 40,000 men—the largest yet recruited in the French-Italian wars—and led them through Alpine passes considered untraversable to swoop down on the Lombardy plain. In Marignano, so close to Milan that the cannons could be heard in the Castello, the battle raged for two days (September 13–14) and ended with a total French victory.

Three years later, Maximilian died and the pivotal question arose as to who was to succeed him as emperor of the Holy Roman Empire. François I and Charles, the Habsburg king of Spain and Naples, both coveted the crown. What should Leo do? On which scale was he to place his papal prestige? He sought Machiavelli's advice, who, after the French invasion, counseled that a conciliatory attitude toward François seemed the lesser of two evils. Yet Leo hesitated to oppose Charles, and he did nothing except play the "balance of power" game, lying and breaking promises right and left. Eventually the determined Charles became Holy Roman Emperor as Charles V and the struggle for Italy continued, with Milan as the symbol. "My cousin François and I," said Charles V, "are in perfect agreement. He wants Milan and so do I."

Early during the French invasion Leo had ordered Francesco della Rovere, duke of Urbino and husband of Isabella's daughter Leonora, to raise an army against the French. Della Rovere refused, possibly because he realized the uselessness of resistance with so small a force, possibly, as Leo claimed, because he was bribed by the French. Leo summoned him to Rome; instead, he fled to Mantua, seeking Isabella's protection. Leo excommunicated him, deprived him of his office, and sent Lorenzo dei Medici with 20,000 men to take Urbino. Leonora and Elisabetta rushed to Isabella, imploring her to intercede for them with Leo, and although Gianfrancesco hated to incur the pope's wrath by sheltering the exiles under his roof, Isabella, relying on her friendship with Leo, sent messengers to Rome with urgent letters begging clemency.

Curious pleas, they seemed more deeply concerned with the fate of her friend Elisabetta than with her daughter's. A strange, dead coldness separated mother and child. What caused so wide a distance? Leonora was in danger, her husband's home and state fallen to the intruder, yet Isabella, who could weep over the misfortunes of one of her ladies-in-waiting, the same Isabella who erected a marble monument to her little dog and wept when her favorite dwarf died, had scarcely a word of comfort for her child. Nor was her indifference due to a sudden chill. Long before and long after the Leo crisis the few letters from Isabella to Leonora—there are very few—read as if they were written to a stranger to whom one speaks politely, but whom at bottom one dislikes. When in March 1515 Leonora had given birth to a stillborn child, Isabella had written not to her—at least no letter from Isabella to Leonora has been found in the archives, though the Mantua-Urbino correspondence has been carefully preserved—but to Elisabetta:

Of the death of the baby born to the Duchess our daughter I have heard with displeasure [*dispiacer*], though I trust in God's will, considering that our daughter is young and able to conceive again and that the premature birth did not affect her health. I recommend myself to Your Excellency and beg you to give my greetings to the Duchess.

That was all—an extraordinary lack of involvement. And the instance was not unique. The following year Leonora almost died after again giving birth to a dead child. Isabella wrote to Elisabetta and to one Margarita Gambacurta, a pretentious and formally worded note saying that she was ready to help, being fast in action and restrained in words. (She was not at all "restrained in words.") And on the same day, February 10, 1516, she wrote Leonora a short conventional note of condolence.

Leonora was a remarkably beautiful girl. We have several portraits* of her, all showing her as a very desirable creature. Could it have been that Isabella was jealous of her daughter's beauty? More probably Leonora was guilty of some transgression which Isabella would not forgive. In 1514 Leonora had given birth to a healthy son, Guidobaldo, but after that her children were stillborn and then her pregnancies ceased altogether. The evidence suggests that Leonora had caught a venereal disease, though the evidence dates from later. In November 1530, Paride da Ceresara, poet, astrologer, physician, wrote two reports to Federico, having been asked to diagnose the cause of Leonora's increasing depression. What ailed her?

---

* One by Lorenzo Costa, one attributed to Raphael, one by Titian, known as "La Bella," though the identification of the sitter has been questioned.

. . . I found the Duchess epileptic and still somewhat abnormal in mind. She has gonorrhea. Her diseases have weakened her very, very much. . . .

. . . the epileptic fits have not recurred, nor have the attacks of depression. The Duchess has become herself again. She will not lose her eyesight, as many have feared.

Francesco della Rovere would not abandon his hope of recovering Urbino. At Isabella's suggestion the ailing Elisabetta went to Rome to beg Leo's mercy. She had hardly arrived in Rome when she received a letter from Isabella, written in a secret code the two women used, which said, "Whatever Leo promises, get it in writing. His word is not to be trusted." The cardinals welcomed Elisabetta with a show of extravagant courtesy, but when she finally obtained her audience with Leo, he and all around him wrapped themselves in silence. She addressed herself to a group as mute as the busts of Roman emperors. "Does Your Holiness not know from your own experience"—she said to Leo, as she later told Isabella— "what it means to be driven from home, do you not know the bitterness of exile?" Elisabetta was referring to the time when the Medici were banished from Florence, but there is no greater mistake than to remind someone of a past misfortune in times of happiness. Leo looked at her through his eyeglass and shrugged his shoulders. More silence. She was dismissed. She had achieved nothing.

At first Isabella advised Francesco della Rovere not to dare a war against the papal forces:

We are inclined to counsel you to try everything possible to avoid open warfare. All terms to avert conflict should be weighed by you, and such caution must be more praised than censured. To conserve the state is to conserve honor. Discuss the matter with the Marchese, with others of your relatives, with your friends. We could not help expressing our opinion, for the love we bear you and our daughter, though we know that you yourself are prudent. But in such a dilemma a man must turn to the advice of others.

No, della Rovere was determined to fight, or die. If that was his decision, Isabella said, she would help him. She offered him an experienced captain, Luigi Gonzaga di Castiglione, and, though she was herself very short of money—she had been unable as yet to repay the sum she had borrowed for her journey to Rome—she pawned 1,000 ducats' worth of her jewelry and gave them to her son-in-law. Alfonso, too, helped, though Gianfrancesco, currying favor with the pope, called the enterprise "insane" and informed Leo of della Rovere's plan. Nevertheless della Rovere was able to raise a sizable army, and with it he stormed Urbino, where the people rose against the dictatorship of Lorenzo dei Medici. Leo countered with another expedition. An eight-month-long struggle wearied both sides and further depleted the already depleted papal treasury. The end was a compromise: della Rovere did not get his duchy back, the pope remaining in possession of Urbino, but the invaluable Urbino Library was returned to della Rovere and he, Leonora, and Elisabetta were allowed to stay on honorably in Mantua. They lived in straitened circumstances: at one time they had to melt down and sell their fine silver dishes, among which were two magnificent gilt plates designed by Raphael. Isabella longed to buy them, but she could not raise the money, her funds having been strained by the defense budget, inflation—and the cost of maintaining young Federico.

4

Federico had been invited to the French court. It was a friendly invitation, not, or not chiefly, a political move, François I having immediately liked the boy when Federico had been presented to him in Milan. François was twenty-one, Federico fifteen. The two shared a love of jousts, hunting, fierce riding, a ball game called *palla* which was a rough kind of football and which the king himself played as roughly as the next, and reading French romances. François in addition loved to play cards for high stakes, but Federico could not afford to gamble. Isabella, though finding it hard to let her darling go, was sensible of the advantage offered the future sovereign of Mantua. She outfitted him in splendid clothes, furnished him with a retinue of forty servants and thirty-five horses, and sent François a gift of four of the noble steeds to the breeding of which her husband had devoted such care. Federico spent almost a year with François, not only in Paris but accompanying him to the royal châteaux, to Amboise, to Avignon, to Blois, which was just being built. From everywhere Isabella received laudatory reports about her son. He was tactful, good-humored, gay, and adapted himself to French customs. One report reads:

If you could see Federico you would conclude that he has been at the French Court forever. Today he had his hair cut *à la française*. He wore a black doublet with a gold medallion, so that he looked quite like a Frenchman.

Her letters to him are a mixture of anxiety, the usual loving maternal caution, and a realization that he was growing up and could be spoken to as a man:

Be a good and religious Christian. Learn from the good examples of the French people and guard yourself against the wicked ones. We heard that the King told you that he wants to arrange a marriage between you and his sister. That pleases me, being a sign that he esteems you. . . .

Go gladly [on a voyage with the king]. . . . I compare you to those antique Romans who marched forth for the salvation of their state with an intrepid heart. . . .

We gave orders to have a pair of shirts made for you, in the German style, more to satisfy you than because it pleases me. Your neck is short and stocky and the style does not become you. It would be sufficient if you wore the shirts two or three times, just to imitate the fashion worn by the King. Then return to the French style.

She was delighted when she learned that Federico was involved in his first love affair:

We are sending you a dozen pairs of gloves and a flask of perfume with which to perfume your mistress. I sent to Genoa and Rome for special oil and other fragrances to satisfy your request. . . . From all sides we hear of your good manners and behavior. Such praise gives life to your father. . . .

A political letter, presumably to be shown to François:

In these times of revolution and tumult you no doubt are beginning to worry. I wish to reassure you, to tell you to be of good cheer and to take heart. The actions of your father are such as can in due time be fully explained to the King. He [Gianfrancesco] is his loyal adherent. If he has given signs of siding with the Emperor [Charles] it was only because he couldn't help himself. This we tell you for the benefit of those who are always ready to utter calumnies and to interpret his moves falsely.

If nowadays neither your father nor I write to you as frequently as before, don't put this down to a lack of our admiration or to boredom. It is because the roads from Mantua are not safe. Letters may be intercepted. And if we do not receive letters from you as regularly as we wish, we will have patience.

A week later she wrote again, trying to justify the father to the son: you cannot judge his actions, nobody can. It will all come out right.

The time came to consider whom Federico should marry. No further consideration was given Cesare Borgia's daughter. It had, of course, to be a political-social alliance, and each candidate was reviewed by Isabella. Six or seven possibilities were discussed, in addition to François's sister, to whom Federico took a dislike. The Marquis of Monferrato, a small but wealthy principality with which it would profit Mantua to be connected, had a daughter Maria, still a child: he proposed marrying her to Federico, and the Gonzagas welcomed the idea. In February 1517 a Mantuan agent was sent to look into the details, and Isabella gave him his instructions:

> Though we might have obtained a larger dowry, we have taken into consideration that the house of Monferrato is as noble and ancient a family as is to be found in Italy, both on the maternal and the paternal side. . . . One may content oneself with the 40,000 ducats [$800,000] of the proposed dowry. They are not 100,000 . . . but what one must consider these days is the safety of the State.

The contract was concluded in April, and Federico visited little Maria on his way back from France; he liked her. Isabella too went to see her and liked her, and she gave the girl a jeweled necklace, ostensibly a gift from her future father-in-law, and from herself two perfumed armbands, set with rubies, a present she used to give her favorites. It was decided that the marriage would be consummated as soon as the bride had reached her fifteenth year. Federico was now seventeen years old, old enough to marry.

That year, 1517, was a watershed year, though hardly anybody could realize its significance. Leo, to whom husbandry was a devil's word, was broke. Several of the Vatican treasures, silver, jewels, tapestries, were pledged to bankers from whom Leo borrowed, sometimes at interest as high as 40 percent. He was no longer able to pay teachers' and scholars' salaries, and the Roman schools were peremptorily closed. All this was disturbing even to the Romans, but intensely shocking to other parts of the Catholic world, especially to Germany. In October Luther fastened his ninety-five theses to the door of a church in Wittenberg.

But in Mantua there was peace. Isabella, still longing to absent herself from her "Illustrious Lord," made a journey as far away as

Provence—how great a distance that was!—and when she returned she entertained wandering poets and scholars. Occasionally she looked in on Gianfrancesco. He had become weak and quiet. She knew there was no hope.

5

In the first months of 1519 Gianfrancesco's condition became terminal. He no longer left his bed. By March he knew he had to die. Carefully and circumspectly he made his testamentary dispositions. His mind was perfectly clear. He appointed nineteen-year-old Federico as his successor—that was a mere formality—stipulating that Isabella was to bear the responsibility of government until Federico's twenty-second year. Isabella was to receive a yearly income of 12,000 ducats ($240,000), his son Ercole as well as his son Ferrante 8,000 each. He left 3,000 ducats as a gift to his two unmarried daughters, Ippolita and Paola. He remembered two illegitimate daughters with an annual stipend of 400 ducats each. His brother Giovanni, his favorite, was to receive a palace and an estate. A special pension of 6,000 ducats was assigned to daughter Leonora and her husband as long as the couple had to live in exile from Urbino.

He called a meeting of his ministers, his treasurer, the mayor of Mantua, and other officials to bid them farewell and to adjure them to perform their offices honestly and devotedly. He directed that all political prisoners were to be freed the day of his death.

On March 19, 1519, he received the last sacrament and then summoned the family. Isabella, the children, his two brothers, and Elisabetta stood around his bed. "My dear son," he said to Federico, "I leave you a fine State and a large revenue. Administer it well, act justly, and keep the love of your subjects." Turning to Isabella, he spoke softly: "I have long recognized your wisdom and ability. I place my trust in you." Isabella sobbed—but no hypocritical words were spoken about happiness or a love which had vanished too long ago to be recalled. Gianfrancesco then asked two Franciscan friars who were present to read some verses from the Gospel of Saint Luke. When they read, "Father, into Thy hands I commend my spirit," Gianfrancesco turned his head and listened no more. He died at 2 A.M. that night.*

* The description of his death is based on Mario Equicola's *Commentarii*, and on Sanuto.

His corpse was taken from the Sebastiano Palace to the Castello, in the loggia of which it was displayed to the people. Eight Franciscans kept vigil, as well as ten young nobles dressed in black cowls and twelve priests bearing torches. With his long beard and emaciated face Gianfrancesco looked like an old, old hermit, though he had barely reached his fifty-third year. The church bells of Mantua were rung continuously for ten hours. Then he was carried to his grave through the streets illumined by torchbearers.

In the same year Maximilian I died, Charles became Holy Roman Emperor, and in the castle of Ambois Leonardo da Vinci closed those eyes which had observed so much so penetratingly. Gianfrancesco's death was not important, since he had ceased to function as soldier, ruler, husband. Yet he was mourned in Italy and remembered for what he once had been. All death, however prorogued, marks a full stop, and Sanuto noted: "I think we will see all sorts of changes, and that quickly. This one or that one who has up to now acted like a bigwig will become a tiny worm."

XI

The Widow

That Lucrezia felt the death of her long-ago lover as a wound the more painful for having to be concealed can be surmised by the letter she wrote Isabella three days after Gianfrancesco died. She tried to write within the formula of condolence, but her sorrow breaks through. "The bitter loss has afflicted me so deeply that instead of being able to comfort others I am in sore need of comfort myself." If Isabella answered this letter, her reply is not extant. Silence reigned between the two women in the three months Lucrezia was still to live.

Another death had touched Isabella's life shortly before Gianfrancesco's: faithful Benedetto Capilupo was no more. As his successor Isabella appointed Mario Equicola, who accepted the post with the stipulation that he was to be given free time for his writing and for travel, but though Isabella valued and respected him the relationship between them never became as close as that with Capilupo. At once she kept him busy, for at once she herself plunged into work.

She made her governmental decisions on her own, free of false piety, her judgment untroubled by the illusion of the widow who believes in afteryears that her marriage had been ideal and her husband an angel. On the other hand, she did not arbitrarily divest herself of her husband's staff, and the only "bigwig" she reduced to a "worm" was Tolomeo Spagnoli, Gianfrancesco's confidential secretary, who had intrigued against her, and whom she accused of misappropriating public funds by forging her husband's signature. Isabella pursued him even after he fled to Verona and then to Rome by going to law and suing him for the restitution of the funds. She did this, she said, to show her people that malfeasance would not be tolerated by their sovereign, but she did it as well because she hated him as a man. A letter to Castiglione, written in July, reveals her true motive:

. . . He [Spagnoli] denigrated us so effectively that we, who in our young years exercised some authority in the state, finally were reduced to nothing. You know that as well as the whole city. You also know that we absented ourself for nine months, four in Rome, because we felt ashamed to live in Mantua as a cipher. . . .

At forty-five she became a devoted head of state, a true ruler, displaying even greater skill than before, more firm of purpose than her husband had been, more "masculine" in decision—and all without losing her femininity, without ceasing to look in the mirror, still finding time to concoct her perfumes and to design her daring robes, fighting against the double chin and the first crow's-feet, and continuing to employ her admiring emissaries in finding another bronze Bacchus at a bargain price. We may believe the French ambassador who wrote François I: "In meting out justice she spends all day giving audience to the various factions. She takes nobody's word without first sifting the matter thoroughly. . . ."

The "various factions" were to be found chiefly among the peasants, and they were important because Mantua's economy was mainly agricultural, producing grain, corn, olives, cheese, fish, and milk for export. The peasant society was divided, the top layer called *contadini grassi,* "fat peasants" being those who owned substantial land. Below them were those with just enough land to support their families, and at the bottom the *lavatori,* who owned no land but hired themselves out to work the farms. A few "middlemen" leased land from the nobles and subleased it to the laborers.* Frequent disputes arose among these groups, while traditionally the peasants as a class opposed the town dwellers.

Almost as important as farming was the production of textiles. Here specialization prevailed. Fleece was beaten by the *battitore,* the wool sorted by the *sceglitore,* oiled and combed by the *petinatore,* spun by the *filatrice,* woven by the *tessitore,* the cloth washed by the *purgatore,* and so forth and so on until it was dyed by the *tintore* (Jacopo Robusti's father was a "little dyer"—hence "Tintoretto"). Quarrels among these "specialists" had to be adjudicated,

* These facts are more fully analyzed by Peter Burke in *Culture and Society in Renaissance Italy.*

as did those among the goldworkers, the stone masons, the wood-carvers, and so on.

Isabella wrote to Federico: "Be assured that I am completely informed about everything which goes through my hands, so that I may all the better serve the ends of justice in our state. . . ." As she had charmed poets and painters, so she was now able to evoke the liking and loyalty of jejune officials. The people of Mantua loved her. At the least, they respected her.

Her immediate problem was to guess which way the fox would jump. In the contest between François I and Charles V—that is to say a contest not only for sovereignty over Italy but for European hegemony—Leo the fox was to be found today in one field, tomorrow in the other. One had to know where he was and what he was planning; to an Italian state the pope's position represented virtually the aye and nay of existence. Isabella now improved her spy system in remarkably short order. Secret messengers traveled the road to Rome and back almost every day, carrying fish or cheese as a cover-up. She wrote her brother Alfonso: "Do not doubt that I have abroad so many people and spies, clandestinely and well placed, that we will find out everything we need to know." It goes without saying that Leo, who declared publicly that he hated all contention, operated a spy system of his own.

Isabella and her son knew exactly what was going on. Leo was apprehensive of the increasing power of the Reformation; he was threatened by the increasingly successful Turks, who after conquering Egypt had overrun Mesopotamia and Syria, and he began to doubt that he could stem the growing Habsburg might, in the person of the young, hard emperor, even though he played off François against Charles. Charles offered Leo most tempting terms, such as the return of Parma and Piacenza as papal cities, help against Luther, the reinstatement of the Sforza family in Milan, and a guarantee of protection for the Medici possessions—and that last included all-important Florence. Accordingly, Leo finally jumped—and on May 8, 1521, signed an alliance with Charles V.

Before that move, while Leo was still ostensibly on the side of the French, Isabella had executed a master stroke. Why should not Federico follow in his father's footsteps and pursue a military career? To be sure, he was inexperienced, but he could be helped by two excellent and proven captains whom Mantua had to offer. The Gonzaga name, she pointed out, would strengthen the papal forces and warn Leo's enemies. Federico was the man he needed. Isabella's eminent friend Castiglione carried the proposition to the pope. Long and difficult negotiations followed. As usual Leo was uncertain, fearing that the choice of Federico might offend François for one reason and Charles for another. In the end, however, he agreed, Federico was appointed "Captain General" to the pope, and the contract was signed in December 1520. But what a contract! The published version contained a clause which stipulated that Federico was specifically absolved from taking part in any altercation between the pope and the Holy Roman Emperor. (This version was shown to Charles.) A separate agreement clearly nullified this clause. (This version was shown to François.) The document states that it was signed in Isabella's "private rooms," indicating her participation. No doubt it was her idea in the first place.

How strange!—this contract which spoke with a forked tongue was probably written, and certainly agreed to, by one of the most high-principled and honorable men of those dishonorable times. Castiglione, now acting as Mantua's Roman ambassador, lived a life of such decency and kindness as to earn him the admiration of adversary as well as friend. He was exceptional even in his relation to women; he had married a girl twenty-three years younger than himself to whom he devtoed all his faith and love. Now, as he worked in Rome, he received a letter from his wife, who had remained in Mantua:

I have given birth to a little girl, of whom I think you will not be ashamed. But I have been much worse than before, with three attacks of high fever. I am better now and hope the attacks will not return. I will write no more now because I'm not yet strong, and I commend myself to you with all my heart. Your wife who is a little exhausted with pain, your Ippolita. [August 20, 1520]

By the time the letter reached him she was dead. He did not know it. Isabella, grief-stricken, shouldered the task of having to inform her friend. She immediately sent a courier to Bibbiena asking him to break the news as gently as possible to Castiglione. And to him she wrote:

My dear one: Well do I know how difficult and indeed impossible it is to set limits to one's sorrow when one loses a being as dear and precious as was to you your sweetest wife, who as you will have heard by now, passed from life to immortality. We do not therefore exhort you not to grieve over so great a loss.

It is only human. With all our heart we, too, feel with you; we, too, suffer bitter distress, because of our love for you and for the love we felt for your wife, a love she merited. Yet we beg you that after you have given vent to your feelings you return as soon as possible to the region of reason. Consider that neither plaints nor tears can repair this terrible damage. Summon patience which will help you to prove to yourself the nobility of your soul. You could do nothing which would please us more. *Bene valete.*

> Isabella, Mantua, August 26, 1520

Castiglione continued to work for Isabella, he completed his masterpiece, *The Courtier,* but he never ceased to long for his Ippolita. When he died in 1529, only fifty-one years old, Isabella said that she had lost "the most faithful of her friends."

Federico, then, became an employee of Leo. And when Leo and Charles finally got together, Federico helped assemble a strong force of imperial and papal troops. In less than three months the task was done; Milan was taken, and Francesco Maria Sforza, a son of Lodovico Il Moro, was installed as duke and vassal of the Habsburg emperor. The French retreated. Federico, who had acquitted himself bravely in the campaign, commissioned Costa to paint a picture celebrating the triumph. Leo ordered elaborate and expensive festivities to begin on November 24, 1521. Standing by an open window to enjoy the tumult, he caught cold. A week later he was dead. He died under the illusion of having won a lasting victory.

Obviously, after Leo's death it became vital to the cause of Mantua to suppress the secret paper in which Federico obligated himself to fight against Charles V should the need arise. Charles would hardly have stomached the deceit. So Isabella went to work through Castiglione, who succeeded, after much trouble, in bribing the secretary of the dead pope. He stole the paper—and it was delivered to Isabella. She wrote to Federico: "We have torn it and burned it with our own hands. We deem it exceedingly dangerous if such a document should become public knowledge, so dangerous that we do not think it safe to preserve it even in our own possession." (Later, when Clement VII, who as Cardinal Giulio Medici had taken part in the contract negotiation, looked for it in order to use it for his own purposes, the theft was discovered. Leo's secretary committed suicide, but nothing could be proved against the Mantuans.)

Immediately after Leo's death, François, back in France, proposed to his erstwhile protégé that he leave the papal services and join him. Federico, still in the field, asked his mother what to do. She answered at once, through Equicola, in a letter written in cipher, addressing her reply to Federico's secretary:

> I showed our illustrious Madama your cipher dispatch. She had already heard most of its contents from Signor Federico himself, who informed her of the eagerness with which the French are seeking our lord's alliance. She feels the greatest pleasure in seeing her son so highly esteemed and sought after by so many great powers, which is a clear sign that both his own merits and the importance of his person and our State are recognized. But she is strongly of the opinion that he should form no new alliance until the creation of the new Pope, because that will best decide our future course of action. Her Excellency hopes that her son may be able to continue in the service of the Church, especially if the Pope is allied with the Emperor, as he has been of late, because the Church will doubtless in the end prove victorious, and, even if defeated, will always be respected, and she considers this alliance to be the safest for this State. Of course, if a new Pope is elected from whom we could not hope for the protection and office which our lord received from Pope Leo, of blessed memory, we must seek for new allies without delay. But Madama certainly thinks that the new Pope, whoever he may be, is sure to esteem the person of your Signor [Federico] highly, because of his past services and because it has been seen in the past how important the Marquis of Mantua is to the Church. This, Madama tells me, is her opinion. . . .

A politically shrewd opinion, indeed! It shows Isabella at her most statesmanlike. It was one of the last occasions on which Federico took his mother's advice.

2

Some years past Isabella had begun plans to move her retreat, her *studiolo*, from the Castello San Giorgio to the Palace proper, that wing of it which was called the Corte Vecchia and where her library and her *grotta* were located. She wanted to consolidate her domain, and now she wished to enlarge the *studiolo*, creating her definitive setting. In the noisy life of the Renaissance such a haven was almost a necessity. Francesco Medici had built an elaborate one which we may still admire in the Medici Palace in Florence, and Carpaccio placed his musing Saint Jerome in a sunny studio filled with books and scientific instruments. Similarly, the German princes were proud of their *Wunderkammer*. Isabella's room was the result of much loving thought to shape it not just into a curio cabinet but into a harmonious unit. It was partly for that reason that she specified the size of various paintings she commissioned, four of which were eventually hung in an asymmetrical arrangement, the two Mantegnas facing each other and the two Correggios to the left and right of the main ornamental door, the work of the renowned sculptor, Tullio Lombardo.

Isabella's suite now consisted of five rooms: the *studiolo*, the *camera dipinta*, which housed more paintings, and the *grotta*, with the overflow of the antique collection in two small *camerini*. Here, then, the widow hoped to live out her life, entertaining her guests, collecting further purchases, and playing an active part in the government of Mantua, in close collaboration with Federico.

Federico would have none of it. Hardly emerged from his teens, he followed the classic pattern, asserting his own will in revolt against his mother. To be the son of a famous mother is a difficult lot; to be the son of a famous mother who would not let the winds of heaven visit his face too roughly was even more difficult. Federico, who had been overpetted and overindulged and who certainly did not lack self-esteem, acted predictably. He didn't need a mother's hand, not anymore. He didn't need a mother's head, not anymore. He had observed enough to do the task on his own. Had he not been as a child the favorite of a pope, as a young man the friend of a king? Why should a woman govern the state which his father had willed to him? It was he, not she, who ought to be sovereign in deed. Abruptly, and without putting up a fight, she relinquished the reins of power.

But in other ways Isabella disapproved of Federico. He had fallen in love, passionately, blindly, completely, with a beautiful, domineering, and unscrupulous girl, Isabella Boschetti. She was married to an unimportant Mantuan nobleman, and she soon left her husband to live openly with Federico. Early she bore him a son, and later two more children. Federico refused to get married, repudiated the Monferrato agreement, cared nothing about the legitimate continuation of the Gonzaga line. Isabella Boschetti meant everything to him; she held him in sexual thralldom for twenty years. At the carnival of 1520, when Federico celebrated the beginning of his reign, a tournament was held to which came knights from France and all of Italy. In the place of honor sat not Isabella the mother, but Isabella the mistress. In May Federico paid an official visit to the doge. Isabella Boschetti, Sanuto notes, went along. The other Isabella stayed home.

Paolo Giovo, in his *Historiae sui temporis*, commented on what was soon general knowledge:

It is useless to pass over in silence the fate of Isabella Marchesana of Mantua. Her people honored her for her magnificent achievements. In various periods of her life she experienced the ups and downs of fortune and she was able to accomplish more than one enterprise. It chanced that her son Federico was seized by excessive love for a lady on whom he lavished all honors and favors, while Isabella remained like one degraded and unesteemed. So much so that the above-mentioned mistress rode proudly through the city with all the nobles following her trail, while Isabella was accompanied only by one or two old men. . . .

Whether or not Giovio was overdramatizing, Federico's turning his face away must have given Isabella many an hour when the hurt sat and mocked her. A hurt to her pride, a hurt to her love, she must have revolved it in her heart as a twice-told tale. Like father like son; here was the rebuff once more. She was reduced to the role of an elegant spectator, now somewhat heavy and slow in movement, surrounded by works of art which testified that man was not altogether evil, but gave their testimony in silence. Isabella, still eager for and capable of action, was forced to fold her hands.

The courtiers did, but her eminent friends did not, forget her. She was in constant correspondence with Castiglione, Bembo, the poet Trissino, and the papal nuncio Francesco Chiericati, who had previously written her lively descriptions of his voyages to Spain, England, and Ireland, and who had pleaded her cause with Charles V. She drew closer again to her brother Alfonso, who had swerved from his martial interests to become enthusiastically involved in beautifying his palace in Ferrara. Isabella advised him, and Alfonso persuaded Titian to paint for his *camerino* a series of pictures in the mythological-erotic mood. Among these masterpieces are *The Bacchanal, The Worship of Venus,* and *Bacchus and Ariadne.* Later Titian painted Alfonso's portrait, which Alfonso may have presented to Charles V. (Federico, not to be outdone, wooed Titian but at this time had to be content with a single painting, though a great one: *The Entombment.*)

Isabella now turned to her second son, Ercole. By tradition he was destined to serve the Church, and as a young man he showed decided intellectual leanings. She asked Trissino for advice:

> One of our sons, Ercole, shows great intelligence and takes much pleasure in study, and what pleases us especially, and we take to be a good sign, is that he delights in the conversation of scholars. We should like you to talk to him of books, and give us a faithful report of the judgment which you form of his abilities, and tell us if it seems to you he is in the right way to attain to some degree perfection in letters, which ought not to be difficult for one of his studious and docile nature. In this we should like to have your advice, which will, we know, be as wise as it is kind.

Ercole was enrolled in the Bologna school of Pietro Pomponazzi, an eminent educator of his age, who was so small in stature that he was nicknamed "Peretto" (little Peter), but so tall in knowledge that the finest minds fought for the privilege of sitting on the benches to hear him lecture. When he taught his whole being seemed transformed, his eyes sparkled, and he stirred his students to the desire to know and understand. Ercole loved him, and when Pomponazzi died he erected a statue to his memory. Isabella was happy when the teacher sent her a good report about the pupil.

3

Leo's successor, Adrian VI, was a misfit of a pope, according to the Romans who hated him. He was guilty of the triple fault of being a foreigner, a true believer, and a stern moralist. Loving honesty and justice, he restored Urbino to Francesco della Rovere and confirmed Alfonso's possession of Ferrara. But the mendacious ministers and the pharisaic priests plotted against and nullified his attempts at reforming the Church. He died after a pontificate of only thirteen months, exhausted in body and lacerated in spirit.* Good riddance, thought the Italians, and so did both Charles and François; it was one point on which they agreed.

After a conclave of seven weeks, during which the cardinals sweated and fought, another Medici was chosen who became Clement VII. He had to meet the same problems that Leo did: the spreading Reformation, the Turkish threat—in 1522 the Turks had

---

* He wrote his own epitaph: "Here lies Adrian VI, who thought nothing more unfortunate in his life than that he became Pope."

occupied Rhodes, the last Eastern fortress against the Ottoman Empire—and the continuing and constantly sharpening conflict between Charles and François. Clement, an irresolute nature, was not up to the task, and he was particularly unfortunate in his timing, which is what often happens to the irresolute. (The Venetians used to call him "Pope I-will-and-I-won't.") At the most unlucky moment he decided to join the French—just before the French army was almost totally massacred in the great two-day battle of Pavia in February 1525. François himself fought savagely, but at the battle's end he was taken prisoner. It was then that he wrote his mother the line so often misquoted: "All is lost save honor—and my skin, which is safe."

All Italy except Rome itself was now under Spanish sway. The harshest imaginable conditions were laid down as the price of François's freedom. He agreed to everything—specifically the renunciation of all his Italian claims—with the most sacred oaths. No sooner had he returned to France than he announced that he had no intention, and never did have, of keeping pledges exacted from him under pressure. Clement, in fear of Charles, now forged with François the "League of Cognac," which Venice, Florence, and Milan joined. And on it went—plots and counterplots, one great prince betraying another, plans to stir up revolution and depose the pope, stripping him of his temporal power, the Turks advancing into Hungary and capturing Budapest, a few patriots ready to fight, many more ready to connive, and half the people trembling lest the horse, the house, or the few hidden ducats be taken away the next day. Where now was Julius's dream of a unified Italy?

However purposefully Federico separated himself from Isabella, he remained his mother's son. He had inherited her skill at keeping out of the fight of the big boys by buttering his bread on both sides. Though Adrian and Clement confirmed his appointment as papal "captain general," he seems to have done little enough soldiering and he managed to keep Mantua uninvolved in the scratching and the clawing. He did go to Spain to confer with Charles and he did fight at Pavia, while Isabella kept the home fires burning at a low temperature, but he behaved amicably (and unconvincingly) both to Charles and to François, as the weathervane of fortune indicated.

Federico had also inherited from his mother a love of collecting and a very real interest in contemporary art, turning from the painters Isabella had known to the younger generation, Titian and, especially, Giulio Romano. And like his father and grandfather, Federico was ambitious to build monuments to affirm Gonzaga permanence. On the site of his father's old stable, on a marshy ground just outside the city, he began to build what was to be one of the finest "compositions" of the Renaissance, an allegretto of a little palace and a garden, the Palazzo del Tè. (What "Tè" means is uncertain; there are various explanations.) It was to design and decorate this palazzo that he summoned to Mantua Raphael's most gifted pupil, young Giulio Romano.* Romano liked his work there so well that he decided to stay. He and Isabella became good friends, and Federico rewarded him with the gift of a splendid house.

The Palazzo del Tè even today, stripped of its furniture and tapestries, offers the visitor a sight at which to exclaim in wonder. Its largest room contains six frescoes of the famed Gonzaga horses, huge and aristocratic inmates of a silent stable. On the ceiling salamanders sport, along with other symbols, bearing a motto in Latin which proclaims that the fire to which those lizards are supposedly impervious "torments me"—an allusion to Federico's passion for Isabella Boschetti. Tè's most spectacular room is the "Giants' Room," whose frescoes—for which Giulio Romano did the original cartoons—depict with a power close to that of Michelangelo the victory of the Olympian gods over the giants. They seem to prophesy the end of the world; they show us a storm of violence, broken columns, hurled stones, muscles and sinews, faces contorted in hate or agony, a Renaissance *Guernica*, which overwhelms the sight of the beholder. The whole palace, including a grotto and a "secret garden," was built for Federico's mistress, and Federico couldn't wait until the palace was finished. He wrote Romano: "We are not amused that you should again have missed so many dates." It is safe to conjecture that Isabella hated it.

She could not stand Isabella Boschetti. She could not bear to be relegated to the role of "queen mother." She could not tolerate retirement. She decided to do what she had done once before, to remove herself from placidity and go traveling. This time she had to ask no one's permission.

---

* It is a curious fact that the *only* Renaissance artist Shakespeare mentions is Giulio Romano, though by the early seventeenth century many of the Italian painters, sculptors, and architects had become famous in England. In *The Winter's Tale* he describes a statue, "a piece many years in doing, and now newly performed by that rare Italian master, Julio Romano" (Act V, Scene 2).

Twice she went to Venice. Twenty-one years had passed since her last visit with Elisabetta. Now she went with Alfonso and Castiglione; brother and sister eagerly sought out the new paintings by Carpaccio as well as Titian's great achievement, dominating the interior of the Frari church, *The Assumption of the Virgin*, whose boldness blew like a windstorm through the art world. They were present at the elevation of Andrea Gritti as doge. The following year Gritti invited her to a private conference, where they talked of the condition of Italy and of the Turks who represented nothing less than a mortal menace to the economic life of Venice. We know all this from Sanuto—how much less would we know without that busy chronicler!—who recorded Isabella's arrival:

Marchesa di Mantova, mother of the Lord Marquis, and sister of the Duke of Ferrara . . . who is lodging in Casa Barbaro, near S. Vitale, with the Mantuan ambassador, and has brought with her, for the use of her household, four *amphorae* and three barrels of wine, twenty sacks of flour, four cheeses, besides meat and vegetables, all of which were declared free of duty by the Signoria.

Sanuto relates that Isabella "enjoyed herself exceedingly" and walked from San Marco to the Rialto, "making an attendant walk on either side of her, supporting her arms, for the sake of her dignity."

What next? She stayed home only a few months before she determined on her next journey. She was going to go to Rome. The voyage was to be not merely a sightseeing tour; she had a double purpose. She wanted to meet Clement and, if possible, inaugurate a relationship with him, as she had done with Leo. More important, she wanted to see if and at what price she could obtain a cardinal's hat for Ercole, just turned twenty. Such at least were the reasons she gave herself. What lay beneath was the desire, the more urgent as her pride continued to suffer, to get away. It is significant that once again she chose the same remedy, and it is perhaps no less significant that Rome was her goal once more.

She began to make her plans.

XII

"Burn All"

Early in January 1525 Isabella sent her personal servants to Rome to get everything ready. In February she herself started out, accompanied by a small suite which included La Brognina, whose indiscretions had been graciously forgiven, a few of her most attractive damsels, her favorite dwarf Morgantino, and a special secretary who was to take care of her correspondence while she was abroad. She spent a few days at Ferrara with Alfonso; then the party took a boat down the Po almost to Ravenna, from where they rode overland to Pesaro, to be met by Leonora and Elisabetta. What Isabella said on seeing her daughter is not recorded, but when she and Elisabetta fell into each other's arms they both wept, and they had so many reminiscences to exchange that Elisabetta persuaded her to stay an extra two days.

On March 2 Isabella arrived in Rome and was quartered at the palace of the Duke of Urbino. She found a noisy and nervous city. After the battle of Pavia, Pope Clement was forced into an alliance with Charles; the emperor would protect Clement and the Medici in Florence and accept Francesco Sforza as vicar of Milan; these were about the same terms he had offered Leo four years earlier. In return Clement would pay him 100,000 ducats ($2 million). This did not prevent that chameleon of a pope from secretly taking part in a plan to liberate Milan from Charles. In turn Charles promoted a conspiracy by the Colonna family: they marched on Rome with five thousand men, plundering the Vatican and Saint Peter's, and were then driven away, not without help from Charles himself, the instigator of the assault. Clement had a few of the least guilty Colonnas murdered. "Treason and murder ever kept together,/As two yoke-devils sworn to either's purpose."

Yet it is characteristic of treason and murder among the great that the yoke-devils are not at once noticed by those not directly involved. Though few Romans knew where they stood—or perhaps because they *did* know—almost all wanted to continue to chase money, mistresses, and merriment. The carnival, Isabella wrote, was gayer than ever. Clement, who had at once welcomed her and sent over gifts of wheat, barley, wine, sugar, wax, oil, and game, invited her on May Day to a strange revel. In the Church of Saints Apostoli, the pope let loose hundreds of fowl; women densely packed in the church snatched at them, fighting for them so greedily that "hardly one of them was able to capture a bird intact." Spectators doused the women with water. The pope approved; Isabella disapproved.

She no longer made her social calls on horseback. Instead she rode in a carriage she had bought; it was an unusual sight and started a fashion. Some of her erstwhile acquaintances were dead: Bibbiena, Raphael, Giulio Medici. Castiglione was in Spain. But Pietro Bembo came to see her and brought to her house the new poets and artists, including Sebastiano del Piombo, whom she greatly admired. She had lost none of her interest in collecting, and she spent hours vigorously bargaining with the antique dealers. She bought a huge number of "ancient marbles" to be shipped to Mantua. If she was not happy, she was content. Only one sorrow clouded her year. Elisabetta, long ailing, died on January 28, 1526. For thirty-six years these two had been the closest of friends. No other could take Elisabetta's place in Isabella's life, and with her a part of herself fell away. Bembo wrote of Elisabetta:

I have liked many excellent and noble women and heard of some who were more illustrious for certain virtues, but in her alone among women all virtues were united and brought together. I have never seen or heard of anyone who was her equal, and know very few who have come near her.

The political clouds darkened and sank lower later in that year of 1526. One of the papal diplomats prophesied gloomily: "The Emperor is master of Italy—he will be the master of the world. Woe to our poor Italy, woe to us who are alive." Federico in Mantua saw the coming events more clearly than Isabella did in Rome, and it is to his credit that he warned her. He realized, he wrote, that she was offended, and if she didn't want to return to Mantua he understood, but by all means she ought to leave Rome. She answered that she knew that Federico's advice was prompted solely by "filial affection," but that he needn't worry about her safety. She could take care of herself. She intended to stay. She stayed, and after many conversations during which Clement attempted to avoid committing himself, she finally, and by sheer perseverance, obtained Ercole's appointment as cardinal. The precious document was in her hands. She had to promise Clement to keep the appointment secret for a while, a promise typical of those demanded by the elusive pontiff, and in return for the appointment, she also promised to try her best to persuade Alfonso to join Clement's cause. Yet, as she was smiling at His Holiness, she wrote home to Federico that if he valued his and Mantua's safety, he should under no condition enter into any kind of alliance with Clement. "Strict neutrality!" That is how we did it when your father was alive. Let the troops of both sides march through Mantua; it doesn't matter. Just keep out of it! Don't commit yourself.

Her business in Rome was finished. Yet she remained and indeed changed her lodging during the summer to a palace situated on higher ground and offering more splendid rooms. "Only rarely do we use our carriage. We have marvelous quarters with a superb garden. There we spend our days in select company. We play and converse. We are careful not to admit everybody to our house." The house was the Palazzo Colonna.

A few months later Charles decided that the subjugation of Italy was moving too slowly to suit him. True, he had swung himself high enough to become its overlord; true, he had conquered. Yet as he reviewed in his mind's eye the panorama of that luscious land, he saw here and there nests of what appeared to him truculent bees, protecting their honeycombs. He must sweep them away. More important—and more difficult—he must capture the richest honeycomb of all, papal Rome. He was sick unto death of scribbling agreements with a pope which neither he nor the pope had any intention of honoring. What was needed here was total victory followed by unconditional surrender. To achieve it he must invade and destroy more effectively than any one had dared to do before him. Who could aid him in the enterprise?

One of his most effective warriors was, curiously enough, a Frenchman, Charles, Duke of Bourbon. He had turned against François, had joined the emperor, fought with his troops at Pavia, and was rewarded by being appointed administrator of Milan. He administered so well that hundreds of citizens committed suicide by throwing themselves from high towers, soldiers deliberately infected nubile girls with venereal diseases, and officials entered private homes at all hours and simply took what they could find. Now Bourbon raised a new army for Charles.

In addition, Charles approached an Austrian condottiere, Georg von Frundsberg, who was known and feared for his *Landsknechte,* mercenaries he had recruited and bound in loyalty to him. Frundsberg sympathized with Luther and hated Clement. Gladly would he join Charles. He pawned and sold everything he owned, including his wife's jewelry, and with the money collected 10,000 men, German desperadoes, quite willing to stick a spike into Clement's neck and more willing to pillage, ransack, and carry home whatever they could find beyond the Alps. Frundsberg promised them that. This motley army descended on Brescia in November 1526. Alfonso revenged himself for the humiliation he had endured from the popes by sending Frundsberg four of his best cannons. Young Giovanni de Medici, the brave son of brave Caterina Sforza, tried to stem the influx of the horde. He called himself Giovanni delle Bande Nere, because he and his soldiers had worn black bands after Leo died. Giovanni fell in a skirmish and died soon after in Mantua.

The way south lay through Mantuan territory; there was the spot where one could cross the Po easily. How would Federico, the pope's general, act? He did nothing, saying that he could do nothing. With cold calculation he folded his hands and permitted the 22,000 men to stream by, even as Isabella had counseled and Gianfrancesco would have approved. Federico possessed no greater political probity than his father did, yet, realistically, he would have been incapable of anything but a show of resistance, the wave being much too strong. So he sat in the Castle and tried not to look out the window. Once again he wrote to his mother, warning her that Rome was in danger of being ransacked; "it is obvious that all the [soldiers] will know that they can find in the house of a Marchesa of Mantua silver, garments, and jewelry." Once again Isabella replied that it was time to leave when and if there would be actual danger; she hoped that the pope and the emperor would come to an agreement.

Such an agreement, uneasy though it was, was actually concluded after the Bourbon-Frundsberg troops had despoiled the fields of Lombardy as effectively as the biblical swarm of locusts.

An armistice was declared, and Clement offered 60,000 ducats as the price for keeping the soldiers away from Rome. It was now the dead of winter; the men had set up their tents near Bologna in a plain which rain and snow had converted into a nightmarish vastness of cold mud. They were hungry, they froze, their shoes had long given out, their clothes were torn to rags. When they heard the news of the truce, they yelled with rage. What, were they to be cheated of the promise of rich booty by a few miserable ducats? Were they to return home to their wives with little to show except chilblains? Was that bastard of a pope to go unpunished? In a general frenzy, made hot by cold, they revolted, chanted "On to Rome," sought Bourbon in his tent and, not finding him, destroyed the tent. Their "father," Frundsberg, tried to call them to order; they turned their lances against him; he suffered a stroke. Lamed and speechless, he was carried to Ferrara. Not even an edict by Charles himself, which Bourbon read to the multitude, could subdue their rage. On to Rome—and so Bourbon, a leader being led, took over the command and gave the order to march. The truce was at an end. The army first turned on Florence, but that city had been so strongly fortified and excellently manned that they could not penetrate it, and they proceeded, filled with the disappointment which feeds the lust to destroy. Nothing could stop them, certainly not Clement's meager army, and by the first of May they were in Viterbo, only 42 miles from Rome. Now at last Clement realized the gravity of his plight. He declared Rome a closed city. Suddenly Isabella was unable to leave.

Wild fears ran through the city. Men dug holes in their gardens and buried their silver. Women ran to buy provisions. The churches were full. Swords and guns were stored under beds. A few fathers still managed to send their children south to find asylum with a relative. Scholars smeared manuscripts with dirt to make them appear worthless. Poison was sold at exorbitant prices.

Isabella was one of the few who remained calm. If she regretted not having listened to Federico's advice, she did not indulge in self-reproach; if she felt fear she suppressed it. She was confident that the worst would not befall her. The Duke of Bourbon was her nephew, and, what was more important, her youngest son Ferrante was serving as one of the officers of the imperial army, which had by now joined Bourbon's mob. Ferrante had become a favorite at the court of Madrid; he was an outgoing, personable young man, good-natured and fond of the mother who had paid little attention to him. Surely he would try to protect her. All the same, Isabella took precautions, turning the Palazzo Colonna into a minor citadel. In an account book she kept she noted that on May 4 she spent "fifty gold ducats to pay fifty armed guards," ten ducats for gunpowder, five for pikes. For the past week workmen had been walling up portals and windows. She had ordered a large supply of food to be laid in. A special guard was assigned to the well in the courtyard.

And now this extraordinary woman did an extraordinary thing. Knowing the general danger, she yet offered her palace to friends and acquaintances. If safety was to be found, she would share it. Her mind, that mind which could be flinty, now forced her toward fellowship. "Come," she beckoned; she could do nothing else. They came. To the unexpected refuge a frightened crowd streamed—the ambassadors of Venice, Mantua, Ferrara, Urbino with their families, twelve hundred noblewomen, hundreds of church officials—all in all more than two thousand people.

During the night of the fifth of May the bell of the Capitol sounded incessantly to call the citizens to the defense of the city. At the last moment Clement fled from the Vatican to the Castel Sant' Angelo with a guard of soldiers and a few favored cardinals. An elderly cardinal was pulled up in a basket, just before the great fortress was closed. The day of the sixth dawned unwillingly, a thick white fog enveloping the Tiber Valley, obscuring defendants and invaders. The attack began near the Porta Torrione, aimed at the Vatican. It was answered by fire from the cannons of Castel Sant' Angelo, and for a moment the horde wavered in fright. The Duke of Bourbon sprang from his horse and, clad in silver armor, seized a ladder and mounted the wall, shouting to the men to follow. A shot from the Castello struck him, and he fell, crying, "Notre Dame, je suis mort." Benvenuto Cellini in his autobiography claims to have fired that shot; it may be so, yet it seems doubtful, for Cellini did not mind flirting with the truth to make himself a hero. Bourbon's fall merely served to infuriate the Spaniards. They rushed the wall with a redoubled thrust, the Prince of Orange having assumed command, and breached it, while the Germans had equal success near the Porta Santo Spirito. In that quarter the massacre began: all the sick in the hospital were murdered, as were all the children in a nearby orphanage. By the end of the afternoon Rome was a captured city, the Germans ensconced at the Campo Fiore, the Spaniards at the Piazza Navona, while Ferrante was guarding the bridge of Sant' Angelo, preventing any communication with the imprisoned Clement.

The Prince of Orange issued an order forbidding plunder. The soldiers laughed at it. Twenty thousand of them now spread over the city. That part of man's nature of which Plato wrote that it is tamed by reason and appears only in dreams now appeared in reality: "the wild beast in us, gorged with meat and drink, starts up and walks about naked." They walked into Saint Peter's and killed those who had sought refuge there. They searched for monks, priests, bishops, old nuns, and slew them. They took everything valuable from the houses of merchants, and when they could find no more they burned the houses. The occupants of palaces were required to pay high sums for "protection," and having bought release from the Germans they were forced to pay the Spaniards in turn. The *Landsknechte* seized babies from the arms of their mothers and threw them from high windows, splattering their blood on the streets. Either a woman agreed to have intercourse with a soldier or a sword was rammed into her vagina. Hundreds of women drowned themselves in the Tiber. Young nuns were auctioned off, violated by one hoodlum after another, then killed. A rich man who put up some resistance saw his sons slain before his eyes, his daughter raped, and was then killed himself. A professor at the University of Rome watched a newly written commentary on Pliny being used to light a campfire and the university itself was despoiled of manuscripts and books. Many artists, such as Marcantonio Raimondi, were tortured by the Lutherans because they had painted pictures of the Madonna. The only reason the Vatican Library escaped destruction was that the Prince of Orange had established his headquarters there. Much of the papal treasury disappeared. Raphael's Stanze were used as stables. The special rage of the soldiers was directed against the cardinals: their wealth was stolen from the poor, they shouted. Guicciardini wrote that cardinals "unable to raise all the ransom demanded were so tortured that they died, then and there, or within a few days." One cardinal was going to be buried alive unless the money appeared at an appointed hour. Fires were lighted under the victims' feet, and one cleric's fingernails were torn off one by one. Almost half the city was in flames. The cry, as in Caesar's Rome, was "Burn all!" and

Cinna the poet was torn for his bad verses. Jean Grolier, a Frenchman who had sought refuge in the house of a Spanish bishop, remembered, "Everywhere screams, the clash of arms, weeping of women and children, the crackle of fires, the thunder of roofs falling." The onslaught lasted seven days. Later Sanuto wrote, "Hell is nothing to what Rome looks like today."

The inhabitants of the Palazzo Colonna spent the first day in a paroxysm of fear, the women weeping, the men cowering in the corners. Isabella, herself overcome with fright, did what she could to comfort them. Where was her son? There was no sign of him. Early that evening one Alessandro di Nuvolara, captain of the Italian infantry in the emperor's army, appeared before the palace. Isabella knew him. They threw a rope down to him from the roof and by that they pulled him up, since the windows and doors at street level had been walled up. He began negotiations to exact ransom. The sum mentioned was enormous, 40,000 ducats ($800,000). He was insistent, but not menacing, the Duke of Bourbon having instructed him before his death that Isabella was to be treated with consideration. Finally, late at night, Ferrante appeared. He had been unable to leave his post at the bridge until he was relieved. The bargaining went back and forth until the early hours of the morning. Its final result was that Isabella would be permitted to leave without paying, but the others would have to buy their release with sums in varying amounts. Yet everyone knew that safety could not be guaranteed, the soldiers being by now quite out of hand. Even five weeks later a report to Charles read: "Nobody can imagine the cruelties committed daily, irrespective of age, station, or nationality. Daily people are abused, tortured, killed." The stench of unburied bodies pervaded the streets, and dogs fed on the corpses. Rome, wrote the Mantuan ambassador, seemed a desert of stone.

The Palazzo was the only house that remained unplundered. But after a few days the food supply gave out. Ferrante begged his mother to leave and chance the consequences. She agreed, and he got together a small detachment of soldiers who formed a protective guard as Isabella left the palace under cover of darkness and proceeded to the Tiber, where several galleys, commandeered by Ferrante, were waiting. Isabella insisted she would not seek safety for herself alone. She took along all her damsels and several friends, including the Venetian Ambassador Domenico Venier, whom they disguised as a porter, carrying an empty trunk. He was so frightened that he never looked up. But all the others, too, were trembling. It was a miraculous escape. "Had Your Excellency remained for another two days," wrote the Mantuan delegate later, "you would have been in peril of your life."

With much difficulty they reached Ostia. There at anchor lay ships provided by Admiral Andrea Doria of Genoa. Yet bad weather, storms, and lightning made it impossible for the vessels to venture on the sea. The whole miserable company huddled together, ill-housed and plagued by hunger. Almost no food could be found; the farmers, themselves frightened beyond reason, were unwilling to help. Ferrante managed to send a few baskets of bread, and after ten days the weather improved, the ships sailed, and they reached Civitavecchia on the twenty-third of May. With all Isabella's troubles and with all the danger, she could not bear to leave her purchases behind. They were loaded on a special ship which sailed northward—only to be raided by pirates. Her precious possessions were gone, and she thought that loss the greatest of her hardships. Later she asked Pandolfo Pico della Mirandola to keep an eye out in case any turned up on the market, particularly the "many antique medallions, very beautiful, which mean a world to us." She was willing to buy them back. A few things were eventually found in Venice, but most were lost forever.

From Civitavecchia the company made its long, weary way to Mantua. When Isabella finally arrived, all the church bells rang and the people streamed out to shout, "Isabella! Isabella!" kiss her hand, and touch her cloak. Federico accompanied her to a solemn offertorium. She was tired, but in joyful spirits, hardly able to believe that she was safe again, and filled with gratitude to Ferrante, to whom she sent a gift of 10,000 ducats—which he badly needed. Her deprivations had not injured her health, but Brognina had become "as thin as a skeleton."

Isabella's generosity was acknowledged as generosity usually is: a few of those she had rescued remembered what she had done, a few forgot, one or two deprecated it. The Venetian ambassador, His Excellency Signor Venier, had obligated himself to pay a certain sum to a Spanish nobleman who had sheltered him before he was able to reach Isabella's house. A contract between the two men had been drawn up, and Isabella herself guaranteed its validity with her own money. The document was lost on the voyage, and

Venier, once safe in Mantua, now denied the transaction, pleaded diplomatic immunity, and refused to pay. This caused Isabella considerable trouble with the Venetian Senate; they wanted to know what the curious transaction was all about. She explained the matter in a long letter and in addition she gave Venier a piece of her mind: "If I were ever to need somebody to explain my affairs to the honorable Senate, I would seek a friend more faithful than you have shown yourself to be. Since you did not honor your agreement, I don't know where to find a speck of honor in you." Venier fled from Mantua to Verona.

Summer came and with it the plague, adding thousands of victims to the ten thousand who had perished in the cataclysm of Rome. Clement remained a prisoner in the Castel Sant' Angelo through the summer months, while the corpses were cleared away and the soldiers, bent by the weight of pillaged goods or with their hats stuffed with ducats, slowly dispersed.

Those Romans who could left the blood-soaked city. Its role as the center of art and learning, as of opulence and immorality, was played out. Aretino, Sebastiano del Piombo, and Sansovino went to Venice; Parmigianino to Bologna; Peruzzi, who had been imprisoned and then ransomed, to Mantua; Cellini back to Florence. Yet nowhere in Italy could one escape the aftermath of the invasion. Small but fierce sieges erupted, in 1528 in Naples, in 1529 in Florence. They were small—except to those who were killed. Famine, atop the black horse of the Apocalypse, rode through the country—in Venice, the years of 1528 and 1529 were the years of the "great hunger"—and Pestilence rode with it. In Mantua in 1528 one-third of the population died from the plague, and Ferrara was almost equally devastated. To relieve the misery of her people, Isabella once again pawned her best jewels, including the famous necklace of a hundred links. Nicolas Carew, en route from England to Bologna, reported to Henry VIII:

It is, sir, the most pity to see this country, as we suppose that ever was in Christendom. . . . Betwixt Vercelli and Pavia the whole country has been wasted. We found no man or woman laboring in the fields, and all the way we saw only three women gathering wild grapes. The people and children are dying of hunger.

Several historians mark the sack of Rome as the end of the Italian Renaissance. "In truth," wrote Erasmus, "this is not the ruin of one city, but of the whole world." It did signal the end of a way of feeling, thinking, creating, although genius, love of art, and money to pay for it were still available. Veronese was born the year after Rome was burned, Titian was still to paint his greatest work, and Michelangelo was to return to Rome to plan the Campidoglio and to paint his *Last Judgment* on the wall of the Sistine Chapel. Isabella resumed her commissions to artists as soon as she was again in funds, and when Titian visited Mantua in March 1529 he was persuaded to paint her portrait.*

The artists who worked after the sack of Rome communicated a new spirit, anxiety-ridden and often violent. The bodies which fly in Tintoretto's *Miracles of Saint Mark*, the wild contortions of the damned of the Sistine *Last Judgment*, the giants of the Palazzo del Tè, testify to a new unrest. The end of the Renaissance? No, because history cannot be written with a bookkeeper's neatness. But the end of a certain contentment with beauty, a full stop to the artistic peace which had shone beneficently on a light-filled country.

2

All Italy was now a Habsburg dependency, though Venice preserved a degree of independence and made a remarkable recovery. Mantua and Ferrara did what diplomacy dictated: they joined Charles, and were left relatively undisturbed. It really did not matter: Italy had become, and was to remain for centuries, a province subject to foreign rule.

Yet there was still the pope. It is difficult in the twentieth century fully to understand the might of the papacy, a force which survived war, contumely, and revolution. One could take arms against a pope; one could not destroy the papacy itself. How well Isabella understood this! Underneath all doubt and scoffing, it still represented the conscience of most of Western mankind. Mystery, fear, tradition, the need to believe—these props upheld Saint Peter's throne. Even the Reformation did not succeed in ending papal power.

* This is not the famous portrait in the Vienna Museum which Titian painted later. The portrait of 1529 is supposed to be in a private collection in France. However, several scholars think it no more than a copy of a lost original, though a fairly good one.

On December 8, 1527, Clement made his escape from the Castel Sant' Angelo disguised as an ordinary merchant. He found refuge at Orvieto in a palace "all naked and unhanged, the roofs fallen down," according to the British envoys who called on him, still trying to get his consent to a divorce for their king. They found him in bed, his sunken face obscured by a long unkempt beard. As the price of freedom Charles exacted from him a fine of 400,000 ducats. Cellini removed the jewels from the papal regalia and melted down gold to help raise this sum. Presently, however, the world's sympathy veered if not to Clement then to what he represented. The Spaniards began to criticize Charles. Catholic Christendom feared that an impotent pope would merely serve to promote the cause of Lutheranism. France, Poland, and Hungary stirred. Charles perceived the danger.

On October 6, 1528, Clement was permitted to return to the Vatican to find a city four-fifths of whose dwellings had been abandoned. Charles now made substantial further concessions to the Church. Florence was to be restored to the Medici, though as an imperial fief, and certain territories were redesignated as papal states. Naples, in turn, became the official property of the emperor. A peace with France was negotiated,* the vanquished François giving up all claims to Italy and paying the fantastic sum of 1,200,000 ducats to ransom all French prisoners. Charles wanted something more: he wanted to receive the gold crown of the Holy Roman Empire from the pope's own hands, confirming not only that he was the *imperator mundi*, the lord of the world, but that the Church approved, blessing his anointed head. Clement agreed—he had no choice *but* to agree—to meet Charles in Bologna.

Isabella, recovered from her Roman experiences but still angry at losing her antique treasures, now took little part in governing Mantua. But the fact that Charles announced he would go to Mantua to make her acquaintance indicates that she had not lost her fame as "First Lady of the world." One may imagine what a stir this news created at the Gonzaga court. Charles landed at Genoa on August 12. It was the first time the man who had conquered Italy set foot on Italian soil. Alfonso d'Este met him and begged him to take the road to Bologna through his state of Ferrara. Charles accepted,

---

* The Treaty of Cambrai, August 3, 1529, sometimes called the "Ladies' Peace," because Margaret, the aunt of Charles, and Louise, the mother of François, were active in negotiating it.

postponed his visit to Mantua, and instead invited Isabella to come to Bologna to be present on the great occasion.

Here she remained four months, witness to a meeting in which an emperor pretended to humble himself before a pope whom he had humbled. It was one of history's unfunny farces, a shoddy ceremony, however purple its draperies. Clement arrived first, after spending a few days with Isabella's old admirer Sabbà da Castiglione; he entered Bologna wearing the triple papal tiara, carried on the papal chair, the *sedia gestatoria,* sixteen cardinals following him. The people received him in silence; hardly a voice was raised in welcome. But they shouted when Charles arrived, hailing the man who had conquered them. Charles and Clement met in front of the great church of San Petronio. Isabella described the meeting in a letter written to her niece, Renée of France; it contains one of the best descriptions of a Renaissance ceremony—and the shameless make-believe of it—that we possess:

Today the entry into Bologna took place about two o'clock, in the following order. First came three companies of light horse bearing lances, all very well armed and mounted. Between them were the artillery and engineers, then fourteen companies of infantry, partly armed with cross-bows, and the rest with pikes and halberds—all very fine-looking men and well armed. In the midst of them was Signor Antonio de Leyva [general of the Spanish troops], unarmed, and carried in a chair by his servants, because he is crippled with gout, and truly there was in him—borne as he was by others—no less vigor and majesty than if he had been in the best of health and armed from head to foot. Behind these companies came the Burgundian knights, all clad in white armor, with velvet doublets of yellow, red, and green. After them rode another splendid company of light horse, armed with lances, and wearing cloth doublets of the same colors, and each Burgundian was followed by a page bearing his helmet and lance, mounted on a fine charger. Then came His Majesty's gentlemen-in-waiting; all in full armor, and doublets and mantles of different fashions and devices, according to their own taste and fancy. Behind these gentlemen came His Majesty's pages, wearing caps of yellow velvet, with velvet suits of these three colors, yellow, gray, and purple, and they rode beautiful and graceful horses, jennets as well as other, all richly draped and harnessed.

At this moment His Holiness descended from his palace, borne in his chair, in full pontifical robes, and surrounded by his chamberlains and gentlemen of the bedchamber. The Ambassadors and all the most reverend Cardinals went on foot before him, walking two and two at a time, followed by infinite numbers of bishops and clergy, and mounted a wooden tribunal which had been erected on the steps in front of the church of San Petronio, draped with white cloth. The floor under the feet of His Holiness and the Cardinals was covered with red cloth,* and the other portions occupied by less exalted personages were draped with different colored carpets. On the opposite side of the Piazza came the royal procession, led by His Majesty's guards, all of them fine-looking men, wearing the same liveries as the court pages. Close behind them were Caesar's [Charles's] greatest and favorite courtiers on horseback, all armed, and wearing the richest doublets and mantles, which made a most beautiful and splendid show. Behind them, under a canopy of cloth of gold, borne by the chief citizens of Bologna, appeared His Caesarean Majesty with one of his no-bles—the Grand Marshal Don Alvarez, Marquis Astorga—bearing his drawn sword aloft before him. His Majesty rode a most beautiful white jennet, and wore a doublet and vest of gold brocade, and was in full armor, only his right arm and breast being uncovered. At his stirrup walked forty young nobles of Bologna in white satin doublets, lined and slashed with gold brocade, with white velvet caps and plumes and rose-colored hose, who met him at the gate by which His Majesty entered, and accompanied him on foot through the streets.

When he reached the steps of San Petronio, His Majesty alighted and presented himself before His Holiness, who stood up to receive him, and after he had kissed his foot, hand, and lips, he was very tenderly embraced by the Holy Father, who made him take a seat on his right hand. The words which His Majesty said to His Holiness were these: "Holy Father, I have come to kiss the feet of Your Holiness, an act which I have long wished to do, and am at length allowed to accomplish, and I pray God that this may be for the glory of His service and of that of Your Holiness." And these words were spoken by His Holiness in reply: "We thank God who has brought us to this day which we have so long desired to see, and hope that Your Majesty may be the means of gaining great things for the service of God and the good of Christendom." After this His Majesty rose to his feet and offered His Holiness a purse filled with gold pieces, among which were two of 100 ducats and a great many others, making in all a sum of 1,000 ducats. Then all who were with His Majesty on the tribunal kissed the feet of His Holiness the Pope. So they spent some time together, but had little opportunity for any private conversation. After that, they descended the steps, and Caesar offered to conduct His Holiness back to the palace, but was induced by His Holiness to remain behind, and he entered San Petronio with four of the Cardinals, Cesarini, Ravenna, Naples, and Ridolfi, who remained in attendance on His Majesty. His Holiness then returned to his rooms borne in his chair, and accompanied by the other Monsignori on foot. And while the Emperor alighted and knelt before the Pope, and entered San Petronio, the procession of his guards continued to advance, chiefly light horse and infantry with a great number of guns. And when he had offered thanks to our Lord God and performed the usual ceremonies, he walked, still on foot, be-tween the Cardinals to the Palace, where his lodgings are prepared. I hear from those who have seen them that they are so near those of His Holiness that only a single wall divides one room from the other.

This spectacle, *Madama mia*, seemed to me so splendid that I confess I have never before seen, and can never expect to see again, anything at all equal to it. And if I had tried to describe all its details to Your Excellency, I should have

---

* Does our custom of "rolling out the red carpet" derive from that?

given you too much to read; but this much I tell you, that through all the streets where His Majesty passed, gold and silver coins were thrown to the people in token of rejoicing and princely liberality. It remains to us to implore God that the conference held by these two great lords who have met together here may produce those good results which we all desire, and lead to the restoration of universal peace in Christendom.

During the following months Isabella's quarters in Bologna became a lively meeting place. Bembo arrived from Padua; Giovio and Guicciardini came to observe history in the making; Trissino the poet was in attendance. Charles himself visited Isabella frequently. She even managed to make him laugh, he who was of a stern and gloomy temperament, forever pursuing vast plans for an empire on which the sun never set.

Preparations for the coronation itself were so elaborate and cumbersome that the ceremony did not take place until almost four months after Charles's arrival. When the moment came, Clement placed a double crown on Charles's head, the iron crown of Lombardy representing his sovereignty over Italy, and the gold crown of the Holy Roman Empire. A Flemish cardinal, Wilhelm Henchener, anointed him. He had been the friend of the unfortunate Adrian VI, had paid all he possessed to gain his freedom in the sack of Rome, and still wore his beard long in sign of mourning. Now he and Clement, Isabella and her sons, Alfonso and the Este, the Sforza and the Medici, the Duke of Bavaria and the Duke of Würtemberg, and innumerable other potentates made their obeisance to Carlo, Imperator Gloriosissimus.* He proclaimed universal peace and forgiveness.

Well, almost universal peace: Florence still held out as a republic. Charles sent Ferrante, who had succeeded to the command of the imperial army on the death of the Prince of Orange, to lay siege to the city. Michelangelo put his sculpting aside to work on new fortifications. Florentine men and women offered their jewelry and household goods to be sold for food. It didn't help. After eight months of fighting and starvation, the city capitulated. The Florentine Signoria was disbanded and the famous bell, La Vacca (the cow), which had summoned so many citizens to meetings, was broken into pieces, "so that," wrote Guicciardini, "we should no more hear the sweet sound of liberty."

Charles, as promised, came to Mantua. Giulio Romano had been

---

* It was the last time a pope crowned an emperor.

kept frantically busy, decorating the city and erecting triumphal arches on which the figures of Mars and Venus, Mercury and Minerva saluted the emperor, spouting quotations from Virgil. On the main square stood a huge statue of Victory; Charles stood in front of it and a laurel wreath was placed on his brow. He was also presented with a gift worthy of the occasion. Federico had commissioned two large paintings from Correggio and "let them be executed in his best manner and be ready as a coronation gift," as Vasari writes in *Lives of the Painters*. They were ready and they *were* in his best manner: a *Leda* and a *Danaë*. Isabella, of course, did the honors; it was for her a triumph of her diplomacy. Her proudest moment came when Charles elevated Federico to a dukedom. Isabella was no longer a marchesa; she was the mother of a duke, her state a duchy. In her pride of place she ignored, or could not admit to herself, that Mantua had become a vassal state.

3

Federico now *had* to get married. It was unthinkable that the Duke of Mantua remain without succession. The Boschetti affair was still going strong, but a dark scandal had risen to becloud it and more than ever Isabella hated to see her son involved. Boschetti's husband was supposed to have instigated a plot to poison her, and the mother of Maria, the girl to whom Federico had long since been betrothed, was rumored to have taken part in the plot. A few people were jailed, and Federico used the rumor to obtain from Clement permission to dissolve the marriage contract. The truth of the whole cloak-and-dagger business is uncertain; it is certain only that Isabella kept urging Federico to shop around for a politically suitable bride. Here, again, each faction sought to bind the Duke of Mantua to its side: François I suggested a sister of the king of Navarra, while Charles proposed Giulia of Aragon, daughter of Naples' last king. Federico still hesitated.

Then on a summer day in 1530, the unexpected happened. The Marchese of Monferrato fell from his horse and died. His brother, a bachelor and a sickly old man, succeeded him. Federico calculated that it was only a question of time, and little time at that, before Monferrato would become a state without a ruler. Here was an opportunity to add the little state to Mantuan territory. Suddenly

Maria rejected became Maria desirable. Federico renewed his suit. Maria's mother, who could discern a "desirable connection" as quickly as any mother, forgot all previous insults and consented, providing an extreme example of a parent permitting politics to make strange bedfellows.

But it was not to be. On September 15, 1530, Maria suddenly died. The messenger who brought the news to Mantua offered Federico a substitute, Maria's sister Margherita. Without thinking twice about it—so little was a human relationship involved—Federico accepted. Three weeks later the marriage contract was signed. Isabella Boschetti was asked to retire, though evidence suggests that she did not entirely abdicate.

Isabella was overjoyed: not only was her first-born son married, the succession fairly assured, but Margherita brought considerable wealth to the shrinking Mantuan treasury. Federico was now sure enough of himself to listen to advice, and after years of estrangement he turned again to his mother. Wanting a gayer and airier house than the gloomy Castello, he asked her to supervise the building of a little palace, to be called the Palazzina della Paleologa, in honor of his bride. Giulio Romano built it; it is supposed to have been a delightful abode, with an open view of the water which framed the city and a terraced garden built on the roof. Isabella, summoning her wonted enthusiasm, furnished it, as an official reported to Federico, while he was visiting Margherita:

> Yesterday *Madama illustrissima* came to the Castello, and wished to see everything. She was much pleased, and went out on the new terrace, which delighted her as much as possible, and stayed there for more than an hour, expressing the greatest admiration for the magnificent view. "If in my time," she exclaimed, "there had ever been such a fine terrace, I should never have complained of having had to live in the Castello!" Her Excellency visited the garden and the loggietta, which she praised greatly as a thing excellently contrived and admirably designed.

Isabella even chose the paintings to be hung. They were, according to the report of the same official, a copy by Andrea del Sarto of Raphael's portrait of Leo X with the two cardinals, Titian's portrait of Federico which Charles V had greatly admired, a Saint Catherine by Giulio Romano, a Saint Jerome by Titian, a Leonardo of which no trace has been found, and in the bride's room, Mantegna's grim and daring masterpiece of foreshortening, the *Dead Christ*, feet toward the beholder—surely a strange choice for the boudoir of a young girl.

The wedding festivities were relatively modest, because shortly before, the Mincio had flooded the fields surrounding the city and the population had suffered. Yet the extraordinary part of it all was that the cold marriage to Margherita, who was described as "of less than mediocre beauty," turned out to be entirely satisfactory. Isabella became fond of her, she gave Federico a male heir, and after some difficulties, which included a revolt in Monferrato suppressed by Charles's army, he was able to add to his title of Duke of Mantua the title Marchese of Monferrato. Isabella lived long enough to enjoy the event.

In the turbulent Europe of those years, a continent hearing harsh tunes piped by the Habsburgs, enclaves of peace and beauty were still to be found and Mantua, small as it was, was one of them. Princes and sovereigns, those in power and those stripped of it, sought a few weeks' respite in the "neutral" city, even as a man seeks a cure for a year's overeating in a fortnight's stay at a spa. Even Charles V, though he had to govern that morn-to-midnight empire, found time to visit Mantua once again and to enjoy Isabella's hospitality. She presented Ariosto to him.

Clement did not come. He did not forgive Isabella her compliant gestures toward Charles. He sat in the Vatican, bitter, inert, sad.

In 1534 he died, five years after Bologna but not before he had committed his final great blunder: he lost Henry VIII as "defender of the faith" and with him England. Virtually nobody mourned him. Guicciardini wrote: "He died loathed by the Curia, distrusted by monarchs, leaving behind him a hated and oppressive memory." Isabella kept silent. His "captain general" Federico, kept silent. A Roman mob threw dirt on his tomb.

XIII

Evening

The evening of Isabella's life followed the familiar course of those who have lived greatly and, not being themselves creators, must now be content as observers. On winter days she drew closer to the fireplace; in the spring she spent more time than before in the garden, aware, as she said, of the benison of being able once more to witness the burgeoning of flowers. She remembered and reminisced and in remembering forgave much. She observed her children and her friends with a gentler look, and sometimes an amused tolerance lay in that look which indicated: I've seen it before. She had little converse with her daughters Ippolita and Paola: they were nuns, and Isabella was more or less content that this be so. "They are brides of Christ," she said, "a son-in-law who won't give me any trouble." She was proud of Ercole, the learned cardinal, who inherited his mother's artistic bent and her love of collecting. Isabella was as enamored of her treasures as ever, and she used to walk among them every day, patting this majolica plate or caressing that little sculpture by Antico. She was overjoyed when Ercole sent her a cast of an antique medallion of Aristotle:

Most illustrious Lady, and dearest Mother, —Since a very ancient medal bearing the head of Aristotle has lately been found here, a number of casts and impressions have been taken from it. After a great deal of trouble I have at length succeeded in obtaining one of these, which I now sent to Your Excellency, so that as it is impossible to obtain the medal itself, which is no longer here, you may at least have a cast that shows the face of this divine man. And certainly, if ever the reverse of a medal was suitable and appropriate, it is this figure of the Goddess of Nature, concerning whom Aristotle reasoned so well that he seemed to penetrate to the very marrow of her bones. I shall be pleased if this cast satisfies Your Excellency, whose hands I kiss humbly, knowing that the sight of my hand-writing will show you that I am in good health, in spite of the excessive heat. [Rome, August 17, 1536]

She learned to love Ferrante, who remained high in the favor of Charles V, having not forgotten how he rescued her in Rome. He did annoy her once in a while, because he was always in need of money and tried to wheedle it from her. Then Ferrante married a wealthy heiress and bought the little principality of Guastalla. When a daughter was born to the couple, Isabella wrote:

I was especially happy to hear that the little one resembles Paola and you. All the same, she'll probably change by and by, as children do change their looks before they grow up. I trust Your Excellency and the Princess won't smother her with too many kisses and play with her too much, tempting though that is with such a sweet thing, particularly now when she is still the only child. I hope that in a few months another little one will come along who will take over the burden of at least some of all those cuddlings.

Yet she was not the conventional grandmother, neither Ferrante's daughter nor Federico's three children occupying much of her thought. As in our feelings for people we often return to the original emotion we felt for them—see Proust—so did Isabella's love for Federico blossom anew. She saw in him a more stately replica of his father, bearing himself "like the Turk, no rival near his throne." Titian's portrait shows him tall and ducal, with dark, deep eyes, his mother's high forehead, a well-barbered black beard, his hand caressing with proprietary gesture a prize dog which begs to be petted. Perhaps a bit of boastfulness mixed with Isabella's love, for Federico was very much the *grand seigneur*. Everything about him was large. His retinue consisted of no fewer than six hundred persons; four hundred horses were tethered in his stables. His collecting of art, to him more a form of aggrandizement than the loving piece-by-piece selection his mother had undertaken, was done wholesale. He bought from a dealer "120 Flemish paintings, including 20 landscapes in which fires burned, so realistically painted that one imagined one would burn one's hand if one touched them."

She attempted, though at a distance, to open her heart a little to Leonora, who was suffering and had gone to the baths of Albano to seek relief. A Dominican friar in Mantua wrote to Leonora:

The other day Madama, your illustrious Mother and my honored mistress, spoke of Your Excellency and of all the miseries and ill health which you have endured, and expressed the greatest distress and anxiety on your account. Twice over Her Excellency repeated these words: "The poor child has really been cruelly tormented by fortune! She has really never had any happiness; I only wonder she has not died of grief!" And she repeated these words, as if she herself shared your sufferings. . . .

Perhaps this letter should be read with some reservations. Yet why doubt the friar? It is believable that Isabella grown old would cast her mind back over the years and experience a pang of guilt over love withheld, the embrace ungiven, the companionship denied her first-born child, the child who had made the mistake of being born a girl.

Turning sixty, Isabella lost none of her personal vanity nor her curiosity about everything fashion decreed, nor was she less assiduous in applying cosmetics to enhance whatever traces of beauty were still left her. She was still considered an arbiter of fashion and was greatly pleased when her niece Renée, wife of Alfonso d'Este's son Ercole, appeared on an important state occasion dressed in a black satin robe in the French style and wearing a gold cap of the kind Isabella had invented. The unconventional attire "greatly exercised the tongues of her guests," a Ferrara gossip wrote. "It is said she wore this cap to hide her ears, or perhaps from fear of a cold," but it is more probable that Renée wore it as a compliment to her aunt.

Isabella's attempts to maintain the illusion of youth did not escape censure. When Pietro Aretino, the most feared satirist of his time, demanded of Federico "two pairs of shirts worked in gold . . . two pairs in silk, together with two golden caps," the Mantuan ambassador advised Federico: "Your Excellency knows his tongue; therefore I will say no more." He got his shirts. Lords, dukes, even kings quaked before his pen, dipped in slime. He knew all the skeletons in all the closets and was ever ready to drag them forth, unless suitably bribed. Federico employed him for a time as court poet, but Isabella would have nothing to do with him. Now, from Venice, where he lived like a prince among an art collection extorted from the studies of blackmailed artists, he launched this bit:

All the signs of the zodiac, all the heavens, all the planets measurable by the quadrant, affirm that the monstrous Marchesa of Mantua, she who has teeth of ebony and eyebrows of ivory, shamelessly ugly and twice as shamelessly made-up, will in her old age give birth, but without benefit of husband.

Isabella was sensible enough not to pay the slightest attention. Or was she flattered by the suggestion that at sixty she could still become pregnant?

From other sources came tributes more flattering and truer. She was, to artists, poets, and princes, the famous lady, a starred attraction one had to visit, representing what the Germans call a *Schöngeist*, a spirit of the beautiful. To many she must have appeared as a reminder of a time when they walked with freer steps and thought with freer minds. Among their tributes, Isabella most prized Ariosto's third edition of *Orlando Furioso*, in which the poet inserted the eulogy of "liberal and magnanimous Isabella" already alluded to. She wrote him a grateful acknowledgment:

Your book of *Orlando Furioso*, which you have sent me, is most welcome in all respects, and most of all, since, as you tell me, you have newly revised and enlarged it. I shall no doubt find new pleasure and delight in reading the poem. I thank you, more than I can express, for your kind allusions to me, and you may be quite sure that I shall always be ready to serve you, whenever an occasion presents itself, because of the great affection and admiration which I have always felt for your rare talents, which are indeed deserving of the highest favor. So, from my heart, I place myself wholly at your disposal.

Titian had become Federico's favorite painter, and at the coronation in Bologna, Aretino and Federico had introduced the artist to Charles V. The emperor sat indifferently for his portrait and paid the artist a single ducat for it, to which Federico quickly added 150 ducats out of his own pocket. But soon Charles recognized the genius of Titian, and during the ensuing sixteen years he was to paint a series of portraits of the emperor which are supreme examples of the portraitist's art. In 1533 Charles compensated for his first miserliness by bestowing on Titian the title and remuneration of "Imperial Court Painter."

The year after, Isabella wanted to have the paragon of painters portray her once again. He accepted the task, but he had no intention of coming from Venice to Mantua to look at the faded features of his subject. Rather, he used as his model a portrait Francia had painted when Isabella was thirty-seven. It is likely that the idea of painting a youthful Isabella at a time when she was in fact sixty came from Isabella herself. At any rate, Francia's portrait was sent, and Titian painted what is a variation on Francia's theme, though it took two whole years before he delivered the picture. On May 29, 1536, Isabella wrote: "Our portrait by Titian pleases us so much that we doubt if we were ever as beautiful as this, even at the age at which he has portrayed us."

This, then, is the famous painting in the Vienna Museum. She appears stately and elegant, the jeweled cap with the dark-light interwoven links lying like a crown on her blond hair, her blue sleeves embroidered with gold and silver.

As she grew heavier and weaker, her travels became slower and shorter. Yet she did not relinquish them, not altogether. She would go to Venice, though she could no longer walk to the Rialto. She again enjoyed seeing the blue waters of Lake Garda, where she and Elisabetta had spent clear carefree days, and she made an annual excursion to Ferrara, even after Alfonso died in 1534. His death touched her deeply. She missed him both as the last link to her parental home and as a confidant. If brother and sister ever spoke of Lucrezia, they left not a whisper of such an exchange.

When Alfonso died, the fact of death, now often observed, came close to her. She consulted her favorite astrologer: when would her own life end? He predicted a date a little more than a year off—he was wrong as usual; she was to live almost another five years—and as usual she believed him, and so she was prompted to make her will. She remembered her servants, her ladies-in-waiting, her grandchildren, and of course her children, though the clause specifying a gift to Leonora is strangely worded: "To Leonora . . . in remembrance of my friend and sister-in-law Elisabetta, who treated and loved her as if she had been her own daughter." Her favorite dwarfs, Morgantino and Delia, she commended to the care of Federico: they were to remain in his service or, if not, be provided with a yearly pension of 50 ducats.

In the spring of 1537 Leonora visited her. Isabella found her looking well and "in the best of health," but that impression is contradicted by Titian's portrait painted around that time, which shows the ravages time and disease had wrought on the once beautiful face of Isabella's daughter. Leonora's eyelids droop, her eyes look weary, and her figure, though covered by an ornate gown, is heavy.

It was the last occasion on which Isabella saw her daughter. She wrote Ferrante on May 30, 1537, that she missed him but was "enjoying the presence not only of Monsignore Reverendissimo [Ercole], but of our dear Duchess of Urbino [Leonora]." But family meetings were not her idea of sufficient entertainment. Quite forgetting her astrologer's prediction, she went to Ferrara at carnival time in 1538 to watch the dancing and to read to a gathering of young people five sonnets she had composed. The Cardinal of Ravenna reported to Ercole: "I do not think an angel from heaven could have written anything more perfect." (A biased opinion, no doubt.) Isabella's damsels made music, and "Morgantino with Delia came in, and jumped and danced together, and did great things with their little persons."

One of the last letters she wrote was a letter-from-home to the absent Federico:

I have just returned from my villa at Belfiore, where I spent some days, with the greatest benefit to my health. I may say, indeed, that having gone there seriously indisposed, I have returned by the grace of God in good health. Yesterday I went to the Castello, and visited the Illustrious Duchess, your wife. . . . All I saw there gave me the greatest pleasure and amusement. . . . I saw Signor Guglielmo [Federico's child], with his fat baby-face looking as innocent and as merry as possible, and both he and his sweet sister Donna Isabella are in my eyes a picture of all the joys the world can give. . . .

In the last autumn of her life, she insisted on making one more excursion to Venice. She stayed there for two months, friends came, she entertained, and this or that "dealer in antiquities" spread his wares before her. On the return journey she was not feeling well; the pains in her stomach, which she had occasionally felt since her youth and ignored, now became insistent. She took to her bed. She did not leave it again. To the last her mind was lucid. Looking back over her life, she is supposed to have said to Federico, "I am a woman and I learned to live in a man's world." She died on February 13, 1539. She died gently; it was almost a swooning away. No medical evidence of the cause of her death is extant. In her will she expressed the wish to be "buried privately without any pomp, in the grave of her husband."

The elegant little princess had experienced a quantity of inelegant pain. She had lived through infidelity and rejection by the man she loved. She had witnessed slaughter and barbarity as well as the creation of masterpieces. As a ruler her guidelines had been tortuous—as drawn by Machiavelli: she had steered a course between Charles VIII and Alexander VI, Louis XII and Cesare Borgia, Clement VII and Charles V, always avoiding collision. She had traversed those days, every one of them, with continuous gusto, unafraid of the winds of chance. In short, she had enjoyed life. She desired fame, power, and love. She had to settle for fame, power, and admiration.

She had achieved a triple triumph: first, Mantua existed; she had left a state which was prosperous and relatively independent and which would endure as such for almost another century. Second, she who once said, "I wish to be as well served by painters as by poets," *had* been well served. As a result of her ambition, her taste, and her persistence, she enriched posterity through a number of works of art which remain vital. Most important, she gave a new meaning to what it was to be a woman. Even if we discount the exuberant praise tendered her by her admirers, praise which was undoubtedly seasoned by the charm of her personality, and even if we see in retrospect that she sometimes acted as if Honesty were a member of her retinue no higher in rank than a pet dwarf—yes, even if she occasionally showed herself a tough morsel, we can admire her enthusiastically for her courage. Her example showed that a woman could climb from the level where she existed merely as playmate, mother, housekeeper.

By 1539, many of the minds which had nourished Isabella's had ceased; Perugino, Signorelli, Sansovino, Correggio, Peruzzi, Ariosto, and Castiglione were dead. She lived just long enough to witness the last French foray wrecked by Charles V. In the year of her death his ambition vaulted the Atlantic, conquering Bolivia and Cuba. Spanish might was to last until another woman smashed it. Six years before Isabella's death, an English baby was born who grew up to be Elizabeth I.

Federico ordered a tomb commemorating his father and mother. He did not live to see it completed; he died only a year after Isabella.

A decade ago the Italian historian Maria Bellonci wrote: "Her real importance to us today lies in the consciousness which she possessed of herself as an individual. That certainty made her feel equal to all, the men of her families, the Gonzagas and the Estes, as well as to kings, popes, emperors, esteemed or not so esteemed, great or very great. The means by which her freedom was won, a freedom which was then rare for a woman to achieve, ought to be employed today by every one of us: that is the cognizance of our own personality. In her that apprehension was elaborated and externalized with a force and in a style which we may well call brilliant."[*]

[*] "Appunti per un ritratto di Isabella d'Este" (*Civiltà Mantovana*, I, No. 4, 1966).

The Fate of the Gonzaga Treasures

It is not a pretty story.

The collection was augmented by Federico and his heirs and remained intact for about a hundred years. By the beginning of the seventeenth century, the art-collecting mania of princes, kings, and cardinals had made it profitable for "picture brokers" and art dealers, not always scrupulous, to operate on an international scale. Paintings by famous artists were copied, attributions were faked, artworks hawked like geese at a fair. It was a thriving business. One of these dealers, and by no means one of the worst, was a certain Daniel Nys (sometimes spelled Nice in British documents) of Venice.

Mantua had fallen on evil days under Duke Ferdinando Gonzaga, a dissolute, profligate, ruttish ruler. He had married a woman from the Medici family, as extravagant as he, who bought art en masse without much caring what she bought. These expenditures, as well as the personal luxury of the couple, threatened bankruptcy to the state. Nys met Ferdinando in 1626, told him that he had worked successfully for so important a person as the Earl of Arundel, and implied that a great deal of money could be made by disposing of the Mantua treasures in England and Spain, where the money was. Let him handle the transaction, Nys assured Ferdinando, and the duke's financial troubles would evaporate. Before anything happened, Ferdinando died. His successor, the homosexual Vincenzo II, was if anything an even more conscienceless ruler and cared more for parrots than for paintings, more for monkeys than for marble. Nys began to negotiate with him in earnest, and Vincenzo lent a willing ear. Charles I, king of England, was a possible purchaser. Like a shrewd salesman, Nys found another interested customer; it was Philip IV, king of Spain, whose ambassador in Mantua, Alessandro Striggi, was empowered to treat with Nys. It so happened that when negotiations reached the final stage, Striggi was ill in bed with severe gout, and could not attend to business, though Nys was actually a guest in his house. Playing England against Spain, and adding to the competition rumors of other contestants such as the Duke of Parma and the Grand Duke of Tuscany, he pressed the British for a decision. Charles decided: he wanted the collection. The contract was signed in September 1627. Vincenzo died in December; he was the last of the great house of Gonzaga, his successor, Carlo di Gonzaga, Duke of Nevers, stemming from a French branch of the family. Carlo, a foreigner in Mantua, and a weak character, made no objection to the denuding of the Castello.

However, a competitor more astute than Nys now came upon the scene. He was a Signor Lopez, agent for Cardinal Richelieu. He could no longer acquire the contents of the main palace, the contract with England having been signed, but he could and did acquire the works in Isabella's rooms, dealing directly with Carlo. Richelieu thus became the possessor of Mantegna's *Parnassus* and *Minerva*, Perugino's *Combat*, Costa's *Comus* and *Allegory*. In 1801 these paintings were sent to the "Central Art Museum" of Paris, the forerunner of the Louvre. There they are now.

Charles I's acquisitions were divided into four portions, the first being valued at 20,000 great ducats (about $600,000 in today's equivalent), the second at 27,000. The second part included Raphael's *Madonna of the Pearls*, which had been purchased for 10,000 ducats only twenty-three years previously. Evidently the king got a great bargain, though the cost of the whole cannot be determined with certainty. Nys claimed that the total sum was 68,000 great ducats. The most spectacular prize was the series of nine paintings by Mantegna, *The Triumph of Caesar*. These were shipped first to Venice, were damaged in transport, and only about two years later reached England, where they are installed at Hampton Court in a building especially constructed for them.

Nys kept on buying for Charles I, and presently he overreached himself, Charles claiming that his additional purchases were bought without proper authorization. Nys himself had purchased the art in question from the Duke of Mantua; to be able to do so he had raised a bank loan, giving King Charles as his "security." Charles was willing to honor the loan, but Richard Weston, Lord Treasurer of England, was either unwilling or unable to hand out the money. Unfortunate Nys!—between his banker and Weston he was squeezed to bankruptcy. He was desperate and had to wait more than two years before relief came. Then an order was issued to pay Nys "in full." The pictures and statues were loaded on a boat in Venice and shipped to London. Nys claimed he had *not* been paid in full and kept petitioning Charles for £3,000, which he asserted were still due him. Eventually this claim was settled. But between the delays and confusion, between Mantua, Venice, and London, a good many works disappeared—stolen or lost.

The Gonzaga collection now became part of the Royal Collection of the British kings. Yet it was not allowed to remain in peace. In 1641 the Civil War began in England, and in 1649 Charles was beheaded. Parliament decided to sell part of the treasures in order to meet the drain on the national exchequer. When this decision was announced, Louis XIV of France, Philip IV, king of Spain, Naples, Portugal, and Sicily (the patron of Velázquez and Rubens), and Archduke Leopold of Austria sent their agents to bid and buy. When they were finished, only a relatively small residue remained in England. That is why Mantegna's

Madonna of Victory can be seen in the Louvre, his *Death of Mary* and a Titian portrait of Federico in the Prado. Raphael's *Madonna of the Pearls* was likewise acquired by the Spanish court and is now one of the glories of the Prado Museum. The two famous Antico statuettes and Isabella's medallion designed by Gian Cristoforo Romano went to the Vienna Museum, where one may compare Titian's portrait of Isabella with Rubens's copy. If, as Edgar Wind believes,* Bellini's *Feast of the Gods* was commissioned by Isabella and only later passed to her brother, we should list it among the Gonzaga treasures. It was owned by various Roman families until the Duke of Northumberland bought it in 1856 and subsequently sold it to Joseph Widener, who gave it as part of the Widener Collection to the National Gallery of Art in Washington.

Isabella's collection of majolica, tiles, and such is of course scattered. One of the most admired pieces, the plate by Nicolo Pellipario depicting the story of Hippolytus and Phaedra, is in the Victoria and Albert; a tile is in the Metropolitan Museum. What treasures remained in England, including *The Triumph of Caesar*, were recovered for the crown during the Restoration in 1660.

London, Milan, Venice, Madrid, Paris, New York, Washington, Berlin—here was a diaspora, indeed!

In 1975 the Louvre held an exhibit, "Le Studiolo d'Isabelle d'Este," in which an attempt was made to reunite the contents and give an idea of Isabella's pride and joy. Although much was shown, much was missing and photographs had to be substituted. An interesting part of the exhibit was the display of works by later artists influenced by the *"studiolo* artists." Degas painted a pastel after Mantegna's *Minerva,* a beautiful study of light, shadow, and movement.

In 1797 Napoleon's soldiers besieged Mantua, and after a long campaign invaded it. They robbed the churches of virtually all that was portable, and then, whether out of revenge or mere love of destruction, they broke the tombs of the Gonzagas to pieces. No trace remains of Isabella's or her husband's monument. No trace remains of her grave.

* Edgar Wind, *Bellini's Feast of the Gods: A Study in Venetian Humanism* (Cambridge, Mass., 1948).

A Calendar of
Significant Dates in Isabella's Life

This calendar does not give a complete documentation of all that happened during Isabella's life. Its purpose is merely to help orient the reader in the welter of alliances, wars, marriages, and political confusion in Italy. It may serve as a frame of reference, and for that reason I have listed certain contemporaneous artistic works and their creators.

DATE	ISABELLA'S LIFE	THE PAPACY	POLITICAL EVENTS IN ITALY	CULTURAL EVENTS
1474	Born in Ferrara	Sixtus IV (1471–84).		Piero della Francesca works in Urbino. Mantegna finishes the Camera degli Sposi in Mantua. Ariosto born (died 1533)
1475	Her sister Beatrice born.			Michelangelo born. Botticelli: *Mars and Venus.*
1476	Her brother Alfonso born.		Revolt against Ercole d'Este, Isabella's father, suppressed.	
1478	Isabella's mother, Eleanora, takes Isabella and Beatrice to visit grandfather Ferrante in Naples.		Pazzi conspiracy. Giuliano de Medici murdered. In resulting war Ercole Este joins Florence, Milan, Naples against the pope. (Peace concluded in 1480.)	Botticelli: *La Primavera.* Giorgione born.
1480 to 1482	Negotiations for betrothal of Isabella to Gianfrancesco Gonzaga of Mantua. Beatrice is promised to Lodovico Sforza.		Louis XI unites France. Sixtus IV wars against Ferrara with help of Venice, then changes his mind and proceeds against Venice. Ferrara is saved. Lodovico Sforza "Il Moro" assumes regency of Milan.	Sistine Chapel, begun in 1473, is decorated with frescoes by various Italian artists.
1483		Sixtus IV dies. Innocent VIII pope to 1492.	Louis XI dies. Charles VIII succeeds.	Raphael born.
1484	Gianfrancesco Gonzaga becomes sovereign of Mantua. Relations between him and Isabella become closer.		Savonarola demands burning of "worldly vanities."	Botticelli: *Birth of Venus.*

1486		Maximilian I becomes German king (Holy Roman Emperor 1493–1519)	Pico della Mirandola publishes 900 philosophic theories. Writes "On the Dignity of Man." Is accused of heresy but exonerated.
1490	Isabella marries and moves to Mantua.	Gianfrancesco is captain general of Venice.	Carpaccio begins painting series on the life of St. Ursula. Leonardo: *Virgin of the Rocks* (circa).
1491	Goes to Milan to attend wedding of Beatrice to Lodovico Sforza. Is attracted to Lodovico. Begins work on her *studiolo*.		Botticelli: 92 drawings for the *Divine Comedy.*
1492	Begins her art collection. Goes again to Milan. Then state visit to Venice.	Lorenzo the Magnificent dies.	
	Innocent VIII dies. Alexander VI, a Borgia, elected pope.		Mantegna honored for *Triumph of Caesar* and *Death of the Madonna.* Piero della Francesca dies. Leonardo designs a "flying machine."
1493	Her daughter Leonora born.	Alexander plans conquests with his son Cesare Borgia. Alexander divides the		

DATE	ISABELLA'S LIFE	THE PAPACY	POLITICAL EVENTS IN ITALY	CULTURAL EVENTS
1494		"New World" discovered by Columbus between Portugal and Spain.	Charles VIII invades Italy. Medici expelled from Florence. Lodovico Sforza first cooperates with Charles, then turns against him.	Matteo Boiardo, poet of *Orlando Innamorato*, dies. Aldus Manutius begins publishing handy books.
1495	Gianfrancesco is appointed leader of the allied troops. Proceeds against Charles. In her husband's absence Isabella assumes government of Mantua.	Alexander forms alliance with Milan, Venice, Spain, and Maximilian I to oppose the French.	July 5: Battle of Fornovo led by Gianfrancesco. The French are forced to retreat.	
1496	Gianfrancesco and Isabella are celebrated as saviors of Italy.			Mantegna paints *Madonna of the Victory,* to celebrate Battle of Fornovo.
1497	After making overtures to Charles, Gianfrancesco is suddenly dismissed by the Venetian Senate; blow to Isabella. Beatrice dies.		Savonarola excommunicated.	Leonardo finishes (?) *The Last Supper,* begun 1495.

1498	Gianfrancesco signs contract with Lodovico Sforza. Then tries to negotiate with Venice. Then rejoins Lodovico and Maximilian. Isabella instrumental in these moves.		Charles VIII dies. Succeeded by Louis XII.	
1499	Gianfrancesco joins Louis XII. Isabella forms friendship with him, becomes "a good Frenchwoman."	Alexander forms alliance with Louis XII. Cesare marries Charlotte d'Albret of France.	Louis XII invades Italy. Deposes Lodovico Sforza.	Leonardo visits Mantua and sketches Isabella.
1500	Son Federico born. Isabella under French influence. Her skill in treatment of Cesare keeps Mantua safe.	Jubilee Year. First of Cesare Borgia's campaigns. Captures Forli and Imola, then Faenza. Lodovico Sforza captured and imprisoned (dies in 1508).		Benvenuto Cellini born. Giorgione: *Castelfranco Altar*. Michelangelo: *Pietà*. Erasmus: *Adagia*.
1501 and 1502	Alfonso d'Este is forced to marry Lucrezia Borgia. Isabella is hostess at wedding in Ferrara. Isabella offers succor to the Montefeltro couple. Gianfrancesco in France.	Cesare proceeds in his conquests. Captures Urbino, deposing Elisabetta and Guidobaldo Montefeltro. Most of Italy now governed by Louis XII and the Borgias.		Isabella commissions works of art from Mantegna, Perugino, etc. Lorenzo da Pavia and she become friends. Correspondence with Giovanni Bellini.

DATE	ISABELLA'S LIFE	THE PAPACY	POLITICAL EVENTS IN ITALY	CULTURAL EVENTS
1503	Daughter Ippolita born. Love affair between Gianfrancesco and Lucrezia Borgia begun.	Alexander VI dies, ending the Borgia power. Pius III elected but dies after one month. Julius II becomes pope (to 1513).	Cesare Borgia exiled to Spain (killed in 1507). Montefeltros reinstated. Other sovereigns return.	Michelangelo: *David* (circa).
1505	Son Ercole born. Leonora is betrothed to Francesco della Rovere of Urbino. Isabella's father dies and Alfonso becomes Duke of Ferrara.			Michelangelo called to Rome by Julius.
1506	Estrangement between husband and wife deepens. Ariosto becomes a friend of Isabella and reads her part of his *Orlando Furioso.*	Julius begins his career as "the warrior pope." Appoints Gianfrancesco as captain.	Plague in Mantua. The papal forces proceed against Perugia and Bologna.	New St. Peter's planned by Bramante. Mantegna dies. Lorenzo Costa appointed court painter of Mantua. Leonardo: *Mona Lisa.*
1507	Isabella visits Louis XII in Milan. Son, Ferrante, born.	Julius allied with Louis XII.	Louis XII invades Italy again.	Raphael: *La Belle Jardinière.*

1508	Daughter, Paola, born. Gianfrancesco shows first symptoms of disease, later diagnosed as syphilis.	Julius forms "League of Cambrai" against Venice.	Guidobaldo Montefeltro dies.	Raphael begins his work in the Stanze (to 1517). Pinturicchio: frescoes in Orvieto and Siena. Michelangelo begins work in the Sistine Chapel.
1509	Gianfrancesco taken prisoner by Venice. Isabella once again assumes government and tries to free her husband. Refuses, however, to hand over her son Federico as hostage.		Battle of Cremona: papal forces and allies defeat Venetians, Maximilian I joins Julius.	
1510	Gianfrancesco freed. But Isabella continues to govern.	Julius turns against the French. Makes peace with Venice. Takes Federico to the Vatican.	Alfonso of Ferrara sides with the French. Julius wars against him.	Botticelli dies. Raphael: *Galatea.*
1511	Isabella politically active in Italian affairs	Julius personally leads his forces. Siege of Mirandola (Ferrara). Forms "Holy League" with Spain.		Giorgione dies. Peruzzi: Villa Farnesina. Statue of Apollo (Roman) placed in the Belvedere.

DATE	ISABELLA'S LIFE	THE PAPACY	POLITICAL EVENTS IN ITALY	CULTURAL EVENTS
		Venice, Switzerland, Henry VIII, and Maximilian I.		
1512	Isabella hostess at "Congress of Mantua" to settle questions of Florence, Milan, etc.	Julius absolves Alfonso, but with heavy penalty. Alfonso flees from Rome.	French driven out of Italy. Medici reinstated. Italy once more intact—more or less.	Raphael: *Julius II.* Statue of Romulus and Remus excavated. Michaelangelo: *Two Slaves.*
1513	Isabella and her husband apart. She goes to Milan and on other excursions.	Julius II dies. Leo X (Medici) becomes pope (until 1521).		
1514	Isabella goes to Rome. She is honored and feted.	Leo inaugurates a new era favorable to the arts and science.		Machiavelli: *The Prince.*
1515	Federico is invited by François to the French court. Isabella lets him go.	Leo proceeds against Urbino. War ends in compromise.	Louis XII dies. His successor, François I, at once makes plans to reconquer Italy. His army successful at Marignano. Takes possession of Milan.	Raphael appointed first architect of St. Peter's. Titian: *Heavenly and Earthly Love.*
1517	Isabella voyages to Provence. Gianfrancesco's health worsens.	Leo financially embarrassed, but Rome has	Luther's theses. Beginning of Reformation.	Leonardo in France with François I. Andrea del Sarto: *Madonna di San Francesco.*

Year	Mantua / Isabella	Papacy	Europe	Arts
		become a center of arts and learning.		
1519	Gianfrancesco dies. Lucrezia Borgia dies. Isabella sole sovereign of Mantua.	Leo hesitates between Charles and François.	Maximilian I dies. Charles of Spain, a Habsburg, succeeds him. He becomes Holy Roman Emperor as Charles V. Opposes François.	Leonardo da Vinci dies. Titian: *Assumption* in Frari church and *The Worship of Venus*.
1520	Federico becomes "captain general" of the pope, through Isabella's recommendation. Castiglione active as her Roman ambassador. Isabella works on the decoration of her new rooms.		Struggle between François I and Charles V (twenty years old) sharpens. Reformation spreads. Turks menace Europe.	Raphael dies.
1521		Leo signs alliance with Charles V. Leo dies.	Papal-imperial forces conquer Milan from the French. Charles deeds German Habsburg lands to his brother, Ferdinand I, and concentrates on Italy.	Michelangelo: *Christ* (statue in Rome).
1522	Isabella enrolls her son Ercole in Pomponazzi's school.	Adrian VI.		Luther publishes his translation of the New Testament. In his essay "Of Married Life" he demands greater equality for women.
1523	Federico strips himself of Isabella's guardianship. Isabella begins to withdraw from	Adrian VI dies. Clement VII becomes pope (to 1534).		Perugino and Signorelli die. Titian working for Alfonso d'Este (*Bacchanale, Bacchus and Ariadne*).

DATE	ISABELLA'S LIFE	THE PAPACY	POLITICAL EVENTS IN ITALY	CULTURAL EVENTS
	government affairs. Visits Venice again.	Vacillates between François and Charles.		
1525		Clement allied to François, just before Battle of Pavia.	Battle of Pavia: great victory of Charles over the French. François taken prisoner.	Giulio Romano at Mantua. Works on Palazzo del Tè for Federico.
1526	Isabella goes to Rome, ignoring warnings that the voyage may be dangerous. Her friend Elisabetta Montefeltro dies.		"Treaty of Madrid": François liberated, renouncing claims to Italy. Once back in France François denounces agreement and forms "League of Cognac" with Clement.	Correggio: *Danaë*. Titian: *Pesaro Madonna*.
1527	Isabella caught in sack of Rome. Obtains cardinalate for her son Ercole. Isabella rescued by Ferrante. Returns to Mantua.	Clement a prisoner in Castel Sant' Angelo.	Charles, impatient, sets out to conquer all of Italy. Sack of Rome: bloodshed and destruction. "End of Renaissance."	Correggio: *Jo. Ganymed*.
1528 and 1529	Isabella goes to Bologna for the coronation of Charles V. He honors Isabella and elevates Mantua to a duchy.	Clement forced to crown Charles V Holy Roman Emperor.	Plague and famine in Italy. "Peace of Cambrai" ends Italian wars temporarily.	Castiglione publishes *The Courtier*.
1530	Federico agrees to marry Margherita Paleologa of		Spain dominates all of Italy, except Venice.	

1531	Monferrato. Charles V visits Isabella. Second visit of Charles. Isabella introduces Ariosto to him.	Ariosto presents third edition of *Orlando Furioso* to Isabella.
Last years, 1532 to 1539	Isabella leads retired life, but frequently goes on minor voyages. Her brother Alfonso dies 1534. Isabella dies 1539.	1533: Titian: *Charles V.* 1534: Michelangelo: Medici Sepulcher in Florence. 1534: Correggio dies. 1535: G. Romano finishes Palazzo del Tè. 1536: Erasmus dies. 1536: Titian finishes Isabella's portrait. 1537: Titian: *François I.*
	1534, Clement dies. Paul III becomes pope (to 1549). Paul persuades Charles and François to a ten-year armistice (1534).	

Bibliography

Ariosto, Lodovico. *Orlando furioso*. Milan, 1965.

Bandello, Matteo. *Novelle*. Milan, 1955.

Bardini, Mario. *Fatti e Uomini della Storia di Mantova*. Mantua, 1944.

Barnes, H. E. *History of Western Civilization*. 2 vols.; New York, 1935.

Baxandall, Michael. *Painting and Experience in Fifteenth Century Italy*. London, 1972.

Béguin, Sylvie. *Le Studiolo d'Isabelle d'Este*. Paris, 1975.

Bellonci, Maria. *Lucrezia Borgia*. New York, 1953.

——, ed. *L'Opera completa del Mantegna*. Milan, 1967.

Bentley, Eric, ed. *The Genius of the Italian Theater*. New York, 1964.

Berenson, Bernard. *Italian Painters of the Renaissance*. London, 1952.

——. *The Study and Criticism of Italian Art*. 2 vols.; London, 1908, 1931.

——. *Venetian Painting in America*. New York, 1916.

Bortolon, Liana. *The Life and Times of Titian*. Feltham, Eng., 1968.

Boujassy, Jeanne. *Isabelle d'Este, Grande Dame de la Renaissance*. Paris, 1960.

Bowen, Marjorie. "Louis XII," in *Sundry Great Gentlemen*. London, 1908.

Brown, Clifford M. *Little Known and Unpublished Documents Concerning Mantegna*, etc. 2 vols.; Mantua, 1968.

——, and Lorenzoni, Anna Maria. *An Art Auction in Venice* [in 1506]. Mantua, 1972.

Burchard, John. *At the Court of the Borgia*. London, 1963.

Burckhardt, Jacob. *The Civilization of the Renaissance in Italy*. London, 1952.

Burke, Peter. *Culture and Society in Renaissance Italy 1420–1540*. New York, 1972.

Canaday, John. *The Lives of the Painters*. 4 vols.; New York, 1969.

Cartwright, Julia. *Beatrice d'Este*. London, 1899.

——. *Isabella d'Este*. 2 vols.; London, 1903.

Castiglione, Baldassare. *Il Cortegiano*. Venice, 1928.

Cellini, Benvenuto. *Autobiography*. London, 1896.

Chamberlin, E. R. *The Bad Popes*. New York, 1971.

Clark, Kenneth. *Civilisation*. New York, 1970.

——. *Leonardo da Vinci*. London, 1958.

——. *Looking at Pictures*. New York, 1960.

Cleugh, James. *The Medici*. New York, 1975.

Crankshaw, Edward. *The Habsburgs.* New York, 1971.

Creighton, M. *A History of the Papacy during the Period of the Reformation.* 4 vols.; London, 1882.

Cronin, Vincent. *The Flowering of the Renaissance.* New York, 1969.

Durant, Will. *The Renaissance.* New York, 1953.

Equicola, Mario. *Di Natura d'Amore.* Venice, 1583.

Fahy, Conor. *Three Early Renaissance Treatises on Women.* Italian Studies, Vol. XI. Milan, 1956.

Ferguson, George. *Signs and Symbols in Christian Art.* New York, 1959.

Garner, John Leslie. *Caesar Borgia.* New York, 1912.

Gobineau, Arthur. *Die Renaissance.* Berlin, n.d.

Goldschneider, Ludwig. *Leonardo da Vinci.* London, 1954.

——. *Michelangelo.* Florenz, 1953.

Gregovorius, Ferdinand. *Lucretia Borgia.* London, 1903.

——. *Werke.* Berlin, n.d.

Guicciardini, Francesco. *Storia d'Italia.* Bari, 1868.

Hale, J. R. *Renaissance Europe 1480–1520.* London, 1971.

Haslip, Joan. *Lucrezia Borgia.* New York, 1953.

Haydn, J., and Nelson, J. C., eds. *A Renaissance Treasury.* New York, 1953.

Jackson, J. Hampden. *A Modern History of Europe.* New York, 1935.

Lane, Frederic C. *Venice.* Baltimore, 1973.

Lang, P. H. *Music in Western Civilization.* New York, 1941.

Larner, John. *Culture and Society in Italy, 1290–1420.* New York, 1971.

Lauts, Jan. *Isabella d'Este, Fürstin der Renaissance.* Hamburg, 1952.

Levey, Michael. *High Renaissance.* Harmondsworth, Eng., 1975.

Luzio, Alessandro. *La Galleria dei Gonzaga.* Milan, 1913.

——. Various essays, such as: "Lettere inedite di fra Sabbà da Castiglione" (1886); "Federico Gonzaga ostaggio alla Corte di Giulio II" (1886); "I precettori di Isabella d'Este" (1887); "Ancora Leonardo da Vinci e Isabella d'Este" (1888); "La Madonna della Vittoria del Mantegna" (1899); "I ritratti d'Isabella d'Este" (1900); "Isabella d'Este e la Corte Sforzesca" (1901); "Isabella d'Este né primordi del papato di Leone X" (1906); "Isabella d'Este e Leone X dal Congresso di Bologna alla presa di Milano" (n.d.); "Isabella d'Este e Francesco Gonzaga promessi sposi" (1908); "Isabella d'Este e il Sacco di Roma" (1908); "Isabella d'Este e Giulio II" (1909); "La reggenza d'Isabella d'Este durante la prigionia del marito" (1910); "Isabella d'Este e i Borgia" (1915).

——, and Renier, Rodolfo. Various essays, such as: "Francesco Gonzaga alla battaglia di Fornovo" (1890); "Delle relazioni d'Isabella d'Este Gonzaga con Ludovico e Beatrice Sforza" (n.d.); "Mantova e Urbino. Isabella d'Este ed Elisabetta Gonzaga nelle relazioni familiari e nelle vicende politiche" (1893); "La cultura e le relazioni letterarie d'Isabella d'Este" (1903).

McCarthy, Mary. *Venice Observed.* Lausanne, 1956.

Marani, Ercolano. *Mantova.* Milan, n.d.

Matarazzo, Francesco. *Chronicles of the City of Perugia.* London, 1905.

Mather, Frank Jewett, Jr. *A History of Italian Painting.* London, 1923.

Matt, Leonard von. *Die Kunst in Rom.* Zurich, 1950.

Maulde, La Clavière R. *The Women of the Renaissance.* London, 1900.

Metropolitan Museum of Art. *The Secular Spirit: Life and Art at the End of the Middle Ages.* New York, 1975.

Meyer, Edith Patterson. *First Lady of the Renaissance.* Boston, 1970.

Mitchell, Bonner. *Rome in the High Renaissance: The Age of Leo X.* Norman, Okla., 1973.

Morris, James. *The World of Venice.* New York, 1960.

Murgia, Adelaide. *I Gonzaga.* Milan, 1972.

Nicoll, Allardyce. *World Drama.* London, 1949.

Oberhammer, Vinzenz, ed. *Kunsthistorisches Museum.* Vol. I; Vienna, 1965.

O'Faolain, Julia, and Martines, Lauro, eds. *Not in God's Image.* London, 1973.

Pastor, Ludwig. *The History of the Popes from the Close of the Middle Ages.* 6 vols.; London, 1898.

Pater, Walter. *The Renaissance.* New York, n.d.

Portigliotti, Giuseppe. *The Borgias.* New York, 1927.

Prescott, Orville. *Princes of the Renaissance.* New York, 1969.

Roscoe, William. *Life and Pontificate of Leo X.* 2 vols.; London, 1853.

Ryan, L. V., ed. Book IV of Castiglione's *Courtier: Climax or Afterthought?* Studies in Renaissance, Vol. XIX. Milan, 1972.

Simon, Kate. *Italy: The Places in Between.* New York, 1970.

Stein, Werner. *Kulturfahrplan.* Berlin, 1946.

Symonds, John Addington. *Renaissance in Italy.* 7 vols.; Gloucester, Mass., 1967.

Tietze, Hans. *Titian.* London, 1950.

Valentin, Veit. *Illustrierte Weltgeschichte.* 2 vols.; Stuttgart, 1968.

Vallentin, Antonina. *Leonardo da Vinci.* New York, 1952.

Various Authors. *Raphael, the complete works of.* New York, 1969.

Vasari, Giorgio. *Lives of the Artists.* Abridged ed.; New York, 1946.

Vaudoyer, Jean-Louis. *Venetian Painting.* London, 1958.

Vaughan, Herbert M. *The Medici Popes.* New York, 1908.

Walker, John. *Bellini and Titian at Ferrara.* London, 1956.

Wandruszka, Adam. *Das Haus Habsburg.* Stuttgart, 1968.

White, John S. *Renaissance Cavalier.* New York, 1959.

Williamson, Hugh Ross. *Lorenzo the Magnificent.* New York, 1974.

Wittkower, Rudolf and Margot. *Born under Saturn.* New York, 1963.

Young, G. F. *The Medici.* 2 vols.; London, 1913.

Index

28   DATE DUE DAYS

SEP 2 7 2012		
GAYLORD		PRINTED IN U.S.A.

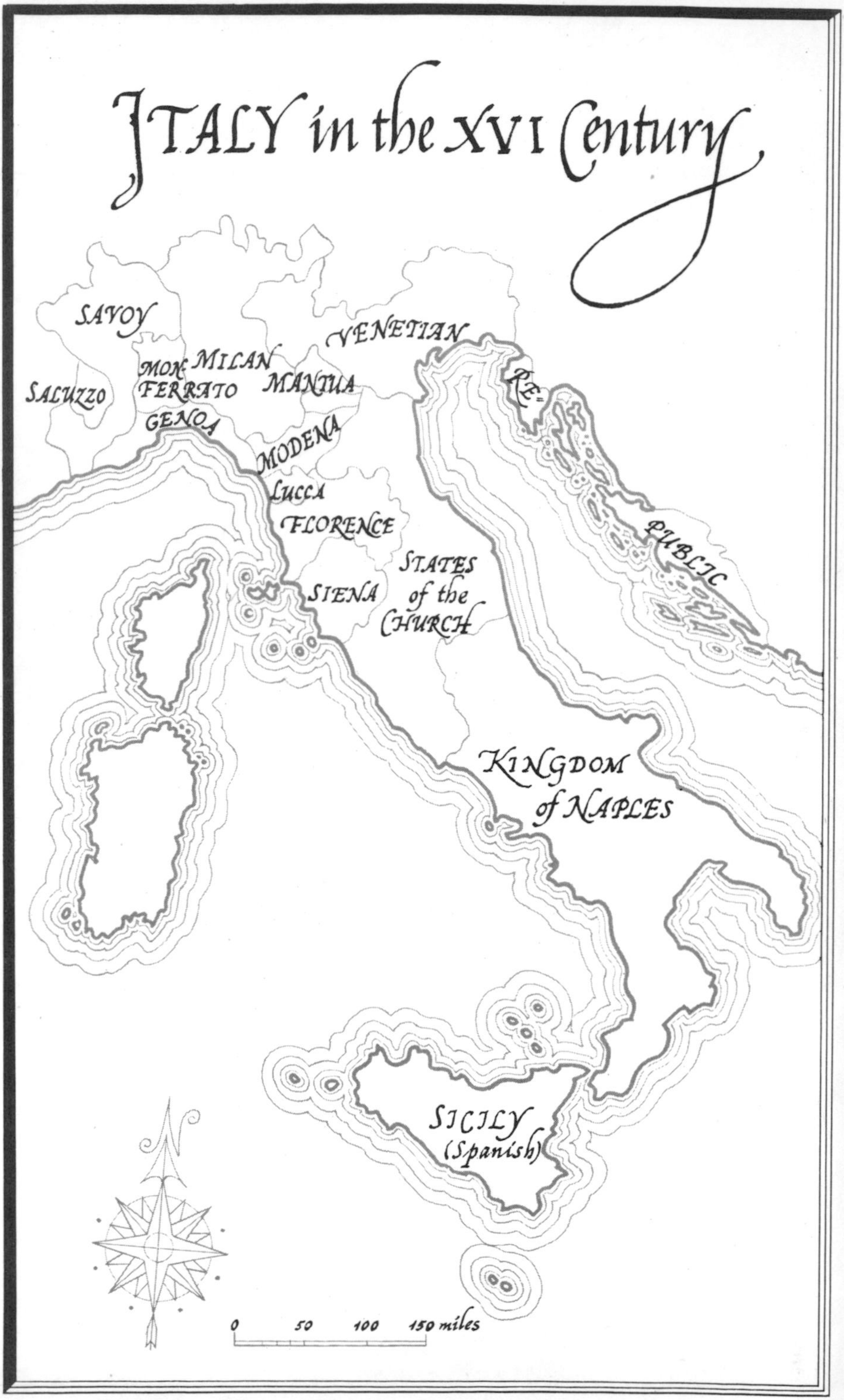
ITALY in the XVI Century
SAVOY
SALUZZO
MON-
FERRATO
MILAN
GENOA
VENETIAN
RE-
PUBLIC
MANTUA
MODENA
LUCCA
FLORENCE
SIENA
STATES
of the
CHURCH
KINGDOM
of NAPLES
SICILY
(Spanish)
N
0 50 100 150 miles